A
Halloween
HOW-TO

A Halloween
HOW-TO

Costumes, Parties, Decorations, and Destinations

**Lesley Pratt
Bannatyne**

PELICAN PUBLISHING COMPANY
Gretna 2001

First printing, July 2001
Second printing, October 2001

The word "Pelican" and the depiction of a pelican are trademarks of Pelican Publishing Company, Inc., and are registered in the U.S. Patent and Trademark Office.

Library of Congress Cataloging-in-Publication Data

Bannatyne, Lesley Pratt.
    A Halloween how-to : costumes, parties, decorations, and destinations /
by Lesley Pratt Bannatyne.
      p. cm.
    Includes bibliographical references and index.
    ISBN 1-56554-774-8 (alk. paper)
    1. Halloween. 2. Halloween costume. 3. Halloween decorations.
4. Entertaining. I. Title.
GT4965 .B29 2001
394.2646—dc21

                                 00-068463

Printed in Canada
Published by Pelican Publishing Company, Inc.
1000 Burmaster Street, Gretna, Louisiana 70053

Dedication

"Let us recognize that we are not the ultimate triumph but rather we are beads on a string. Let us behave with decency to the beads that were strung before us, and hope modestly that the beads that come after us will not hold us of no account merely because we are dead."
—Robertson Davies

For the beautiful beads on either side of me: my late mother Janet Young Richardson, my father David R. Bannatyne, and my daughter, Magdalena Bannatyne Bay.

Contents

Acknowledgments

This was not a solo undertaking. I owe a debt of thanks to the hundreds of Halloween lovers, scholars, and businessmen and women who offered their opinions and expertise to this project, especially those whose stories, opinions, recipes, and photos appear in these pages. I also want to acknowledge the Harvard University libraries and their excellent staff, who made it so easy to do research, and the many people who contributed material to this book: Jackson Braider, Denise Cohen, Ruth and Cheryl Faris, Tim Friesen, Ed Gannon, Sheila Gilligan, Michael Hios, Cortlandt Hull, Ralph and Melissa Mitchell, Michael D. Lee, Marty X. Larkin, Linda Lestha, Scott Messinger, Janet Meyers, Elizabeth Miller, Sue and Dan Oelke, Dave Oester, Liz Pennell, Jeff Quaglietta, Tina Reuwsaat, Chuck Rice, Stuart Schneider, Gary Spahl, Scott Stanton, Troy Taylor, and Maureen Tivnan, as well as the generous and inventive members of Howl 2000 list on the Internet. Others lent their professional expertise to this project, for which I am grateful: Joan Bannatyne, Isaac Bonewits, The Halloween Association, the Humane Society of the United States, Sharon Marzano, J. Gordon Melton, the National Costume Association, Leonard Pickel, Rosemary Ruley-Atkins, Rochelle Santopoalo, Marcello Truzzi, the United States Committee for UNICEF, and last, but not at all least, Dr. Jeanne Keyes Youngson. But most of all, my thanks go to Gary Duehr, whose photographs document so many of our Halloween adventures, and whose thoughtful editing and help with images were essential.

Introduction

Halloween, 1961

I feel exquisitely beautiful. I'm wearing black tights and a leotard, two black-felt ears, and a four-foot-long tail made from a stocking stuffed with newspaper. I have on mittens and my mom's high heels. At eight years old, I'm radiant as I walk with my girlfriends in the smoky dusk of late October.

From out of nowhere Dennis Polaski appears, dressed in a black plastic cape tied Zorro-style. He grabs my head by my cat ears and kisses me. Right on the mouth. Then he's gone, howling, into the bushes that edge the split-level homes in suburban Connecticut.

It is breathtaking.

The girls shriek. I blush, teetering on the edge of Mrs. Kinney's porch steps, my heart pounding. Mrs. Kinney answers the door.

"Yes?"

"Trick-or-treat!" we holler.

She holds out a bowl of Turkish Taffy. My friends and I—a tangle of pink netting, blue eye shadow and pipe cleaners—wiggle through the door. The taffy is an offering, a sacrifice made to gods of Halloween to shield homeowners from the mischief of spirits for the next twelve months. We accept the bribe.

Moments later I'm tearing down the street towards home—hell on heels—clutching my brown paper bag and leaking bits of ripped newspaper through the holes in my tail.

Halloween is the best holiday, ever.

That's how I remember it anyway. First frost in the air, streetlights ringed with haze, the exquisite freedom of disguise. I didn't know then how many hundreds of generations had done these things, felt these things, before mine.

The roots of Halloween are as old as the solstice celebrations. The holiday began in Celtic lands as a fire festival honoring the ancestral dead known as Samhain (sow-en), or summer's end, held on November 1. The first day of winter was the start of the seasonal cycle, making Samhain the ancient Celtic New Year's Eve.

Samhain was believed to be the time ghosts were released from their graves. On the eve of Samhain, Celtic priests, called Druids, used divination to communicate with the spirit world. In the sacred oak groves of northern, pre-Christian Europe, they sacrificed animals and read the future in their entrails. They read omens in the sky, water, and fire to decipher the wisdom of a proposed migration, the right time to make magic, the cure for sickness. No one will ever know for certain the details of the Druids' rituals. But we do know that Halloween's association with ghosts, fire and fortunetelling probably began with these pagan tribes somewhere between two thousand and three thousand years ago.

Since Samhain fell around the same time as the Roman celebration of Pomona, goddess of orchards, the two festivals likely intermingled after Romans invaded Celtic lands. When Christianity swept through the Roman Empire, Celtic and Roman celebrations were recast in a Christian light and a series of church holidays eventually took the place of Samhain: All Hallows' or All Saints' Day (November 1), and, centuries later, All Souls' Day (November 2). All Hallows' Eve became All Hallowe'en, then simply Halloween.

The people of Ireland, Scotland, and Wales kept their ancient November eve traditions alive through age-old games and folkways. They used apples or nuts to divine the future rather than animals or omens in the sky, and asked the spirits about matters of love, rather than questions of survival.

The remembrances of All Saints' and All Souls' Days preserved the essence of Samhain—honoring the dead—throughout the Catholic countries in Europe, but the holidays met their demise in England during the Reformation, when all things Catholic were jettisoned by Protestants. This meant that Halloween was only a faint memory among the radical English Puritans who settled in the New World.

The immigrations of Scots and Irish in the eighteenth and nineteenth centuries brought the Celtic celebration of Halloween to the States. Other immigrant groups added their own cultural layers: the Germans, for example, brought an especially vivid witchcraft lore; Haitian and African blacks, voodoo beliefs about black cats, fire and witchcraft; and the English and Dutch, a love of masquerade.

By the nineteenth century, Halloween in America was as diverse as the young nation itself. In rural New Hampshire, there were barn dances, and in New York City, parades and firecrackers. In the mountains of Virginia, Halloween was when you could hear the future whispered in the wind; in Louisiana, it was time to cook a midnight "dumb supper" and watch for a ghost to join the table. Upper class Victorians reinvented the holiday as a social spectacle, more concerned with romance than death. When this all gave way to twentieth-century realism, Halloween was handed over to children. Its passion and romance metamorphosed into stolen kisses on hayrides recreated for children living in cities, and all that was left of Druidic divining was the fortunetelling booth at the school fair.

By the 1950s, Halloween was synonymous with trick or treating, and the next two decades were its American salad days: nearly every child in the nation celebrated Halloween both at school and in their neighborhood. Soon, adults were back on the scene, and by the 1990s Halloween had ballooned to the second largest retail holiday, right after Christmas. After more than two millennia, the holiday still captivates us.

A *Halloween How-To* sets out to get a snapshot of Halloween today, or rather, several, as the holiday has as many faces as a pumpkin patch in October. It's where you'll find answers to a myriad of Halloween questions: what is the difference between a goblin and a ghoul? Where can you find a decent set of fangs? What's Monster Mud? How do you stage a seance? What's a good recipe for fake blood? Pumpkin soup? Where can you see Elvira? Freddy Kruger's glove? A life-size replica of Frankenstein in his original movie costume?

In these pages you'll find hundreds of Halloween anecdotes, formulas, recipes, how-to's, history, and ideas. Ideas for costumes, parties, indoor and outdoor decorations, movies to rent, CDs to play, good food to cook, unique Halloween destinations and fun things to do. Besides how-to's and ideas for celebrating, *A Halloween How-To* also details what Halloween customs mean, where they come from, and what purpose they serve today, since how-to often leads to but—why?

Halloween 2000

This Halloween I watched a bulky, satyr-like figure walking—no, strolling—up Sixth Avenue in the Greenwich Village Halloween parade, nude. He'd painted his body silver and wore the giant head of a goat. The eyeholes were shining with red light as if there were fire inside his skull. The crowd cheered for him—a pagan icon recast in the glass and concrete of a modern city. The woman in front of me strained against the barriers to watch the naked goat god as he slowly faded into the night. Come next morning, for all we knew, he could be back selling coffee at Starbucks.

An hour later, I stood on a subway platform in Manhattan. A man next to me was wearing a set of wings and a sequined tiara that rose to twice the height of his head. On another day, he'd seem like a perverse Tinkerbell, but it was Halloween. On Halloween, he was beautiful.

"That's a terrific costume," I said.

He nodded demurely. "I love Halloween," he admitted. "Halloween is my last big fling before winter. It's like opening up the fireplugs in the summer."

I couldn't have said it better myself.

A
Halloween
HOW-TO

The Mizell home in Dewey, Oklahoma, where home haunting is a family affair. That's Ricky and Tammy Mizell out front with their daughter draped across the steps in their 1998 "Graveyard Seance" home haunt. Photo by Clifton Hall, Photographic Creations and Illustrations, Kansas City, Missouri.

CHAPTER ONE

Decorating Your House and Yard

How To Plan, Create, Decorate, Build And Light Your Home Haunt

In the early 1960s, when I was a kid of prime Halloween age, it was the night before Halloween we loved. Under cover of darkness, we would soap windows and ring doorbells. Sometimes we picked people we liked, but more often, we picked the crankiest neighbors because, like teasing a little brother, the bigger the reaction, the more fun it was. We were merciless. At some houses we'd ring the doorbell once, twice, up to ten times, hiding in between to watch the guy answering the door get angrier and angrier until at last he'd chase us down the street, the ultimate thrill. This was the kind of sweet victory that Mischief Night was all about.

Kids had power; adults, for once, did not. But things have changed. Now kids have a lot more power in general, and the real reversal at work is that adults, for once, are free to terrorize them. And they do. Each October, fully-grown men and women unpack their Styrofoam gargoyles and sigh, savoring last year's memories of trick-or-treaters running shrieking into the night, relishing this rare opportunity to misbehave.

> "Two weeks prior to Halloween I put up one witch. I call it Witching Day," says Tom Holman from Vancouver, Canada. "The neighbors really get into it. People start coming by the house, and the traffic really picks up. The next day I add two tombstones, and after that, two skeletons coming out of the ground. On the following day, the skeletons are sitting on the roof fishing and having a couple of beers. A day later, they're in the front yard waving to passersby. Three days before Halloween it starts to pick up when I add the gate and fence."

More and more people are spending hundreds of hours turning

used lumber and curbside trash into graveyards, laboratories, torture chambers and dungeons. Yard haunters love the creative aspect of decorating, the challenge of creating a total environment no matter how large or small their yard. These are the people who built dioramas as kids, the post-Dungeons and Dragons folks who like conjuring up fictional worlds, or the baby boomers looking to recreate Halloween as they once knew it. Home haunting hooks the theatrical, the gothic, the moms and dads with an interesting twist, or, some might say, twisted interests.

"When else can you put a serial killer in your yard?" asks Glenn Blinn, home haunting enthusiast, with a grin.

Some spend months planning and executing their decorations, teasing their neighborhoods with pieces and parts of the display, all the while reserving the really big surprises for Halloween night alone.

> "Our house has been closed to anyone but immediate family since August 30," says Ralph Mitchell of Indiana, who has a very strict schedule for his Halloween festivities. "The inside work has been going on since then. The outside mechanics will be done by mid-September. The graveyard fencing and gates should be ready to install by October 1. Strobe ghosts and tombstones follow shortly after. Witches circling over the house will be finished by the second week of October. Flying yard ghosts and outside FCG (flying crank ghost), third week. House-sized spider, the last week in October."

Halloween yard decorators have discovered what Hollywood knows in its dark little soul, if it has one: Americans love a story. Private yard haunts often have a theme or story that ties the decorations together. A couple in Roseville, California ran a bogus alien invasion news story on a video outside their home haunt, then led visitors through the spacecraft they created in their yard. A myth about a sleeping dragon who wakes on Halloween to take one soul, then sleeps again, weaves through the Dragon's Head Inn, Kathy and Mike Marcrum's Sonoma, California haunt. Gary Corb's Hallowed Haunting Grounds in Studio City, California, draws inspiration from T.S. Eliot's *The Wasteland,* where images of spiritless, lost souls are strung together like a tone poem: the ghost of a tiny child calls for her parents, a freshly dug grave inhales and exhales. Motorized mechanics, film projectors, lighting, fog machines, and a host of other film industry toys make people compare this yard to Disneyland or Hollywood movies. However, for Corb and friends, it's all for fun.

There are many answers as to why home haunters do what they

do. They love the creativity. They love the excitement it stirs up. They love to build things. Or they've been doing it since they were thirteen and just can't stop. "For the kids," comes up the most.

Take Debra Eyman-Whitehead from Manchester, Washington, for example. Where most decorators stake out October 1 as the official start to the season, Debra waits until the school bus goes by on Halloween morning. Then she spends the entire day working on her yard. When the same bus comes back that afternoon, she watches the kids' faces as they see her house, transformed as if by magic, with tombstones, flying bats, fairy lights, monsters, and ghosts. She takes the whole thing down late Halloween night and come morning, all is as before.

> "My husband sets up his telescope in the yard and lets people look at the night sky," says Monica Brown, yard haunter from New Mexico. "The response we get is overwhelming, with people often standing in line to take a peek. We've had people get their first look at the moon and planets while standing in our driveway with a full bag of candy."

Kid-wise, yard decorating has an almost instant payoff: trick or treaters flock to home haunts, especially if the yard has been decorated several years in a row and everyone knows about it. Homes that once got fifteen to twenty kids, for example, draw two to three hundred once word gets around. And one good Halloween haunt on the street tends to encourage others, making for a great Halloween street, more trick or treaters, and a more fun celebration for everyone.

The growth of Halloween decorating reflects a booming economy, to be sure. But if the economy were the only factor, Halloween decorations would not only be as plentiful as Christmas, but also as thematically consistent. They're not. There's a weirdness in Halloween yard décor that's truly unique to this holiday and no other. As Halloween scholar Jack Santino said in an interview with the *Detroit Free Press*: "It's the one time of year we recognize the forces that are beyond our control. If people were to put out those decorations any other time of year, the neighbors would call the cops." [1]

Planning Your Yard Haunt

Where you begin depends on who you are. Maybe you're a collage artist at heart, and the only way you can decorate is to throw all the skeletons, pumpkins, cobwebs and writhing rats into a pile in the front yard and monkey with it until it looks right. Or maybe you like to plan, brainstorm—some might even say scheme. In that case, think of your yard as a short series of scenes, much like a play.

First, the introduction. What draws kids in to your house? Extra lighting? Sound effects playing from a speaker in your upstairs window? The light of a dozen jack-o-lanterns? A cobweb gate or fence around your yard?

Then the rising action, used in drama to build tension: what happens along the sidewalk or path to your door. As they come up the sidewalk, what do they see and hear (or almost see or think they hear)? Did something just move in that upstairs window? What was that behind the tree? What's coming up out of the ground? Are those shadowy bats, spiders, or rats in the corner . . . real?

Now, the climax: they ring the doorbell and what happens? Anything right away, or does suspense build? Who answers the door and how? What is that in the candy bowl . . . what's moving just inside the front door, and what's that *CRASH* . . .

The falling action is, in drama, a resolution of conflict: why they did what to whom. For your Halloween home haunt, think of the falling action as what happens as the trick-or-treaters head off your porch and out of the yard. By now they're talking about you and starting to think about the next house. An ideal opportunity for one last trick! What was that *sound?* Where'd *he* come from? Did you feel *that?*

The conclusion ties up the plot and seals the characters' fates. As the kids leave your house, what do you want them to remember?

Come back next year. Bring your friends.

Home Haunting How To's

WALKWAY IDEAS

We set up a fence around the entrance to the yard so that everyone was forced to walk down the path we created. There were five live actors. The first was dressed all in black, wearing this creepy devil mask (I mean really creepy). He actually scared away five would-be trick-or-treaters before they even got within five feet of him! The second was dressed as a dummy with loose clothing and a large ill-fitting mask. This person controlled a buzzer. As people walked past, "BZZZZZZZZ!" We got more screams from that gag than from anything else. Three trick-or-treaters actually dropped their bags and ran away. We had to chase them down to give their candy back to them.

—Michael Hios, Lexington, Massachusetts

Make this wreath with a pair of socks and old boots, a garland of autumn leaves and a few strings of Halloween lights. Photo by Gary Duehr.

Spook Walk   —Courtesy of Jeff Quaglietta, Haverhill, Massachusetts

While many homeowners in this tight grid of suburban streets are happy to display pumpkins and cornstalks, things are a little different at the house that belongs to Jeff and Lisa Quaglietta. Their yard, an ordinary span of green grass and trees throughout most of the year, sprouts a six-foot-tall cemetery fence during October. A life-size skeleton sways from a tree branch over a few dank tombstones. Look closer. There's a phosphorescent ghost beckoning from the downstairs window. A witch on the rooftop slowly rotates her head to glare at you. Out of the corner of your eye, you catch a flickering light. Pumpkins! Jack-o-lanterns that seem to float in space, making a trail that leads around the side of the house and into the deep darkness of the backyard.

"When I first began envisioning my Halloween display, I had the concept of a walkway that guests could follow that not only controlled where they would go, but also contributed to the overall effect," says Jeff. "On the day after Halloween I would scour local department stores and buy whatever fake pumpkins they had left over, since everything was half-off. I was finally able to accumulate fifty of them." The path keeps the guests contained and, Jeff cautions, "as long as they follow the pumpkin faces, they make it out alive."

Materials (makes ten pumpkin posts; adjust up or down for what you need):

30-ft. of 1½" PVC pipe (an inexpensive plastic pipe used for plumbing) cut into ten 3-ft. lengths

20 PVC end caps to fit the pipe size (10 for the top, 10 for the base)

ten 1-ft. x 1-ft. squares of plywood for bases

ten 12" nail spikes (to anchor base in ground)

Screws, nuts, and bolts

50-ft. of extension cord

Ten electric foam pumpkins

Grounded outdoor extension cords

• Make 2" x ¼" notches at the top and bottom of the 3-ft. length of PVC pipe (Figure 1).

• Screw a 1½" PVC end cap onto a wooden base. Secure another end cap to the bottom of the pumpkin. This can be done with glue; however, attaching them with a nut and bolt will hold much better (Figure 2).

• Feed the power cord for the pumpkin down through the PVC (Figure 3).

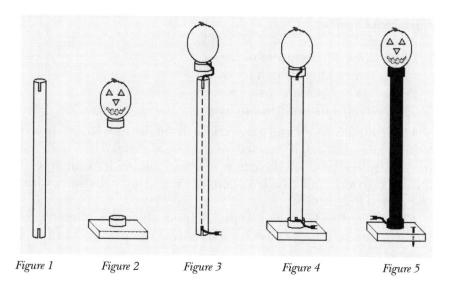

Figure 1   Figure 2   Figure 3   Figure 4   Figure 5

• Place the PVC pipe into the end cap on the wooden base with the power cord passing through the notch. Place the pumpkin on top of the PVC pipe with the power cord passing through the notch. The pumpkin and base should be aligned with the notches to the rear (Figure 4).

• Paint the post black. Oil-based paints tend to work better on PVC since they will not scrape off as easily. Drill a hole in the wooden base and secure the post to the ground with a 12" nail spike (Figure 5). Plug the pumpkin into an extension cord.

Important: Make sure you use heavy-duty, grounded, outdoor extension cords and plug them into a grounded (3-hole) outlet.

Shop Vac Surprise

This trick is inspired by the leaf-blower scare created by Malcolm Little and Ed Otero.

Duct tape a hose extension onto a shop vac and hide the machine around a corner of your house. Hide the hose with leaves or bushes and bury the end in a big pile of leaves. Put the vac on blower mode and plug it into a power strip that you can turn on and off from inside your house. When you see a group of trick or treaters about to pass by, turn on the switch! The noise, leaves and air will take them completely by surprise. Again, be sure to use heavy-duty, outdoor, grounded extension cords. And make sure the hose stays on the ground, aimed at their ankles, to be safe.

Halloween Luminary

Materials:

Large can, coffee can size or larger
Awl or large nail to punch holes
Primer, gloss black and orange paints
Thin wire, for hanging luminaries

• Strip off any labels and glue residue from the can. Draw a jack-o-lantern face with magic marker on the outside. Make big, bold features: simple is best. Fill the can with water and put it in the freezer until it's frozen solid (the ice keeps the can from collapsing when you punch holes in it).

• Use an awl and hammer to punch holes along the marked lines about ³/₄" apart. Punch holes for a handle if you plan to hang your luminary.

• Let the ice melt. Dry the can.

• Paint or spray both the inside and outside of the can with primer (read the paint can labels to make sure it adheres to metal).

• Once it dries, paint the inside of the can gloss black. Paint the outside orange. Paint gloss black inside the eyes, nose and mouth, and let it dry.

• Spray (outside, please!) with polyurethane or any brand of clear coating. Dry, then spray again.

For hanging luminaries, cut a length of wire and thread it through the handle holes. Knot the ends, and wrap any sharp points of the wire with tape. For standing luminaries, pour a little sand or kitty litter into the bottom of the can to give it some weight. Place a votive candle inside and light!

Tricks with Treats: the Candy Bowl

I used to put two card tables side by side with enough room between them for me to fit my fist through. I covered the front and top of both tables with a paper tablecloth and cut a small slit in it so I could poke my hand out. The candy bowl was right behind that. When kids came to the door, I got under the table and pulled the door open with a string. They would just look at the bowl for a while, not knowing what to do, then I'd pop my hand through the slit with a Turkish taffy in it! Most of them would laugh, but I did scare some kids.

—Home haunter in Arlington, Massachusetts

Think of your candy bowl as center stage in a drama. Decorate the table it sits on: try dead flowers, books with creepy titles, candles,

An altar made entirely from items purchased at garage sales greets visitors on Halloween at the Haunted Chamber, an elaborate home haunt near Pittsburgh. The Chamber combines story line, sleight of hand, and mind reading effects to scare visitors. Photo courtesy of DeceptionsUnlimited.

skulls or bones, instruments of torture (rusty tools are great) or objects used for divination like crystal balls or tarot cards. Set the stage for the bowl of treats.

The Galloping Ghoulish Gourmet's Body Part Buffet

Since 1986, Dr. Rochelle Santopoalo has been creating a grotesque fantasy in her yard each Halloween. The first year she had just a few things: a dummy's arms and legs busting out of the dirt, some spooky music, and spotlights trained on a few handmade tombstones. She and her brother dressed up and animated the scene. Word spread quickly, and about one hundred trick-or-treaters came by that night. One year later, she got close to four hundred kids and there was a line outside her yard to get in.

The good doctor created a special Halloween persona for herself: the Galloping Ghoulish Gourmet. The buffet includes Jell-O molds of a brain, heart, and hands ("I like to put a ring on the finger—it adds creepiness"). It also features intestines from the local butcher ("you've got to throw in one thing that's real"), bottled toe jam (peanut butter, cottage cheese and applesauce in a jar), and a host of other hideous delectables.

Try assembling any or all of these on your porch this year, put your candy bowl smack dab in the center of the buffet, serve up your candy and see what happens.

Animating the Porch and Yard   —Bob Cronin, Boston, Massachusetts

"One Halloween, my cousin Pete dressed up one of those dummies people make out of stuffed clothes and put on their porches to decorate. He wore jeans, a plaid shirt, and work boots, all stuffed with newspaper. Then he put a paper bag on his head, with a face drawn on it, and sat on the front porch next to the candy bowl. He taped a note to the bowl that said, "Please help yourself," but when kids did, he'd grab their arms. There's a girl in his neighborhood who still won't speak to him."

Scared-Stiff Fluorescent Ghosts

These are "life-size." It takes about a half-hour to make one, start to finish.

Materials:

An old bed sheet

Bottle of liquid starch

Rit Laundry Whitener (makes the cloth fluoresce under black light)

Felt or marker (for the face)

Foil

Plastic bags

Metal coat hanger

Black light bulb

• Stuff a plastic bag full of other plastic bags to form a head-sized ball. Cover it with a layer of aluminum foil so that the ball keeps its shape.

• Untwist a coat hanger, but leave the hook intact to hang the ghost. Push the coat hanger down through the head, then bend it outward in a triangle to form shoulders.

• Find the center of the sheet and cut a small hole in it. Pour several capfuls of Rit Laundry Whitener into a bucket, then add a whole bottle of liquid starch. Soak the sheet in the starch mixture for about five minutes, then wring it out.

• Thread the hook through the center hole of the sheet and drape it over the head and shoulders. Hang the hook on a clothesline and pin the ghost's "arms" to the line. The sheet will dry stiff as a corpse.

- Use paint or markers to make a face, or cut eyes and mouth out of black felt and glue them on.
- Place the ghost close to a black light.

Hint: Hang these somewhere they won't get wet. Rain will rinse out all the starch and your ghost will dissolve back into into a lifeless, soggy bed sheet.

Body Parts in Unlikely Places

You can have fun with these props just about anywhere. Stuff an old pair of pants with newspaper, two-liter plastic bottles, Styrofoam peanuts, plastic bags, or rags. Pin or hot glue socks to the legs of the pants, stuff them as well, and tie on a pair of old shoes. Or stuff an old shirt and attach a pair of stuffed gloves.

- Attach legs to the bottom of your automatic garage door so that they ride up and down each time you trigger it.
- Hang legs from your upstairs window, as if somebody's gotten stuck halfway in.
- Close legs in the trunk of your car and drive around with them all day.
- Close a stuffed arm in the passenger window of your car.
- Stuff a glove and tape it to the inside of your mailbox, reaching out.
- Stuff a garden glove with newspaper and bury it halfway down in a flowerpot as if it's breaking through the dirt. Or, partially bury a mask in the pot.
- Stuff a life-like latex mask with plastic bags to add some dimension, then run a garden hose behind it and let a trickle of water spill out from the mouth, gargoyle-style. Rig the set-up over your front door.

Chuck's Cauldron—Courtesy of Chuck Rice, Campbell, California

Chuck has been haunting his front yard for only a few years. He builds things all year long, but like many other home haunters, does not set anything up in front of his house until October 1. Then he installs his tableaux piece by piece throughout the month to build anticipation for the big day.

Materials:
Real logs
Red and yellow cellophane paper
White holiday lights

Chuck's cauldron. Photo by Chuck Rice.

Plastic cauldron
Plastic skeleton (about 3-ft. tall)
Length of cheap black nylon fabric to shroud the skeleton
Black light bulb
Two yellow highlighter pens
Flashlight or glow stick
Dozen Ping-Pong balls
Thumbtacks, hardware nuts, water-resistant glue

• Start with the fire: stack real logs, like in a fireplace. Crinkle red and yellow cellophane paper and tuck it among the logs. Thumbtack the cellophane if you need to. Loop a string of white holiday lights in, around and through the cellophane to animate the fire.

• Buy a plastic cauldron from the Halloween section at any large store or order one from a catalog (see Resources).

• Fill the cauldron with water. Break open a couple of yellow highlighter markers and dump them in. Screw in a black light bulb nearby to make the water glow green.

• Paint or draw eyes on a dozen Ping-Pong balls and glue a hardware nut (as in nuts and bolts) on the back side so the eyes are weighted to float looking up at you. Goop-brand glue will work for this, and so will Super Glue.

• Hang the skeleton over the cauldron. Tape a flashlight or glow stick to the inside of the rib cage.

• Drape a swatch of cheap, black, see-through nylon fabric around the skeleton as a kind of grim reaper robe with a hood. The light should shine through the fabric to silhouette the skeleton ribs. You can also buy cheap, black, child-size robes in the Halloween section of most stores—the cheaper the better, because you need to see through it.

• Light the scene very dimly, or not at all. The holiday lights under the cauldron, the black light, and rib cage light should carry the illusion. To add sound, plant a speaker nearby and play a tape of a bubbling pot; record your own tape loop by blowing air through a straw into a glass of water.

Last year we used our neighbor's baby monitor and put it at the entrance to our haunted yard. A grim reaper character would talk to the kids and get them to say their names and where they were from. During their walk through our yard, the person hiding in the shed would call out their names (overheard through the monitor). He was talking through flex pipe, so it made his voice sound like he was talking from a deep tunnel and sounded really eerie.

—Lindalee Flessas, home haunter

Dancing Lawn Ghosts
—Spotted on a lawn in Arlington, Massachusetts

These just make you smile. They look especially mischievous grouped around a tree, birdbath or lamppost.

Materials:

Two old bed sheets, cut in half to make four pieces

Four ¾" diameter 3-ft. wooden dowels

Duct tape

Plastic grocery bags for stuffing

String and black marker

• Wad up several plastic grocery bags inside one plastic bag to make a head shape.

• Duct tape this head to the top of a wooden dowel.

• Cover the whole structure with a piece of white bed sheet and tie a string around the neck. Draw on a face.

• Make three more.

• Mark four spots on the ground. If the ground is soft, you can drive each dowel right in the earth. If you have harder ground, pound a stake or metal rebar into the lawn, then tape each mounted ghost to the spike with duct tape. Angle the dowel to make the ghost lean back a bit.

• Knot the ghosts' arms together as if they're holding hands in a circle.

The Crashed Witch
—Courtesy of Sue and Dan Oelke, Elk River, Minnesota

You may have seen her smashed into a telephone pole, porch, or tree. The black hat's a bit bent; her arms and legs akimbo. She's Wile E. Coyote plastered against a cliff in that one long moment before he falls to the rocks below. Although you can buy one at a Halloween store these days, the crashed witch can easily be made by hand and, in my opinion, looks much more realistic.

Materials:

Two 1-ft. x 2-ft. boards for legs, each cut to 38" long

Two 1-ft. x 2-ft. boards for arms, cut to 28" long

One board for the backbone, cut to 34" long by however wide you need it; this board must be slightly wider than the pole you are

Sue and Dan Oelke built this crashed witch for a telephone pole near their home in Elk River, Minnesota. Photo by Sue Oelke.

working with, so that the witch's legs can fit on either side
Pair of long gloves (any kind)
Pair of long striped socks
Old black dress
Store-bought witch's hat
Old broom
Wig or skein of yarn for hair
Saw, hammer, coat hangers, glue and nails

• To make the feet, untwist a coat hanger and bend the wire into a U shape. Duct tape it to the end of the leg (38") board. Make two.

• Bend a piece of coat hanger wire into the shape of a hand and duct tape it to the end of the arm (28") board. Make two.

• Glue/screw the legs to the sides of the backbone board at the bottom corners and the arms to the top corners.

• Fill each glove with a little stuffing and staple a glove to each arm.

• Fill each sock with a little stuffing and staple a sock to each leg.

• Slit the old black dress up the front center and wrap it around the witch structure. Staple it back together in the front. Make sure it's long enough and big enough to cover the frame.

• Nail the whole structure to your pole, or, if you're working with a metal pole, strap the backbone to the pole with long cable ties.

• Arrange the broom so that half sticks out behind your witch and half in front; nail or tie the broomstick to the pole.

• Staple the wig to the top of the backbone.

• Stuff the witch's hat with fiberfill or plastic bags so that it retains its pointy shape. Staple or wire the hat to the pole so that it sits on top of the wig.

TURN OFF THE LIGHTS

Darkness is at the heart of Halloween. People who haunt their yards will tell you the less light, the better. Never underestimate the ambient glare of a nearby street lamp or the reflective halo of a big city. It's brighter than you think out there. Keep your lights as low as you possibly can to be safe, and it will give the effects you create more punch. Shadows, black light, and colored light can all add a lot of drama to your yard.

Shadow Plays

Turn your front windows into a shadow theater. Pull down the shades, hang a skeleton, bat, or any Halloween prop in the window, and turn the room lights on. As long as the object is between the light and the shade, you'll have a silhouette when it gets dark. Get bizarre, if you like, and hang knives, chains, rag dolls, or any of the morbid objects you would find in an Edward Gorey book.

Using Black Light

With a black light (also called an ultraviolet light, found at a building supply or party store), many effects are possible. You can make ghosts come alive by soaking the cloth first in extra-strength laundry detergent powder (the bluing agent makes them fluoresce) and hanging the ghosts close to a black light. You can also use Rit Laundry Whitener/Brightener, mixed with water, on any fabric or surface you want to glow under black light (this will stain, so be careful you don't get any on your hands, or they'll glow too). Water it down in a spray bottle and coat cobwebs and tombstones, or write with the solution on the sidewalk. The words will look normal under ordinary light, but as soon as you add the ultraviolet light, they'll glow. And anything covered with fluorescent or luminous paints will glow.

Black lights are available in bulbs or tubes: the bulbs don't give off much light, but they're cheap. The tubes cost more, but are more efficient, burn cooler, and produce a stronger light. Which you need depends on how large an area you want to cover.

Hint: Black lights burn hotter than ordinary bulbs. Be careful handling them, and keep them out of direct contact with flammables.

Monsters and Tombstones

Monster Mud

Anyone thinking of building his or her own large-scale yard decorations should know about Monster Mud, an inexpensive joint compound mixture that dries into a hard and durable shell. Home haunters use this stuff to build a myriad of monsters and props they can use year after year: cauldrons, tombstones, grim reapers, and even faces in the trees.

People generally agree on this recipe:

• One gallon latex house paint, the cheapest and darkest you can find. It can be indoor, outdoor, gloss, semigloss or flat; it depends on how you want your project to look.

Hint: Ask your paint clerk for mis-mixed paints. They usually sell them extra cheap and, if you ask, will make the paint black for free.

• Five-gallon bucket of premixed joint compound from a hardware or building supply store.

The recipe is 5:1 mainly because the materials are usually sold in 5-gallon and 1-gallon buckets; 4:1 works equally well and you can use a 1-gallon bucket of joint compound and 1-quart of paint when building smaller creations.

To build a monster, you'll need chicken wire (the kind with small openings, 1" or smaller) to make the armature, and burlap to cover the wire. Burlap can be scrounged from a supermarket or bought at the gardening department of a building supply store, which is also where you'll find chicken wire. Here's a how-to for building monsters drawn from the experience of home haunter Michael Hios:

• Mold and bend the chicken wire into the shape of your monster or prop.

• Mix the paint and joint compound in a bucket until slightly runny.

• Cut burlap into 1-ft. x 2-ft. pieces. Saturate the burlap in Mud, strip off the excess (just like working with newspaper strips for papier-

mâché), and put the wet burlap on the chicken wire frame.

> "Burlap doesn't necessarily need to be cut into strips," says Hios. "Sometimes I cover my chicken wire armature with burlap, using wire ties to secure the burlap to the frame, and then add Monster Mud with either a paint brush or my hands. This is especially helpful when working with very large creations. I built two 7-ft.-tall grim reapers and this method probably saved me about eight hours. I also like it because once the burlap is attached, you get a better idea of what the finished creation is going to look like."

You can color Monster Mud by mixing in other latex paints, but hues are muted. Paint the sculpture after it's hardened for better color results. By using "rubberized" floor paint, you can add the color and a protectant in one step.

To waterproof Monster Mud creations, cover them with polyurethane (spray or paint outside—polyurethane is toxic!) or any clear acrylic spray in a matte or satin finish.

Tombstones

—Courtesy of Scott Messinger, home haunter and fake tombstone artist from Plano, Texas

They're like the training wheels of home haunting—most avid Halloween yard decorators started with a few tombstones in the front yard. They're relatively quick to make, store pretty easily, and can last for years. There are two basic types: foam and plywood.

Foam Tombstones

Use DOW brand insulating foam board. This is the pink or blue material used for house insulation and is sold in building supply stores. It comes in 4 x 8-ft. sheets; buy the thickest you can find.

Make your tombstones as tall and wide as you want. You can cut the foam* with any thin, sharp blade. Good foam cutting tools can be found in craft and hobby stores, as can the "Wonder Cutter," a battery-powered tool that cuts with a hot wire.

If you can only find thin foam, glue three layers together using scrap pieces from around the edges for the inner layers. You can fill the partially hollow middle with expanding insulating foam from a can (again, you need to be outside and away from all flames—follow the label instructions!). Use any waterproof glue such as Liquid Nails (many glues will eat away the foam, so check the label to make sure the glue is waterproof and can be used on foam board). Fill in any cracks on the outside with wood putty. Use 120 grit sandpaper to smooth the wood putty and finish shaping the foam. You can also use a block of the same foam to smooth the cut edges.

To attach your tombstones to the ground, you can also use any sort of metal spike—like a tomato stake—that you press into the ground then up into the tombstone. Be careful, as too many holes will weaken the foam. If your tombstones are made of foam layers: (1) cut a channel out of the middle layer, (2) insert a length of PVC pipe into the channel, (3) pound two lengths of ½" rebar into the ground, and (4) slip the PVC pipe over the rebar.

The advantage of foam tombstones is that they're lightweight. The disadvantage is they're lightweight—if wind and rain are common in your part of the country, and if your tombstones need to stand up for more than a week or two, you might be interested in plywood tombstones.

*Important: Don't cut foam indoors. It's toxic and very harmful to inhale. Always cut Styrofoam in a well-ventilated place like an open garage or yard and wear a good quality breather mask.

Plywood Tombstones

The advantage of plywood is that mice don't eat it over the winter, and your tombstones could last a good ten years. However, you must be skilled with a jigsaw.

Cut tombstone shapes from ½" plywood with a jigsaw. Screw two pieces of pipe strap (U-shaped metal straps with screw holes on either side) to the back of the plywood "stone." Drive two spikes or poles of any sort into the ground, and slip the plywood "stone" right over it, fitting the poles into the pipe strap.

Painting Tombstones

On wooden tombstones, you can sponge-paint a granite texture. Use a sea sponge (from a craft or building supply store) and mix three shades of gray from dark to light. Sponge on the darkest color first and let the paint dry. Do the medium color next, let dry, then do the lightest color. Repeat until you get the effect of granite-speckled stone. Paint a black shadow along the top and one side to give the illusion of depth.

On foam stones, the kind of paint you use is important. An oil-based paint will eat away the foam for a weathered look—try it first on a scrap to see if you like the effect. Auto primer will also slightly melt the foam, and looks good if you prime the top, sides, and front of the stone. Water-based latex paints will not break down the foam and are good for lettering.

You can also paint your tombstones (wooden or foam) with a mixture of half white textured ceiling paint and half gray latex house paint for a convincing look and feel. Covering the stones with Monster Mud will also work, and because there's paint in the mixture you won't need to paint them again. Paint and Monster Mud both work as weatherproofing under most conditions, and water-based polyurethane will give extra protection if you need it.

Hint: If your insulation board has a plastic film on it, peel it off before you paint.

Tombstone Epitaphs

You can carve, paint freehand, or use a computer to write epitaphs on your tombstones.

To carve an epitaph into a foam tombstone, write the letters first with a marker. Then cut *V*-shaped grooves on each letter using a sharp hobby knife. Many folks recommend a rotary or "Dremel" tool (a small, hand-held device like a fat screwdriver that rotates interchangeable tips). Once you've carved the letters, darken the inside of each one with black paint. Remember: carve foam outside.

For typeset tombstones, use a computer to print out your epitaph in a large font (it may take several 8½" x 11" sheets tiled together, depending on the size of your tombstone). Glue the epitaph to the foam with a light coating of spray adhesive, then carve the letters through the paper. Peel off the paper and voila!

If knives and power tools give you pause, create your epitaphs on either foam or plywood with a wide paintbrush.

Lighting Your Tombstones

Use spotlights, flashlights, floodlights, any outdoor light, but location is everything. Light the stones from the side, or from very low to the ground in front. Or carve a nice, big hole in the back of a jack-o-lantern and station it so that it throws an otherworldly, flickering light on your stone.

Ideas for Epitaphs

These have been compiled from graveyards, history books, and the imaginations of friends and home haunters (see Resources for more epitaph sources).

Humorous Epitaphs

She always said her feet were
   killing her
But nobody believed her.
Sh-h-h

I.B.Crisp
Fixed the toaster with a knife
And got the shock of his short
   life.
—Courtesy of Scott Messinger

Here lies the resting place
Of Abraham Lincoln.
Took his wife to a musical,
What was he thinkin?

Here lies
A French existentialist.
Pass by unless
You know what is, is.

Pass by
And fear no harm,
I am not here
I bought the farm.

Remember always
To smell the roses,
If you dig here
Hold your noses.

What is life
But a shadow?
And what is death
But a really big shadow?

Here lies Lizzy Borden's father
And here
And here
And here.

I told you I was sick.
Your name here.

C. Dracula
1236
1458
1527
1703
1823
2001

Here lies Jonathan Yeast.
Pardon me for not rising.

Here lies Kelly
We buried him today,
He lived the life of Riley
When Riley was away.

Here lies an atheist.
All dressed up and nowhere to
   go.

Here lies Butch
We planted him raw,
Quick on the trigger
But slow on the draw.

Proper Names:

Restin Pieces
Barry M. Deep
Ben Dover
Candy B. Goode
Dawn Under

Barry Dembones
Dianne Rott
Robin Graves
Justin Pieces
Otta B. Alive

Will B. Back
Willy Rott
Yule B. Next
Ted N. Buried
Yetta Nother
Dr. Izzy Gone

Fester N. Rott
I.M. Outtahere
Just Restin
Asa Wormturns
A. Lotta Dust

Poetic Epitaphs:

Cast a cold eye
On life, on death
Horseman, pass by!

Death is a debt to nature due,
Which I have paid, and so must
    you.

Dear happy days, forever fled
I too must wither, and be dead.

Remember man, as you walk by
As you are now, so once was I.
As I am now, you soon will be
Prepare for death and follow me.

And the response:
To follow you I'll not consent
Until I know which way you went.

Hope for the Last Minute Haunter

Run out of time? Didn't think about Halloween until it was too late to get to the store? It doesn't take much effort to transform your house and yard into a "Halloween House" that kids will remember. Here are last-minute yard haunting ideas that take less than an hour to accomplish.

• Never underestimate the power of the imagination. Just lighting your porch with jack-o-lanterns and opening your front door extra s-l-o-w-l-y can send some trick-or-treaters over the edge. Answer the door in a mask or costume and ham it up. Turn off all the lights in the house and answer the door with a flashlight.

• Find your creepiest music tape or CD and play it from a car parked in the driveway, loud. Crack the car windows and lock the doors to keep your equipment safe.

• Pull down your shades and move a lamp close to each one. Hang objects that will make spooky silhouettes: knives or cardboard bat shapes.

• Run an extension cord out of your house and place a flood light at the base of a tree, pointing upward. It will cast weird shadows and give the tree a very menacing look. If you have a colored floodlight, all the better.

• Don't use the front door. Lead trick-or-treaters around to the back door (if it's darker or spookier) with luminaries, jack-o-lanterns, or even a string of holiday lights. Lead them to a basement window or garage, and hand out treats from there.

• Hang yellow caution tape (available from building supply stores) around your yard as if it's a crime scene. Draw outlines of bodies in chalk on the pavement near your house or driveway. You'll be surprised how creepy these simple sketches can be.

One Final Note on Safety

As a homeowner, you are responsible and liable for your guests. Light your steps sensibly; cordon off areas of your yard where you don't want folks to walk. You may need to guide groups of kids or guard your props in person to ensure that trick-or-treaters are safe from tripping, especially if they're distracted by your decorations.

CHAPTER TWO

A Pumpkin Primer

Everything You Need To Know
About Pumpkins

For those who are curious about the pompion, the gros melon, the curcurbitacae, the giant orange orb, here's everything you need to know about pumpkins: why we carve them, how to carve them, and how to protect, preserve, light, photograph, display, and, not least, cook them.

Pumpkin FAQs

Why Do We Carve Pumpkins?

The jack-o-lantern has origins in history, folklore, and even science. Like many Halloween symbols, its origins intertwine like tendrils of smoke from a snuffed out candle.

The carved face is, at bottom, the face of death. It goes back at least to the Middle Ages, to when they say folks in the British Isles lopped off the top of a turnip, hollowed out the insides, carved a skeletal face, and lit a flame inside. It was an icon for the dead, for spirits present in the dark, or for souls released from Christian purgatory or hell.

Country folk came to use these lanterns to protect their homes against malicious spirits. They also carried them to ward off demons in the dark when they went out visiting on the Eve of All Hallows. If you glimpsed a flickering, fierce-faced lantern through a copse of trees, it was likely a group of neighbors making their rounds.

But a flickering light in the distance had another connotation in earlier times. Curious lights were witnessed out in the bogs and fermenting swamplands; lights that appeared rootless, wandering, like

Chadds Ford Pumpkin Carve, 1998. Photo by Al Webber, Sr., courtesy of the Chadds Ford Historical Society.

damned souls locked out of both grave and grace. These lights, called among other things, will o' the wisp, corpse candle, spittle of the stars, Jack with a lantern, Jack ma' lantern, or just Jack, were believed to trick men into bogs and holes. This jack-o-lantern was swamp gas.

> A wandering fire,
> Compact of unctuous vapour, which the night
> Condenses, and the cold environs round,
> Kindled through agitation to a flame,
> Which oft, they say, some evil spirit attends
> Hovering and blazing with delusive light.
> Misleads th' amazed night-wand'rer from his way
> To bogs and mires, and oft through pond or pool.
> There swallow'd up and lost from succour far."
>   —Milton, *Paradise Lost* (1667)

Ignis fatuus, or foolish fire, is a spontaneous combustion of gas that produces an otherworldly light, usually around marshlands, old churchyards and rivers; anywhere rich, composting soil is found. The burning gas rises out of the warm, wet muck, meets colder air, and is buffeted on wind currents. Travelers would mistake the light for that of a distant window, head towards it, and end up lost in the swamp. In poetry and folklore, this phenomenon refers to both an elusive light and the idea of being led astray or tricked.

Some folks said the light was a soul from purgatory, while others said it was an omen; sightings of will o' the wisps could mean imminent death. In the American South, you could protect yourself from the light's spell by turning your pockets inside out, or by stabbing a knife in the ground. Stories about this jack-o-lantern pre-date any regular celebration of Halloween in America.

The Legend of Tricky Jack

In Irish folklore, the jack-o-lantern took on the persona of Jack, who, like the flickering will o' the wisp, was a trickster. Jack was a nasty, small-minded sot who was drinking at a bar when the Devil came through the door. He was after Jack, whose time was up, but Jack convinced the Devil to have one last drink with him before they went off to Hell. The Devil obliged, and afterwards, Jack went to pay. He had no money. The Devil had no money. Jack convinced the Devil to change himself into a sixpence—just for a moment—so that he could pay for their drinks. The Devil did it. Jack grabbed the sixpence, stuffed it into a coin purse with a cross on the catch, and trapped the Devil. Jack promised to let him go if he promised not to come back for his soul for ten years, and the Devil made the deal.

Jack felt safe. After all, he thought, I'll surely sober up by then. I'll reform, and God won't let me go to Hell.

In ten years, nothing changed. Jack was walking down a dirt road and the Devil appeared, ready once more to take him away. Jack agreed to go, but just as he was about to take the Devil's hand, he pointed up to the apples in a nearby tree.

Those would taste awfully good, Jack told the Devil, especially on a long trip. The Devil squinted at the apples, which were in fact delicious-looking, and bolted up the tree to pick a few. Jack carved the sign of the cross on the trunk with his pocketknife. The Devil, once more, was trapped. This time Jack made him promise to never come for him again. And again, the Devil made the deal.

After another few years, Jack's body wore out. His heart stopped and his bones collapsed. His soul rose and went to Heaven, but they would have nothing to do with him. He traveled to Hell, but the

Devil glared at him and bolted the gates. The Devil had promised not to come for him, and he was going to keep that promise.

"Get out!" barked the Devil, and threw Jack a lump of burning coal to light his way back to earth.

So Jack wanders, to this day, welcome nowhere, with only an ember from Hell to light his way.

The essence of a trickster may still be there in the winking eyes and crooked grin of American jack-o-lanterns. But our modern carved pumpkin doesn't wander, lost between worlds on Halloween. It sits on the front steps as a welcome, more like the lanterns of the early Celts—a beacon in the window to frighten off evil spirits and lead friendly ones home to visit a while.

From the First to the Biggest

Native Americans taught white European settlers how to raise pumpkins. Colonial farmers in New England used them as a junk crop; they planted pumpkins on leftover land and used the fruit to feed the animals (pumpkins are genetically related to pickles and melons and are technically fruits, not vegetables).

Different climates account for differences in pumpkins: some orange, some yellow or white; some tiny, some large, and some very, very large. Pumpkin breeding has been going on since the beginning of cultivation, and farmers have always harvested seeds from the heartiest, sweetest, or biggest of their crop. But it wasn't until 1893 that William Warnock grew the first giant pumpkin—all three hundred sixty-five pounds of it. Now, growing the world's biggest pumpkin has become a passion for many. People pamper, feed, groom, shade, and de-bug their fat beauties with the obsession of pro sports coaches. Up to a few years ago, no one believed you could grow a pumpkin over one thousand pounds. Since that barrier's been broken (Paul and Nathan Zehr of Louisville, Kentucky weighed in at the World Pumpkin Confederation with a 1061-pounder in 1996), no one really knows how large pumpkins can grow. Like other rarefied breeds, they exist for one purpose: to put their owners in the record books. But unlike some designer plants, giant pumpkins can reproduce; their seeds are treasured for their genealogy, and occasionally hoarded, prompting accusations of foul play at weigh-offs.

We're still inventing what to do with these behemoths. At 700-lbs.

or more, they can't really be lifted, cooked, or even preserved. But American ingenuity being what it is, they've been turned into, of all things, boats.

On October 22, 1997, the World's First Pumpkin Regatta captains competed in cucurboats—vessels carved the day before from 800-lb. pumpkins and driven by car battery-powered electric trolling motors—in New York City's Central Park. The course was a quarter of a mile. The competitors were: Stew Leonard, Connecticut dairy-store owner; Henry Stern, New York City Parks Commissioner; and Wayne Hackney, creator of the cucurboat. Stern won the first race (it was a fix); his pumpkin sank during the second.

Choosing, Carving and Preserving Your Pumpkin

Choosing Your Pumpkin

Experts suggest finding a pumpkin with no bruises, dents, or spots; one that stands up straight and matches your design idea. But choosing a pumpkin is just as idiosyncratic as finding the right Christmas tree or picking out a valentine. Since we've been carving them for generations, we can't help but see pumpkins as faces, and the reasons we pick one over the other are, well, personal. You may be after the pumpkin your father always found: the perfect, round, fat pumpkin he would carve into a grinner. Or you may be looking for the bumpy, odd-shaped pumpkin that needs a home. At Halloween, they're not just pumpkins anymore, inert and squat: they have personalities, a life span. They become a temporary extension of the family.

The main thing to remember when choosing your pumpkin is to be gentle. Bruising or dropping will shorten the life of a pumpkin, no matter what the size.

Prepping your Pumpkin

Professionals use utility knives, all shapes and sizes of tiny saws, and a host of ordinary kitchen tools. Here are just a few items you might have sitting around the house that make excellent carving tools for jack-o-lanterns:

• Double-edged serrated knife: good for small areas because it can carve in both directions (this is the tool that comes in most pumpkin carving kits).

  • Xacto knife/utility knife: cuts big pieces quickly and easily.

  • Boning knife or paring knife: carves smaller details.

• Apple corer: makes holes for polka dots or freckles. Use the curved, sharp edge to "score" the pumpkin, rather than carve it.

• Cookie cutters: tap the cutter all the way through the pumpkin rind with a hammer and punch out the designs.

Gutting

Cut the top of your pumpkin in a five or six-sided shape. Angle your cuts to leave a slanted lip, so the top doesn't fall inside the pumpkin. Cut a notch on both the lid and pumpkin to match them up.

Got an uneven pumpkin that sits cockeyed? Cut straight across the bottom rather than the top. Another advantage to cutting across the bottom is that you can place your pumpkin over a lit candle rather than singe your fingers trying to light from the top.

Professional carvers suggest you scoop out the guts to leave a rind that's one inch (small and medium pumpkins) to two inches (big pumpkins) thick.

Patterns

Have your own idea for a carving? Great. Sketch it on paper first, then use a non-permanent marker or crayon to draw the design onto the pumpkin. Or coat the sketch with artists' spray adhesive, slap it on, and cut right through it. If your pattern won't lay flat, soak it in water, smooth it on the pumpkin, and let the paper dry before you carve.

Carving

Marty X. Larkin once carved Elvis and Marilyn faces in pumpkins on San Francisco's Fan Pier for tourists. But that was years ago. Now he's the Rock & Roll Chef, with a TV show behind him, several original products for sale (including a pumpkin carving kit), and miles and miles of touring under his belt. Larkin, a professional musician and chef, is front man for the Rock & Roll Kitchen, a band that plays food-related songs like "Brown Sugar" and "Bad to the Bone" in between cooking sets at corporate events. Having sculpted hundreds of pumpkins over the last several years, Marty has a few ideas about what to do and not do:

"Always make your mistakes on paper! That's where I work out the design first. When it gets to where I want it, I attach it to the pumpkin (usually with adhesive spray or a glue stick), and start carving. I use an Xacto knife—it lasts a lot longer than the little saws you get in most kits. No pumpkin is too small to carve. If it's real small like a pie pumpkin, a good approach is use the whole pumpkin and scrape

Flexible paring knives are the tool of choice for the folks at the Great Jack-o-lantern Festival in Oxford, Massachusetts. They score their pumpkins—scrape just a little layer off the rind—to create designs that glow when lit from inside. Photo courtesy of the Great Jack-o-lantern Festival.

off the outside surface, scoring it, rather than cutting all the way through. Every design, simple or complicated, has one rule: no islands. Meaning: everything must be connected to the pumpkin. And always start from the middle, then work your way out."

Anyone who's been to a pumpkin festival knows that when you line up pumpkins carved by different people, no two look exactly alike. There are probably as many face-carving possibilities for pumpkins as there are faces in the world.

Experiment with winking eyes, howling mouths, teeth, freckles, angry eyebrows, crooked features, any variation you can think of. Simple scenes, such as a moon or cat, work well for beginners. If you want to create something different, try to think differently: imagine your pumpkin as a canvas, rather than a head. Try polka dots, for example, or stripes. Or stars, maybe even just one big star. Or cut a repeating pattern all the way around the pumpkin. Cut your pumpkin in half lengthwise, put both halves cut-side down next to each other on a step, and carve them into giant eyes. Make letters, icons, warnings, or wishes.

Cut too far? Forget about the islands? Reattach broken pieces with toothpicks or straight pins.

Preserving Your Pumpkin

Uncut pumpkins kept in a cool place but protected from frost will keep for an average of two months. Depending on your weather (cold is good, hot is bad), a carved pumpkin will last from one day to one week. Carved pumpkins that are preserved can last two weeks. To preserve them, you must slow the natural process of decay and dehydration.

Pumpkins shrivel because they've lost moisture. You can make your pumpkin last longer by dunking it in cold water for a few seconds after you've carved it. Dry it off, then cover every cut surface with petroleum jelly. Not only does the goop help the pumpkin keep its moisture, it also works to keep pumpkin thieves away. If they can even get a grip on your Vaseline-covered pumpkin, they'll likely change their minds once they get slimed. You can also apply clear furniture wax to seal in moisture, or brush on vegetable oil. Some expert pumpkin carvers spray their finished carving with several coats of lacquer or hair spray, which gives it a glossy finish.

Frost, sun, animals, insects, and bacteria will speed up the decaying process, so the more of these you can avoid, the longer your jack-o-lanterns will last. And keep them cool: when you're not using them, put them in the refrigerator or cover them with a damp towel.

Finishing Touches

Painting

Acrylic paints won't wash away in the weather, and if you paint your pumpkin, chances are good it will last quite a bit longer than a carved one. Here are a few painted pumpkin ideas to get you started:

Grim Reaper

Paint the front of your pumpkin white. Let it dry. With a crayon, draw two black eye holes, a triangular nose hole, and skeletal teeth right on the pumpkin. When you're satisfied with your sketch, use black paint to darken the lines and fill in the eyes and nose. Take a yard of black fabric and pin it around the face like a hood.

Pumpkin in Chains

Draw two evil-looking eyes, a nose, and a twisted grin in black paint on your pumpkin. Stretch several feet of thick chain around the pumpkin as if it were bound to the porch steps. Shroud the sculpture in cobwebs.

Voodoo Pumpkin

Paint a frightening face in grays and blues and pin a ratty black wig to the top. Puncture the pumpkin with barbecue skewers, just like pins in a voodoo doll.

Demon Pumpkin

Put your pumpkin on its side so that the stem becomes the nose. Paint your pumpkin green and make slanting eyes and a wide-open, crooked mouth. Use wisps of matted cobweb to make hair and a beard, and glue them on the pumpkin. For horns, pin parsnips to the top of your pumpkin.

Decorating

Porch steps aren't the only place you can plunk a pumpkin. Think about what other locations in your yard can double as a display stand. Got a birdbath? Plop in a pumpkin. Hanging planter? Stick in a jack-o-lantern for the night. How about unscrewing the finials on your fence posts so you display pumpkins there? Try a few along your stone wall, in an above-ground cellar window, jammed in the crooks of trees, or lined up on a swing on the front porch.

You can also stack them: carve five pumpkins of varying sizes, from large to small. Balance your pumpkins on top of each other in a totem pole with largest on the bottom. Keep them in place by driving a wooden dowel through each of them and into the ground, just like a barbecue skewer. Decorate with a string of holiday lights.

Lighting

Many professional pumpkin carvers suggest candles in small glass votives or small oil burning candles, because they don't tip over and last a long time. But the traditional standing candle will work just fine. Dig a hole halfway through the rind at the bottom of the pumpkin using the tip of a long carving knife, and fit the candle in it. Plain white candles give off the most light.

To make your jack-o-lantern last longer, carve a chimney hole so that smoke can escape. Jack-o-lanterns get mushy and rot mostly because once the lid is on, the pumpkin becomes an oven and cooks from the inside out. To mark the place for a chimney hole, light the candle, place the top on your pumpkin, and see where black soot marks the lid. Cut a hole there to let out the heat.

A strand of holiday lights or a cheap flashlight can be effective if you don't want to worry about flames.

Photographing

Take pictures of your jack-o-lantern outside at dusk, when there is dim light outside and a strong light inside the pumpkin. Three candles will brighten the inside; if you miss dusk or are photographing inside, a sixty-watt bulb in a lamp will provide the right room light.

Most pocket cameras don't focus closer than three feet. If you want an extreme close-up, do an enlargement later from your snapshot. Use fast film, four hundred or eight hundred speed, so you don't have to worry about a tripod. You want to achieve a tricky balance of light where you can see the outside of the pumpkin, a glowing interior, and maybe some of the yard or house. Cover your bases by taking some shots with flash and some without.

Cooking Pumpkins

There are carving pumpkins and there are eating pumpkins. The smaller ones, called cheese pumpkins, are what you want for pies, cookies, soups, and stews. The big ones, called stock pumpkins, are really just for carving.

When choosing a pumpkin to cook, look for a small one that's heavy for its size. You want a hard rind and no bumps, warts, or bruised spots. A three and a half pound pumpkin yields about one cup pumpkin puree. To puree, cook the pumpkin, scoop out the meat and process in a blender until it's thick and smooth. Drain the excess water and use as you would pumpkin from a can. If you can't find sugar pumpkins, butternut and hubbard squashes can be substituted in most pumpkin recipes with good results.

Cooking Methods

Microwave: Set on high, cook seven minutes per pound.

Oven: Cut into large chunks, remove seeds and strings, and bake in a covered baking dish at 350 degrees for 1½ hours, or until tender. The pumpkin will scrape easily from the peel, and you can mash it into a thick puree. You can also roast it whole, punctured, in a little water.

Stovetop: Gut and cut pumpkin into pieces, then simmer for about 25 minutes in a covered pot with enough water to cover. When cooked, it's easier to remove the rind.

CHAPTER THREE

Do-It-Yourself Halloween Costumes

50 Costumes To Die For Plus Patterns, Makeup, and Masks

As I got on the subway, I dabbed at the dribble of blood making its way down my forehead. I was worried it wouldn't dry before I got there. I spotted an empty seat and squeezed through the crowd. My ankles ached. I hadn't anticipated how hard it would be to walk with cement blocks on my feet. Just my luck—a bunch of grapes nabbed the seat when I was within two feet of it. I grabbed a pole for balance, and checked out the grapes. Nice costume. She looked up at me, and I couldn't help but grin. We were obviously both headed for the same kind of place. So was the Count, a few seats down, and some sort of Mother Nature creature with a wreath of blinking battery-powered Christmas lights on her head. It was Halloween night in the city, and there were costumes everywhere.

Two Hundred Years of Costumes

If there were any folks out on Halloween two hundred years ago, they were likely Scottish or Irish people going door to door singing and begging for drinks and food. Most people—if they celebrated anything like Halloween at all—were huddled at a neighbor's house playing fortune-telling games, eating, and telling ghost stories. Costumes were not a big part of American Halloween celebrations until the early twentieth-century, when Halloween became, for the first time, a holiday for children.

The first children's costumes were the classics: pretty little pixies and maids (as in sweet young girls, not French domestics) and ghosts made from sheets and pillowcases. The renegades came in

The pet parade at Key West Fantasy Fest, a part of Halloween in the Florida Keys for more than twenty years. Photo courtesy of Stuart Newman and Associates.

the 1920s: burglars and wild Indians for boys, gypsies for girls. Hobo and tramp costumes grew popular in the 1930s in response to the Depression. In the early 1940s, Halloween was all but overshadowed by World War II. Halloween costuming, like Halloween itself, really took off in the 1950s, when the entertainment industry got into the children's costume business. As a result, prefabricated costume characters like Mickey Mouse and Tinkerbell took over the display windows of corner stores. Although it's true that costumed grownups would often accompany their kids in town parades, seeing an adult in costume at a party or parade *without* kids was rare.

That began to change in the 1970s. Halloween costume parades for adults popped up in gay enclaves, notably San Francisco's Castro District (the first adult Halloween gatherings were in the late 1960s), Greenwich Village (first parade in 1973), and Key West, Florida (first Fantasy Fest parade in the late 1970s). The large-scale costume parade had been the province of the small-town Halloween celebrations for decades; now it was a magnet that brought urban adults back to Halloween. To a certain extent, the gay community nudged the celebration of Halloween back into the realm of adults.

By 1980, one out of every four adults wore a costume. And not just to a party—adults in costume worked the tollbooths of turnpikes and the lunch lines of school cafeterias.

"The licensing craze really took off then," recalls Richard Dick of Castle Blood Haunt Couture, a Halloween costume business. He added,

> "I don't mean the little plastic Casper-in-the-box costumes that we all remember, but costumes that would actually look like favorite movie characters. I partially give credit to the world of science fiction for this. Fans of that particular genre have always been starved for things to wear from favorite movies and TV shows. There were Star Wars characters first, then the resurrection of Disney animation studios in the late '80s. Horror, that had taken a back seat through some of those times, was brought out again big time, for us as least, with the release of Michael Jackson's 'Thriller.'"

By the mid-1990s, adults were willing to spend big money on Halloween get-ups, especially for costume rentals and makeup. According to the National Costume Association's recent polls (1997-1999), medieval or Renaissance costumes fly out of the stores at Halloween; so do flappers and gangsters, harem girls, anything from *The Wizard of Oz*, and superheroes. History is in; people like to rent

Antony and Cleopatra or *Romeo and Juliet.* My own poll of costume rental shops found that the current president and first lady are always popular, as are characters from whatever movie was hot the spring or summer before. Anything sexy or exotic is always popular, and anything in drag.

When I asked one hundred non-costume industry folks what they thought about Halloween costumes, I discovered a few more trends. Sheet and pillowcase ghosts are out. Cheap packaged costumes are out. Wearing a hooded sweatshirt and calling it a costume is definitely out. Wax lips too—most people hate the way they disintegrate once you chew them. Pet costumes are in (one of eight households dressed their pets in 1998). Dracula-style fangs are definitely in, since now you can have them custom fit for your mouth. Aliens and psychopaths are in for all ages and both genders. The classics are, and always have been, in: Wolfman, Dracula (or any vampire), and Frankenstein. The most often-worn costume in 1999? A witch.

So what about you? What are you going to be this Halloween?

Fifty Haunting Halloween Costume Ideas

CONCEPT COSTUMES

The following ideas were collected from costume parties, contests, Halloween lovers, and Halloween parades over the past ten years. The good thing about a concept costume idea is that it often inspires a better one. Use these ideas as they are, or use them as a springboard for your own.

Brilliant Five-Minute Costume

This one is so simple it's almost too good to be true.

Dress in black. Attach a lightweight mirror—about 5"x 5" would be good—to a wire or a strip of fabric. Hang the mirror around your neck so that it faces out at chest level. Go as everyone else at the party.

Floor of a Movie Theater

For the adventurous, here's one that was spotted at a costume party in Boston on Halloween, 1998.

Start with a black leotard or black T-shirt and pants. Pin, stitch, or glue at least a dozen candy wrappers to your shoulders, chest, knees, etc. The more, the better. Crumple up a few empty soda cans and hang them around your neck. String a few around your waist as well. Use a large popcorn bucket as a hat. For the final touch, spray bubble gum pink silly string all over your outfit and glue on a smattering of popcorn.

Wrapped Meal for a Spider

You know how a spider catches its prey, then wraps it up in webbing until it can come back later and dig in? That's the effect we're after here.

This costume is done mostly with fake spider web—the kind you see for a dollar or two in stores around Halloween. If you've used this stuff before, you know it takes a little patience to get it right, and the more money you spend on it, the easier it is to work with.

Dress any way you like. Make a set of antennae for yourself out of pipe cleaners glued to a headband. Just before you head out, have a friend wrap you up in the spider web material. One package of web should do it—stretch the material out so it goes around your body several times. Covering part of your face will look creepy. Wrap only down to the mid-thighs so you can walk, and leave one arm free so you can eat and drink.

Head on a Platter

Courtesy of Pat Williams, Panama City, Florida. This is for the gourmand among us. You'll need a box big enough to fit over your

Halloween in the Castro, San Francisco, 1998. Like Head on a Platter, this costume requires only a box and some imagination. Photo by Wes Cherry.

head and torso, some extra cardboard, assorted plastic food, foil, an old tablecloth and lots of parsley.

Cover the top and sides of your box with the tablecloth. Hot glue the cloth to the box in several places so it doesn't slip. Measure a hole in the center of the top of the box big enough for your head to fit through (about eight inches in diameter) and cut a hole in both the cloth and the box. Try it on to make sure it fits. Cut a round platter shape out of cardboard with a hole in the center just large enough for your head and cover it with foil. Glue the platter to the 'table top.' Arrange parsley on the platter, then add plastic food—carrots, radishes, tomatoes—anything you like. Dabs of hot glue should keep them all in place. Stick your head up out of the box and through the platter to become the main dish of a truly ghoulish meal.

Bag of Trash

Collect and wash soda cans and Styrofoam containers until you have a stockpile of clean trash. String a few cans together. Tie together a trail of old yogurt containers, Styrofoam take-out cartons, whatever you have. Make a crown of crumpled paper and tin foil, plastic forks and coffee filters. When you're ready to go out, take a large, durable, drawstring trash bag and cut leg holes. Fill the bag with other clean plastic bags until it looks stuffed. Step inside, and pull it up to your chest, just under your arms and tie it tight. Decorate your head and arms with the strings of trash you've already made. Buy a few fake flies at a novelty or Halloween store and glue them to your forehead and hair.

Galaxy/Milky Way

You'll need two packages of gold foil star garland from a craft or stationery store (they usually come in twenty-five-foot lengths), three strands of small, white battery-powered holiday lights and a belt-size scrap of fabric to make this.

Start with a black base: it can be anything: a velvet dress, a tuxedo, a leotard, or black jeans and a T-shirt. Loop strands of the star garland through your hair, then decorate your whole body with stars. Keep looping the stars until you're out. Put a few safety pins or tacking stitches here and there to keep the stars in place. Save some to lace up your shoes.

Make a belt to hold the battery packs by sewing them to a six-inch wide swath of cloth with heavy-duty thread (the plastic pack usually has a few holes you can sew through). Tie this cloth belt tightly around your waist. Be forewarned—the battery packs will be bulky. Wind the three strands of lights around your body (they're completely harmless) and pin the ends onto your clothes. Pop in your batteries just before you go out and camouflage them with a scarf or sash. Use new batteries and you should be good for several hours.

Daylight Savings Time

Courtesy of Bill Ryan, Wayland, Massachusetts. Basically, the front of you is "spring ahead" and the back is "fall behind." You'll need a spring of some sort, leaves, pins or hot glue, and any basic black outfit. The shirt should be a throw-away.

Take your springs—a slinky or two, a few coils of lightweight wire, or several coiled pipe cleaners—and attach them to the front of your shirt. You may need to sew, hot glue, staple, or pin your springs, depending on how heavy they are. Hot glue real or artificial autumn leaves all over the back of your shirt.

You may need to explain this costume to some, but most people will get it. Even those who need an explanation will have a good laugh when they finally see it.

Voodoo Doll

Put on a funky skirt and mismatched sweater. Braid your hair so that it sticks up all over your head in lots of tiny braids. Poke wooden barbecue skewers through the sweater to give the illusion someone has stuck pins in you—a little hot glue will keep them in place.

Bomb Squad Trainee

Buy a second-hand suit at a thrift store. Burn holes in the sleeves, lapels and pants but be careful, and always have baking soda nearby in case the flame gets out of hand! Go outside and "dust" the jacket unevenly with a thin layer of black spray paint to make it look scorched (spray painting needs lots of ventilation). Wear a name tag with "Bomb Squad Trainee" written on it. Buy a pair of used eyeglasses and break them, but not so badly that you can't wear them. Spike your hair straight up and out with a strong gel—the finger-in-the-socket look—and smudge a little black makeup on your face as soot.

Titanic Survivor

Courtesy of Zach Holmquist, South Jordan, Utah. For a male survivor, buy a dark suit and pants and a white dress shirt from your local thrift store. Muck it up a bit (see Distressing, below). For a female survivor, wear whatever you think someone on a ritzy cruise might be wearing, be it ball gown or nightgown.

Create a life preserver from a Styrofoam hoop (the kind used for making floral wreaths, available at craft and fabric stores). Make sure it's big enough to easily slip over your head. Glue several layers of cheesecloth over the Styrofoam by soaking the cloth in a mixture of watered-down white glue. Dry it overnight; it will stiffen. Use black electrical tape to spell "RMS Titanic."

Attach glittery pipe cleaners to your hair for icicles (craft or art stores have these). Sprinkle a handful of glitter confetti or Christmas tree glitter on your hair and cover it with hairspray; hairspray fixes the glitter (and works on glittery shoes, too).

Cover your face, neck, and hands with pale white makeup. Paint a purplish-blue color around the eyes and in the hollows of the cheeks, as well as on your neck and hands. Color your lips blue and dust your face with powder to set the makeup.

Finally, sprinkle a little silvery glitter on your face and clothes. Sling the life preserver over your head and you're done!

Knife in the Back

Here's a classic of a different kind.

Start with a large rubber knife from a joke shop or toy store. You'll also need a small piece of thick cardboard—about 8"x 6"—an Ace bandage, and a shirt or suit jacket cut with a small vertical slash in the back for the knife to poke through.

Push the knife tip about five inches through the cardboard and attach it to the board with duct tape. Tape the knife on the other side of the cardboard as well. If you're having trouble getting the knife to stick straight out, make a wedge of folded-up cardboard and tape it to one side of the knife to prevent it from flopping sideways. Attach the cardboard-and-knife mechanism to your back by wrapping the Ace bandage around it several times. Fit the slit in the shirt or suit jacket over the knife handle and slip your arms in the sleeves.

Post -it Note

Cut a 3-ft. x 3-ft. piece of cardboard and paint it yellow (or cover it with a big piece of yellow posterboard). Sponge a stripe of diluted green paint across the top to look like glue. Write a huge note across the surface in magic marker and tie the cardboard "post-it pad" around your neck with a string.

Bag of Red Hots

Start with a red leotard and tights, the brighter the better. Take a sturdy, see-through trash bag that's big enough to wear and poke holes for your arms and legs. Reinforce the holes with packing tape. You can also use a sheet of plastic (like the kind used for insulating windows in winter) and make the bag by stapling the sides and bottom. Leave gaps for your arms and legs. Then, fill the bag as full as you can with red balloons. Close the bag gently around your neck with a ribbon.

Self-Portrait

Find an empty, ornate picture frame from a thrift shop. It has to be large enough to "frame" at least your head and shoulders, but not so big that it's too unwieldy to carry around all night.

Dress formally, as if actually sitting for a portrait. If you can put together a look from another time period, great. If not, your most elegant look will do. Don't skimp on jewelry, scarves, hair decorations, or hats. The more extravagant you look, the more portrait-like you'll appear. To secure the frame, tie a half-inch piece of black elastic from the middle of one side to the other as if it were picture wire. Hang the frame from your neck and adjust the elastic so that the rectangle frames your torso and head. If it leans too far forward or too far back, you can add stability by looping pieces of elastic from the frame around each shoulder.

Yard Sale

Gather junk like costume jewelry, old clothes, hats, stuffed toys, mittens, slippers, and lightweight kitchen utensils. Tie a small tag to each item and write a price on it: "all earrings, $1," etc. Fasten each item to your clothes with a safety pin. Wear a hand-painted sign ("Yard Sale, address, time, etc.") taped to your back.

Swim with the Fish

This is a mob deal gone bad. You'll need to make fake cement blocks for your feet and scare up a good-looking suit.

Find two shoeboxes big enough for your feet. Cut a hole in the top of each shoebox big enough to slip your foot through. Now glue the top of the shoeboxes to the bottoms with strong glue and paint the boxes to look like cement. There is a stone textured spray paint that will work (available in hardware or paint stores), but it's pricey. You can paint them yourself by using a white base, then sponging on repeating layers of black or dark grey paint to create a speckled granite-like look.

Next, dress up. Wear a dark, pinstriped suit, black shirt, thin black tie, and sunglasses. Slick your hair back and tie your hands loosely together in front of you (so it looks like you're tied, but you can still use your hands) and put on the cement shoes. *Hint:* If you have to walk anywhere first, wear ordinary shoes and save the cement shoes until you get to the party; they don't wear very well in the real world.

Where's Waldo

If your friends are going to the same party, you can try all dressing similarly with only slight variations so that there's only one Waldo.

Collect striped clothing throughout the year or scour thrift stores for striped socks, a shirt, hat, and a scarf. What you don't find, you can make. Waldo's shirt, for example, can be a white turtleneck with stripes made of red electrical tape. Alter a white hat or scarf with the same treatment. For Waldo's glasses, twist two black pipe cleaners into large circles and attach them to each other with a short piece of pipe cleaner. Twist two more pipe cleaners onto the side of each circle as ear pieces and bend them to fit your own ears.

Freudian Slip

Courtesy of Bruce Gellerman, host of "Hear and Now," WBUR radio, Boston's NPR station.

It's simply a pun, but he had a lot of fun with it. Find a slip at a thrift store. Photocopy images of Dr. Freud from books, cut them out and pin (or adhesive spray) them to the slip. Wear whatever you like underneath.

Catch of the Day

This is the grown-up version of Ariel the Mermaid. You'll need a fishing net, either real (sold in sporting stores) or decorative (sold in party supply stores), sea creatures or shells, an 11"x 14" piece of green posterboard, and a 4-ft. length of flimsy green fabric.

Use hot glue to attach plastic fish, shells, and sea creatures to the net. If you don't have the real stuff, or even the plastic version, make them from brightly colored posterboard. Create a fish tail by folding the green posterboard like an accordion and stapling one end shut to create a fan. Knot one end of the green fabric and staple the fan-tail to the knot.

Put on your best bikini top. Wear a pair of stretch pants or tights. Tie the green fabric around your waist so that your tail drags behind you on the ground. Lastly, cover yourself with the net so that you look caught, but can easily move and see.

For a mermaid with attitude, try this instead: wear the same tights, bikini top, and tail as above, but draw cartoon breasts on a flesh-colored leotard and accessorize with a wide-brimmed straw hat and sunglasses.

Out-of-Work Superhero

Overweight, out-of-shape, and unable to do most anything—that's this guy. Dress in a pair of tights and matching long-sleeve jersey. Pull a pair of men's briefs over the tights. Make "muscles" by filling a nylon knee-high stocking with rags or foam and knotting it. Stuff a couple of these fake biceps underneath your jersey top and keep them in place with duct tape. You can also use balloons for muscles if your top is so snug they can stay in place by themselves. Cram a pillow under your shirt for a paunchy stomach and keep it there with a wide belt or sash. Customize for whichever superhero you're impersonating: you can carry a silly string dispenser for an out-of-work Spiderman, for example, or add a cape with an *S* for an over-the-hill Superman. You can also make up your own superhero. I've seen Dustbuster and Captain Viagra so far. . . .

Roadkill

Muck up a used suit: use any or all of the distressing tips described below! Get an old white dress shirt and rip it up. To create the tire treads that ran over you, lie the damaged suit and shirt down on a flat surface (with the shirt tucked inside the jacket as if you were wearing it) and paint a tire tread (horizontal series of tire-width lines) down the front using black acrylic paint. Even better, apply several layers of black acrylic or latex house paint onto a section of your car's front tire. Make it really thick because the rubber will absorb a lot of the paint. Spread your suit out underneath the tire, drive over it once, and you'll end up with a perfect tire print! For an extra touch of realism, add lots of fake mud or blood.

PERSONAS WITH PERSONALITY

If you have the least bit of actor in you, a persona costume might be the best choice. Personality adds more to a costume than any number of gory details. It's also tons of fun to go over the top and transform yourself totally into a character you'd run from in the light of day.

Medusa West Coast style. A little bit of wire gives these snakes their height. Photo by Wes Cherry.

Medusa

Medusa was such a hideous gorgon that she turned men to stone when they looked at her; she was so evil she chewed up heroes for breakfast. Medusa was actually a serpent-goddess of the Amazons. She ultimately lost her head—literally—under Perseus' sword, but he needed the help of major Olympian gods to do the deed. Medusa was one powerful lady.

The main element in Medusa is snakes. Pick up about ten cheap rubber or plastic snakes at any toy store (or pick through a child's toy box for them—just about every kid has a few tucked away somewhere). Vary them: get some five-inch ones as well as several longer ones. Rubber snakes are best because of the way they bounce when you walk. You'll also need an ordinary bed sheet.

Wrap the white sheet around you toga-style, and secure it with safety pins. Criss-cross a long piece of rawhide (bootlaces will do) or fabric strip around your waist to give the toga a little shape. Now for the snakes. Attach each one to your hair using twist-ties or pipe cleaners. Twist the shorter snakes into the front, like bangs, and the longer ones into the sides and back of your hair. Tie strips of fabric around your feet sandal-style. Although the real Medusa had wings and a body covered with scales, the toga and sandals will carry the Greek myth part of the costume. Paint your lips and nails black.

For a fun twist on the classical, put the snakes up in big curlers and wear a bathrobe.

Tippi Hedren (from Alfred Hitchcock's **The Birds)**

Originally I saw this costume on a man coming back from the 1987 Greenwich Village Halloween parade, so I know it works beautifully on either sex.

Tippi played the ingenue Melanie Daniels in the 1963 film about a California town plagued with gruesome attacks by ordinary birds. Scour closets or a thrift shop for a two-piece suit—a skirt, blouse and short jacket set that looks like it's from the 1960s, preferably green, pink, or some innocent pastel color. If you can find one, great. If you fit into an old one from the attic, even better. If neither of these options work, you can alter a regular suit with a few quick tricks.

To transform a regular suit into a 1960s style, start with any thrift store suit. Cut the jacket to waist length and use the extra fabric to add patch (fake) pockets and wide cuffs. Add large "mod" style buttons down the front of the jacket. Pin the lapel together up to neckline and cut what's left of the top of the lapel to a Peter Pan curve. Glue contrasting color trim to jacket edges and pockets, collar or cuffs.

Once you have a suit and blouse, you need to muck it up with a bit of blood (dark red acrylic paint or fake blood) and add a few rips here and there. Tear a shoulder seam and rip off a button. If your suit still looks too pristine, do what my theater friends do: lay it down on the driveway in the mud and run your car back and forth over it a few times.

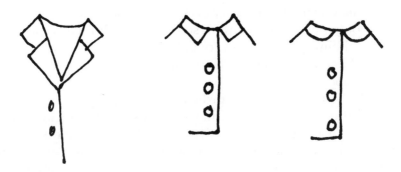

How to construct a '60s-style suit.

As a final touch, cut little *V*'s here and there in the suit for beak bites.

Now accessorize. Wear an old pair of hose (or buy some, guys) and fill them with runs and snags. If you can manage them, put on high heels. Dirty them up. One shoe on and one shoe off is good. If you're a guy or a girl with shorter hair, you'll need a shoulder length blonde wig. You'll also need a 1960s-style pillbox hat, à la Jackie Kennedy. But don't haunt second hand stores, they're easy to make (see below).

Put on makeup, then smear the mascara and lipstick and add a large beak-shaped cut and a little drizzle of fake blood to your forehead in red lip liner.

Most importantly, buy several small birds from a craft, floral or bridal supply store—they're usually inexpensive. Sew or hot glue them onto the shoulders of your jacket and your hat. Attach them to your wrist, your hair or to the back of a pair of gloves (so you can "shoo" them away).

No 1960s female character went anywhere without a purse. Clutch yours desperately. Tissues might be nice to carry for recounting your horror when folks ask you who you are. Although many people will know instantly, those who haven't seen *The Birds* may ask. Camp it up. You can also add a telephone to reference the scene where Tippi is attacked by birds in a phone booth or carry an oar to reference the first attack, when a bird bites her forehead while she's out rowing in the lake.

How To Make a Pillbox Hat

Cut a strip of cardboard three inches wide and long enough to fit

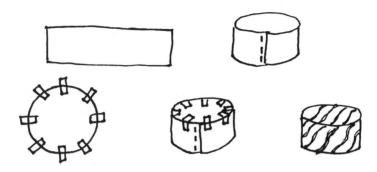

How to make a pillbox hat.

around your head like a crown. Cut a strip of fabric—match your suit if you can—five inches wide and a few inches longer than the cardboard. Using spray adhesive, glue the fabric to the cardboard, being sure to fold it over the edges just as if you were wrapping a present. Tape down the ends with duct tape. Form the cardboard into a circle and staple the ends together. Decorate the "hat" with a flower, or glue a bit of netting to the front. Add an elastic chin strap (staple it to either side of the hat) or secure the hat to your hair with bobby pins.

Lizzie Borden

Lizzie Borden took an ax
And gave her mother forty whacks.
When she saw what she had done,
She gave her father forty-one.

She was never proven guilty, but everyone knew she did it. Lizzie was a '90s girl—1890s that is—so start her with a long dark skirt and white blouse reminiscent of the late Victorian era. Add an apron, a large prop hatchet, and carry a chalkboard with "mother" (make forty hatch marks) and "father" (forty-one) written on it.

Isadora Duncan

Isadora Duncan was a famous American modern dancer known for both her innovative ideas (she danced barefoot to complex music early in the twentieth century) and her flamboyant outfits. Just as theatrical was her manner of death: she was strangled by her own scarf when it wrapped around the wire wheels of her touring car.

Wear a loose fitting, gauzy dress. Add scarves: tie them around your wrists, your waist, and your head. Wrap one end of your longest scarf around your neck, and tie the other end to a bicycle wheel. Carry the wheel with you. To add to the look, wear driving gloves and goggles.

Mother Nature

Buy a wedding or prom dress from a thrift shop. Tear off the sleeves and top layer of the skirt (there are usually more than one) and attach this fabric to the back of the dress like a cape. Add a crown of cheap silk flowers and ribbon, or of fall colored leaves for a forest nymph. Accessorize with a wand: wind decorative gold star garland around a branch or wooden dowel, then glue a gold Christmas ornament to the top.

Edgar Allan Poe

Nineteenth-century poet and father of the modern mystery story, Poe is the American pioneer of the gothic style, and most easily identified with his famous poem, "The Raven."

Wear a dark suit and white ruffled shirt (you can add lace ruffles to any white dress shirt by gluing them on). Make a quill pen of a single white feather and carry it in your breast pocket. Wear a short cape. Carry an old book (any appropriately gloomy subject). Last, add a raven: they can be found at stores around Halloween time and are surprisingly inexpensive. The birds usually come with extra wire around the claws; you can twist this wire around your watchband and have the raven sit on your wrist. Or you can sew the wire to the suit at the shoulder and have the bird perch there.

Pumpkin King

Borrow, rent, cobble together, or scavenge a good-looking suit. The closer you can get to formal, the better. Tails would be perfect. Paint your fingernails black or wear some of those extended claw-type nails sold in stores in October. Find fake vines (available at crafts or floral supply stores), wind them around your arms and shoulders, and pin in place.

The headpiece is what makes this costume: a real jack-o-lantern. Find a pumpkin that's larger than your head. Cut straight across the bottom, scoop out the guts, and carve an opening in the front big enough for your face. Line the inside of the pumpkin with a double layer of brown paper bag and then foil to protect you from any slimy parts of the rind (you can wear a cap or helmet too). Try it on; adjust until you can see, hear, and balance the pumpkin head.

A pumpkin-headed clarinetist marches in the parade at Salem Haunted Happenings, Salem, Massachusetts, 1999. Photo by Gary Duehr.

Use makeup to accentuate your own evil features.

Zorro

(or the dread pirate Roberts, if you're a fan of *The Princess Bride*)

Find a white blouse that's way too big for you. Rip the sleeves from the cuff to the elbow and knot them up to make ¾ sleeves. Leave the shirt untucked and tie a wide piece of fabric around your waist as a sash. Wear black Lycra stretch pants, or the closest thing you can muster. And if you have black boots, great. Buy your sword and black half-mask from a costume shop or store, and add a cape. If you don't have a mustache, draw one with black eyeliner pencil. Tape a piece of chalk to the tip of your sword so you can scrawl your signature *Z*s here and there.

Ophelia

Shakespeare's maddened Ophelia drowned herself, unable to cope with the intensity of her Danish prince of a boyfriend and the blunderings of her dotty dad. They found her floating in the river covered with wildflowers.

Find an old wedding or prom gown (white if possible) at a used clothing store. Tear off any extra sheer fabric and save it for the headpiece. Make a crown of flowers by attaching real or fake flowers to a length of elastic that fits comfortably around your head. Gather the extra sheer fabric and pin it to the back of the flower crown. Attach a few more flowers to the fabric trailing down your back.

Since no one wants to wear a costume that's really wet, the trick is giving the illusion of being wet. Slick your hair back with shampoo, and add a sprinkling of silver glitter. Add makeup that's bluish-white to give a drowned pallor. Buy some Spanish moss (sold at craft stores and very inexpensive), tie it in bunches, and spray paint it a dark seaweed green. After you're all dressed, arrange patches of "seaweed" in your hair, tuck some of it in your sleeves, your bodice and even your shoes.

COSTUME CLASSICS

"I always go for authenticity in my costumes and a lot of detail. I study pictures, books, films and videos. I am always scouting second-hand, antique, thrift, consignment and vintage clothing stores, auctions, estate and yard sales for clothing, accessories and props that look real. I can't emphasize enough how many wonderful items you can find for next to nothing!"

—Morticia, Baroness Reuwsaat, Mistress of Darkwing Manor, Manassas, Virginia, and diligent collector of Halloween props, accessories, Victorian Halloween objects and funerary items

You can buy, rent, or create a costume. Alternatively, you can acquire one, as the Baroness suggests, in the bins of thrift stores, at yard sales or on curbs come trash day. Here are a few suggestions for second-hand classics: vampires, witches, monsters, the undead, the invisible, and the headless.

Female Vampire or Witch

Scour your local thrift shops for a formal party dress that looks as classic as possible: think nineteenth-century (full skirt, fitted on top) and look for dark colors like purple, dark blue, deep green, red, rust, or basic black. Then have fun adding to it. Here are some things you could try:

Gothic Witch

Distress the garment. Tie up part of the skirt in a knot to expose a leg. Cut a bodice down the front of the dress (see Patterns and Tips, below) and lace it up with black ribbon. Rip your sleeves up to the elbow. Hot glue a layer of distressed tulle or cheesecloth to the waist. Wear fishnet stockings, black lace gloves, and a necklace made of plastic spiders strung on a ribbon or chain. Or wear a choker made of a velvet ribbon with a jewel glued to the center.

Medieval Witch

Add tatters to your dress made of fabric scraps cut into odd shapes and pinned, sewn or glued to the hem, waist, shoulders, and neckline. Redo the bodice to add a ruffled insert (see Patterns and Tips). Tie one shawl around your shoulders and another around your hips. Hang a garlic string from your waist and pin fake mice or rats to the bodice.

Gypsy Witch

Cut the collar of your dress into a shallow scoop and glue on fake gold coins or gold trim. Wear large hoop earrings and cover your hair with a scarf. Tie several scarves around your waist. Wear necklaces, an ankle bracelet, tons of bracelets on your arms, and stick a few tarot cards in your bodice as decoration. Carry a fake dagger in your waist-sash and paint your nails bright red.

Undead (Male or Female)

Take an old suit or dress from a thrift shop and dirty it up as best you can. Bury it in the backyard, cover it with mud or paint, or try any of the ideas from the Distressing section of this chapter. Tear off a sleeve; if you're working with a dress, rip the skirt.

Women can wear one earring, torn-apart beads, one shoe, and torn stockings. For guys, shred a tie, turn your pants pockets inside out, and add some dirt to your cuffs.

Mousse or spray your hair straight up and out. Add a hospital ID bracelet or a morgue toe tag, a boutonniere or corsage of dead flowers, glue on a few fake bugs, and work a plastic worm into your ear. Wear a noose looped around your neck, and just before you go out, dye your tongue and teeth black. Put a few drops of red and blue food coloring on your tongue and swish it around like mouthwash. The effect is dramatic, but it wears off gradually, so bring the food coloring bottles with you and reapply from time to time.

The Invisible Man

Wear a dark suit with a dark shirt and tie. Use a pair of black gloves to cover your hands, and wear black socks and shoes. To cover your features, take an old pair of thick black tights (not pantyhose) and cut off one leg at the hip. Take this leg and cut it again at the knee. This thigh-to-knee length piece will make a tight-fitting black hood that you can still see through. Sew the top of the leg closed and pull it over your head. There should be enough length left so that you can tuck the extra fabric under your shirt collar. Button the top button of your shirt. Wear a fedora and pair of sunglasses on top of the hood. This costume does not work if you're going to be doing any eating or drinking!

Vampire Baron

There are vampires of folklore: anemic, prone to fainting, short of breath. They have sores that won't heal. At night, they scratch their way out of the earth with long, hideous nails. Not so much fun for a party. Then there are the vampires of literature, the sexy, sophisticated, alluringly dangerous night creatures that inspire lust and loyalty. Here's how Morticia costumes this kind of Baron:

"If you can put your hands on a ruffled white shirt and brocade-type vest at a thrift store, you're halfway there. Add black dressy pants. Find or make a cape, or substitute a used tuxedo coat with tails. These can be found quite reasonably at tuxedo rental places—when they are just a bit too worn or shabby, rental shops will often sell them as costumes at a bargain price."

"Peruse your local second-hand shops for a piece of costume jewelry you can pin or glue to the costume at the throat. To make a widow's peak at the top of the forehead, use black washable hair

Vampire Baron, put together by the Baroness Reuwsatt with imagination and cast-offs rather than any perceptible sewing skill. As she says, "I'd rather take a beating than sew on a button."

spray (cut out a template to cover all but the peak if you're new at this). Use vampire makeup and find good quality fangs at a costume shop." (See vampire makeup, below.)

The Headless Horseman

Here's another classic from the Baroness:

"Find a long blue women's coat and a pair of white pants at a thrift store. Buy several feet of golden braid; sew it onto the shoulders and cuffs to simulate military braid (the Headless Horseman was rumored to be the ghost of a Hessian trooper, whose head had been carried away by a cannon ball in a Revolutionary War battle). Sew the braid down the pant legs as well. Sling a wide black belt over your shoulder and fasten it to a costume shop sword. Wear white gloves.

"To appear headless, find a cardboard box that covers your head and rests on your shoulders. Cut semicircles that fit over your shoulders and a hole for your face to see through. Fasten the coat over the box and hot glue it in place. Add a scarf around the "neck" and hot glue that in place as well. The scarf should cover your face but be transparent enough for you to see through. Add a cape and the highest black boots you own.

"Lastly, carry a carved-out jack-o-lantern as your head."

Bride of Frankenstein's Monster

"I used this costume with great success in my home haunt," admits the Baroness.

"Buy an old sheet from a thrift store, stain it in a tea bath (steep twelve teabags in your biggest pot of water and let sit for an hour). Fold the sheet in two and cut a simple A pattern: the top of the A should be as wide as your shoulders, the bottom flares out just like the letter. You should now have two identical A-line pieces of sheet. Sew or hot glue them together at the shoulders and sew up the sides (big basting stitches will do—you could also hot glue them if you don't want to sew). Tear the remaining sheeting into long, narrow strips and wind them around your hands and arms like a mummy.

"Add a scar to your forehead (see Makeup, below) and draw dramatic, deeply accented eyes and mouth against pale white, powdered skin. The 'Bride' wig can be found at a costume shop or you could rat your hair up, spray with black washable hair color and add a white washable hair color streak above the ear."

PROFESSIONS

Think of all the professions that lend themselves to Halloween costumes, from the obvious—undertaker, exterminator, hangman, or gynecologist—to the obscure—blues singer, fur trapper, gigolo, census taker, Wal-Mart greeter, or toxic waste transfer station attendant. To make a profession-based costume more Halloween-themed, simply add the word "dead" to the profession you choose, as in dead snake wrangler, dead accountant, dead air traffic controller . . . you get the picture.

Perfume Sample Girl
Wear your most stylish dress or suit. Accessorize with the biggest, most sparkly earrings, bracelets, and necklaces you can find. Put on lots of makeup and douse yourself with perfume. Carry a perfume bottle and offer to spray people's wrists.

Telemarketer
Wear a suit plus a headset and carry a clipboard; spend the night reading a thirty-second script of your own invention. Remember, no pauses, and don't take no for an answer—have lots of annoying questions as follow-ups.

Tourist
Search your local thrift store for a brightly colored flowered shirt. Add Bermuda shorts if you have them. Wear sunglasses and cram maps and brochures into your pockets. Carry a camera around your neck (you could even take flash pictures). Wear a wide-brimmed hat and cover your nose with zinc oxide. Ask directions loudly and often.

COUPLE COSTUMES

There are hundreds of famous couples in history, such as: Bonnie and Clyde, Morticia and Gomez, Herman and Lily, Jekyll and Hyde, Betty and Veronica, Sonny and Cher, Tweedledum and Tweedledee, Sacco and Venzetti, the Mario Brothers, the Blues Brothers, the Smith Brothers—and that's just the tip of the iceberg (oh yes, Jack and Rose, too). If you're thinking of going out on Halloween with a friend or partner, here are a few ideas to get your imagination going.

The Mertzes
Fred and Ethel Mertz were the bickering neighbor characters in *I Love Lucy*. They were consummate straight men, flawless foils for Lucy's harebrained schemes.

Ethel needs a 1950s dress: a floral print, below-the-knee length, with short sleeves and a belt buckled at the waist. Set your hair into a '50s do, off the face and done up in tight curls. Red lipstick and a vintage purse complete the outfit.

For Fred, wear plain brown or black dress trousers with suspenders and a short-sleeved, light-colored dress shirt. Pull the pants up higher than your waist, and hitch them up with a belt. Add stomach padding if you're thinner than Fred. Wear a wide necktie with a bold pattern.

Becoming Ethel and Fred is in the details. For example, Fred shoves his hands in his pockets and Ethel whacks him in the shoulder with the back of her hand. Watch a few reruns before you hit the streets.

The Odd Couple: Felix and Oscar

Here we have the quintessential neatnik and the incurable slob. For Felix Unger, the neat one, try a simple long-sleeved white shirt and black pants. Tuck in the shirt and iron a crease into the pants. Wear an apron, rubber gloves, and carry a bucket full of cleaning supplies. To become Oscar Madison, wear a big, baggy sweatshirt and sweatpants, a baseball cap, and untied sneakers. Make sure a T-shirt hangs out underneath the sweatshirt. For props, carry a cigar, the sports pages, and a bag of Cheetos.

John and Yoko

Capture John and Yoko at their 1969 bed-in honeymoon at the Amsterdam Hilton. You'll need two identical long black wigs, one for each of you, and little round sunglasses for John. Wrap one sheet around both of your torsos and pin it in place. Carry a hand painted sign that says "Give Peace a Chance," the song they recorded at the bed-in.

Adam and Eve

Start with a body suit or a bathing suit, whichever you feel more comfortable in. Buy a few green leaves for each costume from a craft or floral supply shop, and pin them onto the appropriate areas. Add a rubber snake around Eve's shoulders and a half-eaten apple for Adam.

Ventriloquist and Dummy

There are famous dummies in running suits and denim vests, hippie dummies, even Howdy-Doodie look-alikes. You and your partner can both wear the same brightly colored flower-print shirts; or white shirts, black vests and bowties; even tuxedos like Edgar Bergen's infamous Charlie McCarthy. You can also dress in opposite colors (one in a white top and black pants, the other in a black top and white pants, etc).

The most important element is making the dummy look like a wooden doll, which can be as simple as drawing a thick black line from the corners of the mouth straight down to the jaw line with a good black makeup pencil. Add a cheap wig and draw on big, bushy eyebrows to add to the "fake" look of the doll.

Practice a few moves together so that you can actually perform a short routine should the right situation arise. Check your library for old vaudeville routines.

Each Other

Here's another costume that's tons of fun and as simple as raiding each other's closets. You go as each other.

Paper or Plastic

Paper is made entirely of brown paper grocery bags, plastic of white plastic ones. Cut holes in big bags and wear them as shirts, and cover your feet with bags and keep them on with elastic bands. Make bags into a skirt, shorts, hat, gloves, purses, backpacks—anything!

LAST-MINUTE COSTUMES

You promised yourself you'd do better. You wouldn't leave your costume to the last minute and have to drag out the fairy godmother outfit you've worn three years in a row. But first there was your daughter's meltdown over the wings that weren't exactly right, then the moment when you realized you were three bags short on candy, followed by the bathroom emergency of your son who got his mummy costume stuck in his fly. Or maybe you got out of work late and by the time you got home there were already trick or treaters leaning on the doorbell. Now it's 7:00 P.M. on Halloween, and despite all those promises, you don't have a costume yet. Don't fret. There are a number of simple, last-minute costumes easily assembled with everyday items.

Here are three quickies from someone who makes it her business to know, Rochelle Santopoalo, Ph.D., Publisher/Editor of *Happy Halloween Magazine.*

One Night Stand

Dress in dark pants and white turtleneck. Cover the top of a cardboard box with a brown paper bag. Use glue or tape to attach an empty cigarette pack, matches and small box of tissue to the top. This is your nightstand. Strap on a waist purse with the pouch in front to make a ledge for the nightstand to rest on. Attach the stand to the pouch with extra large binder clips. Place a lampshade on your head.

Dirty Laundry

Dress in long underwear. Cut a cheap plastic laundry basket so you can wear it around your waist. Fill the basket with clothes, softener sheets, and an empty bottle or box of laundry detergent.

Traffic Light

Dress in black pants and turtleneck. Cut out five-inch-round circles of green, red and yellow construction paper. Stick them to your shirt. For an extra effect, wear white gloves, white shoes, and sunglasses and carry a whistle.

Theater Short-Cuts For Costume Construction

Costume Patterns and Tips

Courtesy of Maureen Tivnan, a professional theater artist in Boston.

Most of the costumes that follow are the quick "I have to make it today" costume and will not require any machine sewing. They can be glued or stapled, but in some cases, require some quick hand sewing.

Things You Should Know Before You Sew:

• All measurements can be done with a string or cloth measuring tape.

• Most fabric measures 45" wide, although some will measure 60" wide, and some less than 45" (usually expensive woven textiles or silks).

• Patterns should be made first from paper (brown paper or newspapers), since most simple paper patterns can be tried on and fitted before you buy and cut your fabric. This also ensures you buy the right amount of cloth.

• All raw edges of fabric can be sewn or glued to make a finished edge, or covered with trimming.

CAPES, COLLARS, AND HOODS

Basic Cape

A basic drawstring cape can be made from sheets, curtains, large towels, shower curtains, fabric, or old skirts. Hem any large rectangular piece of fabric, but leave the ends of the seam open. Then pull a cord

Fold edge

Basic

With stiff collar

With soft collar

These basic, soft-collar and stiff-collar capes are easy to make and require almost no sewing.

through and gather the fabric to fit.

To close your cape with clasps, snaps or buttons instead of a cord, make a basic drawstring cape. Rather than run a cord through the hem, gather the top of the cape together and pin the gathers in place with straight pins. Sew a single length of ½" elastic along the gathers. Remove the pins. You can then close your cape with a clasp, snap or button. Two buttons sewn on either side of the cape can be tied with shoelace or cord.

Cloth shower curtains work well as capes if you thread a cord through the holes in the top of the curtain. A skirt with a waistband makes a nice stiff-collared cape: just open it up at a seam and remove the zipper.

Soft-Collared Cape

For a soft collar that falls over your shoulders, make your hem wider—five to six inches—and sew another channel one inch below the hem to pull a cord or elastic through.

Stiff-Collared Cape

For a cape with a stiff collar, cover a piece of cardboard or poster-board with fabric, then sew or staple the bottom edge of the collar to the inside of the cape—this variation works well for a headless horse-man since it can sit on top of your head.

Grim Reaper-Style Hood

For a roomy, grim reaper style-hood, you'll need at least ½ yard of 18" fabric. Fold the fabric as shown, and cut along the gentle curve indicated by the dotted line. Sew or glue the two pieces together along the curved edge. Open the hood and sew or glue its bottom straight edge to the top straight full edge of cape. Pull the cord through and gather. *Hint:* If your cape is larger than your hood, you can slightly gather the cape before attaching the hood and fin-ish gathering after it is attached. Be careful to leave the ends open so you can pull the drawstring through.

Pointed Hood

Buy ½ yard of fabric. Fold the fabric and trim to an 18" square. Mark the *A* and *B* spots on the fabric in chalk: *A* marks the center of the square—nine inches from the fold and nine inches from either side—and *B* is six inches directly above this center. Using these as your guides, outline the hood in chalk on your fabric. Cut along the chalk lines, then glue the two pieces together.

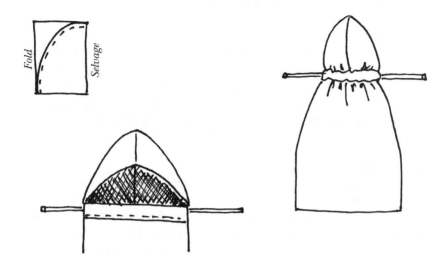

Grim Reaper-style hood.

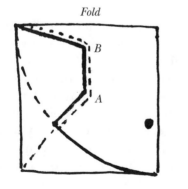

Pointed Hood.

Separate hood piece works well with a tunic.

BODICES AND SASHES

V-Cut Bodice

Cut a V from the neckline down to the waist of your dress. Poke four to six holes along each of the edges of the V and lace it back up with cord or ribbon. You can also create this look with two pieces: an old skirt and an old shirt. Remove the sleeves from the shirt, cut the V and lace up. Hide the fact that the top and bottom are two pieces with a wide sash.

Ruffled Bodice

Cut a small piece of cotton or sheer fabric, about twice the length of the front of your dress. To make ruffles, run two rows of large basting stitches along top and bottom of your piece of fabric. Pull the threads to gather the fabric. Iron these gathers flat, then sew or glue them to the inside of a scoop-neck dress. This bodice also can be done with an old shirt or tank top.

Sashes

Measure a thick band of fabric around your own waist. Poke several holes in each end and lace them together with a ribbon or cord. To give a sash some shape, fold your fabric and draw a chalk line as illustrated. Cut along the line. Sashes can be tied, velcroed, snapped or buttoned.

TUNICS

You'll need twice the amount of fabric for the length of your tunic: for example, a 36" long tunic that comes to just about your hips will require 72", or two yards, of fabric.

Open your fabric up and fold it so that the salvage (unfinished) edges are perpendicular to your fold. Cut a small hole to stick your head through. A short slit down the center of your head-hole, either in front or back, will help you get your head through. You may sew, staple, or glue the sides, leaving room for your arms. Or you can leave the sides open and use a belt or sash. Cut a jagged or curved bottom, depending on what sort of character you're costuming.

To add sleeves, measure from the top of your shoulder to your elbow. This is a comfortable width measurement for any sleeve. Take twice that amount of fabric, fold it in half, and cut the length of

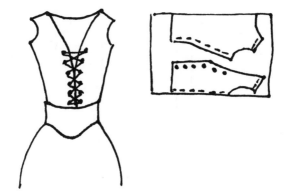

Laced-up V-cut bodice.

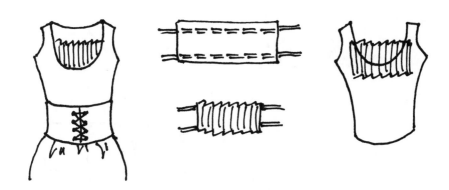

Ruffled bodice.

Shaped sash.

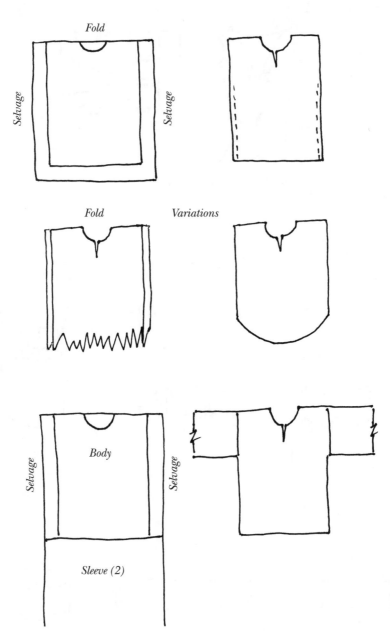

Fold

Selvage *Selvage*

Fold *Variations*

Selvage *Body* *Selvage*

Sleeve (2)

Tunics.

sleeve you want. Lay your tunic out flat and fasten your sleeve to the edges of your tunic, keeping the fold of your sleeve in line with the fold of your tunic. Now glue, sew, or staple the bottom edge of your sleeve and close up the sides of the tunic.

WIGS

Matted wigs can be made from poly-fiber fill or the cobwebs available around Halloween time. Tease them out and glue them to the inside of a hat or bathing cap. You can color these wigs with RIT-brand dye or watered-down paint (use a color wash the consistency of very dirty water).

You can stiffen regular costume wigs with spray adhesive to make them easier to shape and work on. Let them dry a while before styling.

FAKE BOSOMS

According to guys who spend a lot of time in drag, the best material for constructing a fake bosom is birdseed. Buy a pair of nylon stockings, not pantyhose, and fill one of the stockings with a few handfuls of parakeet seed. Tie the stocking, then pull the nylon back over the knot and tie it again. Do this until you're at the end of the stocking. Repeat for the second stocking.

DISTRESSING COSTUMES

Theater artisans and movie costumers have many techniques for aging, or distressing, fabrics. Some require multiple layers of paint, dye, or un-sewing; others are simple, quick, and use items you'd normally keep around the house. Here are a few distressing tips from veteran theater artisan Janet Meyers.

Coffee or Tea?
White or light-colored shirts and pants can be easily aged by soaking the garment in a dye bath of coffee or tea; it's a particularly nice color for mummy wrappings or dead brides. Add one full pot of coffee or twelve teabags to the biggest spaghetti pot you have filled with hot water. Leave the garment for an hour, then wring out and dry.

Just Back from the Dead: Cheese Graters, Awls, Sandpaper and Sneakers
To make your costume look ancient and worn, take an awl or

seam ripper and slash the fabric in different areas. Fray the edges by pulling the cross threads out. For variety, make a hole with your seam ripper, then rip it bigger with your fingers. Hack up the bottom hems of the garment with scissors.

Not damaged enough? Tape coarse sandpaper to a wood block and sand your costume in the parts you want to look extra worn, like the knees, elbows, or seat. If you sand enough, you can wear holes in the fabric and it will look like you've crawled from the crypt on your knees.

Wash your costume with any extra-strength detergent and add a little Clorox for extreme aging. For an uneven, faded look, wet part of your costume, dunk it in a bleach solution (a cap or two of bleach to a dishpan of water), and then wash it (beware: silk will disintegrate). To increase the battering of the cloth, throw a sneaker in the washing machine with your costume. For a really ragged look, rub your cheese grater over the fabric in one direction, just like you were grating cheese. Got a wire brush? That works too.

Mud- or Blood-Splattered Clothing

Lay your garment flat. Mix up good mud colors—brown, black, dark red—using either acrylic or fabric paints (poster paints and tempura paints are water-soluble and won't last). Dampen an ordinary household sponge with water and dab it on the fabric where you want the mud to go. Then dip the sponge in your mud color and dab it on the wet area. It will bleed a bit from the wetness and look more realistic. Let it dry.

To look like a semi roared past you spewing mud all over your clothes, try this: dilute your mud color with water, then dip a wet paintbrush in the mixture and flick it at the fabric. Either of the above techniques can be used with red paint to simulate blood. You can also squirt the paint directly onto the costume for a trickle or stream of blood, or just paint it on. Acrylic paint will stiffen the fabric, which is fine for jackets and some shirts and pants. But if you're working with a more flowing fabric like a T-shirt or silky dress, you'll need to use fabric paints instead. Buy the kinds that come in jars and bottles rather than tubes—tubes are often dimensional and don't work as well for this purpose. Red nail polish can be used if you need just a tiny bit of blood (on your costume, not your face!).

Wounded?

For a wound, mix up blood-colored paint: red with a little brown or blue. Using a spray bottle filled with water, squirt a concentrated stream at a spot on your shirt or dress and let the water drip down. Dilute the blood-colored paint with water and dab it onto the wet spots with a brush. Try to get the paint in the center of the wet spot so that it bleeds by itself to the edges, creating a realistic-looking ring of blood. Then run your brush down the wet outline of the drip. Let it dry. If you need a darker color, repeat.

Dust, Mold or Just Plain Old

To age a costume, say, a hundred years or so, you can use a dry brush technique to overlay faded color. Buy acrylic paint in a lighter color than the fabric you want to distress. Using a dry brush (any old paintbrush will do), dip it in the paint, then wipe the brush on newspaper to get the moisture out of it, and paint big, dry streaks of color on the fabric. The drier the brush, the better the result.

For mold, dampen the whole costume piece with water and turn it inside out. Lay it flat on a piece of plastic. Dilute white paint and streak it on the garment using an old brush. Check to make sure it's runny enough to go through the fabric and show on the outside. Let it hang dry inside out. Wet a few spots on the costume with water. Then, using a sponge, dot on an ugly mold color like yellow with a bit of green. Let it dry, then repeat, making blotchy areas that look like cauliflower florets. When you turn the garment right side out, it should have a mottled, blotchy, worn look as if it's been up in the attic or down in the grave for quite some time.

To make a costume dusty from centuries in a mausoleum, you can use baby powder or talc (wear a dust mask for this one, though). Hang your costume on a hanger outside. Make a dust ball out of a square of cheesecloth filled with powder, tap the ball against your costume, and streak it. Shake out the excess. You can also use any white wash-out hair coloring spray and cover your costume with a fine mist. This gives a dusty illusion without the dust.

COSTUME BLOOD

Blood is an often-used Halloween costume accessory, and can be made in the wink of a thirsty vampire bat's eye. It can be mixed, cooked, or designed specifically for spreading or trickling. Note: Most of these formulas probably won't come out of clothing. They may stain, but won't harm, your skin. To get rid of red stains on your skin, make a paste of baking soda and scrub—it lightens the stain and sometimes removes it completely.

Quick and Easy Blood

—Courtesy of Janet Meyers

1 cup corn syrup

About 5 drops red food coloring

Add chocolate syrup a squirt at a time and mix until you get the blood color you want. Need more than just a touch? Here are the ingredients and amounts for a bigger batch, about two cups:

1 pint light corn syrup

2 tablespoons red food coloring

10 drops blue food coloring

1 tablespoon vegetable oil

MB2 Blood Formula

—Courtesy of Murr Rhame

For a soaking and spreading blood, try this. As an added plus, there's no sugar and very little food in this formula, so it's less attractive to bugs.

Flour base:

2 teaspoons of all-purpose flour

1 cup water

• Mix the flour into water completely before heating.

• Bring to a boil, then simmer for 30 minutes. Stir frequently. Mix in any surface scum.

• Let cool.

• Add food coloring: 2 tablespoons (1 oz.) red plus ⅛ teaspoon green.

Cheap Blood

To produce runny blood, add a few drops of red food coloring to dishwashing liquid. Mix in a drop of blue food coloring or concentrated coffee to get a more realistic color.

MAKEUP

—Courtesy of Edward Gannon

As Director of Attraction Development at the Spooky World haunted theme park in Foxboro, Massachusetts, Ed Gannon supervises makeup artists, oversees the park's haunted operations, and helps design new attractions. Here are a few of his favorite makeup designs, along with some tricks he's learned on the job.

Brushes and Brands

No matter which makeup you're doing, use a good makeup brush, not a pencil: one that holds the bristles tightly in a straight line. Round brushes are useless for most makeup techniques. A good brush can be used to fill large areas, but also turns sideways to draw a thin straight line. And always pull, never push, makeup.

Good makeup is worth the money; buy yours at a costume shop rather than a department chain. But if you do have to buy from the big chains, the pots (with a good brush) are better than the makeup sticks or crayons. Just don't switch: if you start with a stick, stay with it. Don't mix makeup on the same job.

Powder every finished makeup job to set the makeup, otherwise it will run right off your face as soon as you sweat or itch. Baby powder is OK, but if you sweat a lot it's worth getting the professional makeup powder, as baby powder absorbs moisture and may ball up. Makeup comes off easily with baby oil. If you've used liquid latex, cold cream will take it off. The longer the makeup has been on, the easier it is to remove. Liquid latex, spirit gum, Rigid Collodian, and good quality makeup can all be found at a costume shop.

SKIN TREATMENTS

Dead Skin

- Clean skin with astringent.
- Lay down a coat of liquid latex on the area you're treating. Use a cotton ball to apply the latex, and try to use de-ammoniated liquid latex—it's easier on the nostrils.
- Stick a few cotton balls on the latex layer and let dry a minute or two.
- Pull cotton balls off—this leaves a wispy texture of cotton ball fibers.
- Paint latex over cotton fibers; let dry.
- Cover area with makeup.

Rotting Skin

- Clean skin with astringent.
- Lay down coat of liquid latex.

• Stick raw oatmeal on area; let dry for a few minutes.

• Paint a few coats of latex over oatmeal with a cheap brush (once you dip it in latex it's no good anymore).

• Cover area with makeup.

Wrinkled Skin

• Clean skin with astringent.

• Lay down coat of liquid latex.

• Pull skin taut and lay down tissue paper over the stretched skin.

• Let dry a minute (the tissue will wrinkle when you release the skin).

• Add another coat of latex.

• Cover area with makeup.

JOHNNY DEAD MAN MAKEUP: A STEP-BY-STEP HOW-TO

"Blythe Spirit," "Frankenstein Grey" or "Vampire" are all good base makeup colors for undead designs.

• Stipple base color (any shade of white) makeup all over face with a textured sponge.

• Blend, using the sponge.

• Stipple blue around eyes and blend.

• Mix blue and white makeup, then paint like eye shadow over eyes.

• Stipple whole face with dark blue.

(Dark blue gives a "dead" look. Dark red looks like broken blood vessels and green looks like mossy fungus, especially with bits of yellow.)

• Stipple yellow and red to add dimension.

• Paint lips blue with a brush.

• Draw blue accent lines along the natural lines of the face.

• Dust on a layer of cornstarch or powder to set makeup; brush off extra powder with big makeup brush.

Warts

To make a wart ahead of time, wad up a tiny bit of cotton and place it on a piece of wax paper. Paint it with liquid latex, shape it a bit, and let it dry (decorate with a hair if you like). When you need it, peel it off and glue it on your face with latex or spirit gum. To build a wart on your face, dab your skin with liquid latex. Take a few flakes of oatmeal and stick them to the latex, then cover the mound with another coat of latex. Let dry and apply the same skin-color makeup you use on your face.

Cotton ball fibers covered with liquid latex give the illusion of dead skin.

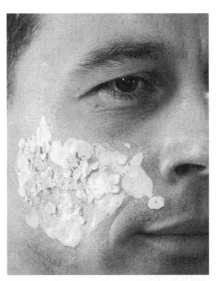

Oatmeal and a coat of liquid latex make "rotting" skin.

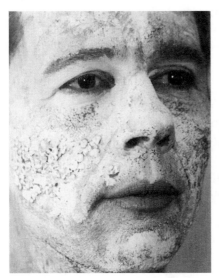

Stipple dark blue over a white base and draw accent lines.

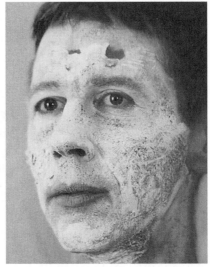

Finished "Dead Man" makeup includes wound made of peeled latex.

Blacked-out Teeth

Use any tooth black sold at costume or makeup stores. Dry your tooth first with tissue, then paint the stuff right on. Tooth black comes off with toothpaste and a toothbrush.

Bruises

Buy a makeup palette that includes the colors purple, black, and yellow. Using a sponge to apply the color, put one color on each of three corners of the sponge and dab yellow, then purple, then black on the area you want the bruise to appear. Repeat. The different colored layers will eventually look very realistic.

Cuts

Paint on a layer of liquid latex slightly larger than the size of the cut. Let it dry. Apply skin-colored makeup over the area. Tear a hole in the latex patch with the tip of a makeup brush. Paint dark red and yellow inside.

Scars

A scar is really quick and easy. You need to buy a substance called Rigid Collodian at a makeup or costume store (it's inexpensive and there's enough in a small bottle to last through lots of scars). Paint it on your face in a series of parallel lines; it shrinks the skin and creates a puckered scar-like appearance. Dab a bit of reddish-brown makeup into the deepest parts of the scar. Put the scar wherever there's extra skin, like a cheek; it won't work nearly as well on top of bone or cartilage.

VAMPIRE MAKEUP: A STEP-BY-STEP HOW-TO

Think of a face as a pattern, a collection of shapes. The same base makeup colors listed above for Johnny Dead Man work for vampires.

• Cover face with astringent.

• Smooth on white base makeup with a sponge.

• Paint purple on the eyelids, all the way over the eyebrows, and under the eyes.

• Paint a thin line of red under each eye (but not too close—red makeup stains and you may need to scrub hard it to get it off).

• Paint purple lines under the cheekbones and blend all the way down to the jaw line.

• Paint purple shading under mouth and around the nose; blend it in.

Sponge on white makeup and blend.

Paint purple around eyes, cheek hollows, and along lines of the face.

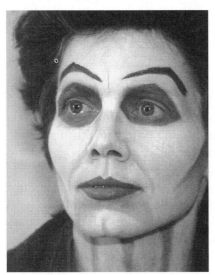

Draw dark eyebrows above real ones; accent lips and trachea.

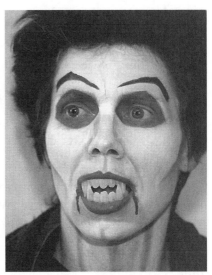

Add fangs and lines of red makeup at the corners of the mouth.

• Draw black eyebrows above the natural brows.

• Draw throat lines, following the trachea (you can also shadow the collarbones, and cleavage for females, depending on what costume the vamp is wearing).

• Paint the lips purple.

MASKS

Latex masks come in every size and type—if you need a high-quality, long-lasting mask, it may be best to buy one. Although you can make your own latex masks, the process involves molds, patience, and some trial and error. It's also expensive, especially at first when you're assembling materials. But almost anyone (including kids) can make a papier-mâché or plaster-gauze mask in a relatively short amount of time. Although they're not as flexible as latex masks, they are durable and can be made, in the case of plaster-gauze masks, to fit your own face.

Papier-Mâché Masks

Mix up papier-mâché paste. For a simple recipe, use watered-down white glue mixed with a little cornstarch. To make enough paste for one mask, mix a tablespoon of cornstarch with ½ cup white glue; stir to make a thick paste, then add water, stirring constantly, until it's the consistency of soup. For "professional quality" papier-mâché paste, try this recipe:

1⅓ cup water

3 tbs. flour

1 tsp. liquid bleach

• Boil one cup of water.

• In another bowl, combine 3 tbs. flour and ⅓ cup cold water; stir until smooth.

• Add flour and water mixture to boiling water; stir until thick.

• Pour paste into plastic storage container and stir in one tsp. liquid bleach to prevent spoiling.

Figure out what you're going to use as your mold: a mannequin head (can be found cheap at yard sales or, sometimes, at wig and makeup stores), a clay form you've sculpted, or any number of head-like forms such as a plastic skull, hockey face, or even a helmet. You can't use an actual face for papier-mâché masks because the drying time is too long.

• Cover the surface of the mold with petroleum jelly so the mask will release once it's dry.

• Tear strips of paper from a grocery bag or newspaper. Dip one piece into the paste, squeeze off excess liquid by pulling the strip between two fingers, and lay it on the mold. Lay the next strip to overlap the first. Smooth each one flat throughout the process. Continue covering your mold with overlapping strips until you have covered the whole mask area. To make a stronger, more durable mask, lay down one layer, dry the mask on a radiator for an hour, then add another layer, dry, layer, dry, etc. until you have the thickness you need.

• Let the mask dry overnight.

• To remove your dry mask from the mold, gently insert your fingers between the papier-mâché and the mold and tug at the forehead, chin, and both sides. When you feel the mask release, carefully reach your fingers underneath and ease it off the mold.

• Wipe the inside to remove the jelly.

• A papier-mâché mask can be painted with almost any kind of paint. To extend the life of your mask, paint or decorate it, then paint on a layer of acrylic gel or medium. Let it dry thoroughly—overnight is best. Poke a hole on either side of the mask. String thin elastic through the holes, measure it to your face, and tie knots in the ends.

Plaster-Gauze Masks

Plaster masks can be made of a substance called Pariscraft (found in art supply stores), or any brand of plaster cloth (found in craft stores). It's plaster-impregnated gauze that resembles the plaster used for casts, but is especially made for crafts and contains no dangerous chemicals. Don't use regular plaster—it burns! Plaster-gauze is sold in long rolls, like an ace bandage. For the purposes of this how-to, let's assume you're using a friend as a model.

• Lay down newspapers on your work surface; this material is goopy once you get going. Cut about twenty plaster-gauze strips, six inches in length. Cut another fifteen strips, two inches in length. Cut a dozen very thin strips about four inches long. Fill a bowl with lukewarm water for dipping the strips.

• Cover your model's face with petroleum jelly. Pay particular attention to the eyebrows, hairline, and any facial hair.

• Have your model sit in a chair and cover his hair with plastic wrap. Cover his clothes with a garbage bag.

• Dip a six-inch strip of gauze into the bowl of water, squeeze the strip between your fingers to get rid of the excess water, and lay it

Mermaid mask cast of the artist's face in plaster-gauze. Mask and photo by Janet Meyers.

on your model's forehead. When you lay down the strip, you'll see tiny air holes in the gauze. Rub the strip gently until all these holes fill with plaster and the strip is completely creamy white. Then, take your next six-inch strip and place it on your model, being sure to overlap part of the first strip. Smooth out the air holes and go on to your next, overlapping and smoothing each time.

• Use the different length strips to fit different distances and widths as you cover the face. If you're making a half-mask, cover the top of the nose, most of the cheeks, and stop there. If you're making a full-mask, cover the whole face. *Never* cover the nostrils and mouth; leave one or the other open so your model can always breathe easily.

• You can cast the eyes open or shut. If you cast a mask with your model's eyes shut, be very gentle smoothing the plaster strips over the eyelids. You can cut the eyes out later when the mask dries, or paint them, then cut slits below the mask's eyes just big enough so you can see out. If you cast the mask with your model's eyes open, carefully lay your thinnest strips around the eyes and in between them.

• Once you've covered the entire face, give it a final smoothing.

• Add a second layer, laying new strips over the first layer. Don't worry about edges of the mask being uneven because you can simply trim them with scissors when the mask is dry. Check for weak spots by lightly tapping your finger on different parts of the mask. Wherever you feel movement—if the plaster is wiggly or caves in—add yet another layer of strips. The plaster will probably already be hardening by now—it will feel slightly warm on your model's skin.

• Let the finished mask dry another three minutes. Then have your model bend his face towards the floor and make faces—the more he contorts his face, the easier the mask comes off. Work your fingers under the edges of the mask and help it wiggle free. The bits of plaster left on your friend's face come off easily with soap and water.

• Set the mask in a dry place for twenty-four hours. Although it may appear dry to the touch, the mask will take a full day to dry thoroughly.

• Trim the mask with scissors and cut any uneven edges. If you want to cut eyeholes at this point, use a utility knife. Paint the mask with acrylic paints, or acrylic medium or gel so it will be mold-proof.

• Spray your dried mask with fixative. Poke two holes in the sides of the mask and use knotted elastic thread or colorful ribbons for ties.

There are as many different kinds of masks as there are faces, and you probably have one lying around the house you're completely unaware of. Think differently about masks. A loosely woven burlap sack with felt features makes a great scarecrow mask. A knit cap, nylon stocking, paper bag, flower pot, cardboard box—anything you can pull over your head (and still breathe)—can make an interesting mask.

HOW TO BE A COSTUME CONTEST CONTENDER

"I come into the room screaming and yelling. I'm wearing the electric chair and have fake legs that kick out when I spin, a Moog for special effects, and an overhead prison-type light that flashes. People love it!" says Tim Friesen. His Ted Bundy costume was so popular he wore it eight or nine years in a row and built up quite a reputation. So much so that he started to see his costume in other places, most memorably on the *Today* show.

Tim has won around thirty thousand dollars in prize money since he started hitting the costume contests about sixteen years ago; he remains virtually undefeated to this day. His secrets?

• Comedy sells! Be outrageous. More than anything, people like to laugh.

• Do timely topics. The costumes that really pack a punch tend to be current. White House scandal? Newsworthy criminal or international enemy? These are the themes you want to make into costumes. Case in point: in 1996, Hurricane Andrew ripped through Tim's native southern Florida, so that was the year he dressed as a hurricane. He built a fluffy cloud complete with a carbon dioxide canister that blew wind. A sound system pumped out cracks of thunder; light bulbs inside the cloud flashed as lightning and his windshield-wiper squeeze bottle made it rain. Tim took home another first prize.

• Be a ham. Make yourself known in a crowd. Start with a grand entrance, work the audience, introduce your character or theme, and bring gags to entertain.

• Have a few surprises tucked up your sleeve for the judges. Things like silly string, smoke, and pulling out fake body parts can steal the show.

• Make your costume comfortable and lightweight. There is nothing worse than being miserable for an entire evening.

• A great costume doesn't have to take forever to make. Tim says, "I've seen costumes that take only a day or two to construct win thousands of dollars. On the other hand, I've seen monumental efforts spent constructing such things as 'a shoe.' Excellent-looking costume, but no pizzazz."

CHAPTER FOUR

Halloween Party How-To

Invitations, Decorations, Games, and Themes

What a Great Night For A Party

A rat and skull greet me on the front stairs. Inside, the rooms are dim. Down one hallway, a line of six-foot-tall luminescent ghosts twirl in midair, and a room in the distance glows with a light I vaguely remember from junior high school dances. Inside the living room, the curtains are tattered and full of cobwebs, tiny bats flitter in the lampshades, and a bunch of dead roses sits nearby in a vase. The punch bowl bubbles and cascades of fog hug the buffet table, parting only to expose Meat Head, a life-size sculpture made entirely of food, who grins at me with egg-yolk eyes. I open the front closet and a skeleton lifts its chalky white hand to take my coat. That does it. I jump, drop the coat, fall backwards into a massive spider web and the sound of maniacal laughing comes out of the dark. I scream. Not once, but many times. "Alright!" grins my host. "It's working!"

Nearly one-quarter of us planned to attend a costume party in 1999. [1] One out of four! That means that pretty much wherever you are after dark on Halloween, someone nearby is cooking up a gathering. You can, too. As the Wicked Witch of the West said when she was pondering Dorothy's demise, "the only question is . . . *how* to do it."

In this chapter, you'll find lots of things to get you going, from invitations and decorating ideas to games and themed party ideas. Suggestions for Halloween music and video rentals follow in chapter five; recipes in chapter six.

The Baron and Baroness Reuwsaat at their annual Halloween haunt, Darkwing Manor, in Manassas, Virginia. Photo courtesy of Tina Reuwsaat.

Invitations

Handwrite your invitations using a fountain pen on antique-looking stationery. Roll up the paper, tie it with a black velvet ribbon, and mail it in a tube. If your guests live close by, print your invitation on a strip of paper, tie it around the stem of a miniature pumpkin, and hand-deliver it. Or use any of the verses and phrases below on an invitation of your own design.

Greeting:
Carpe Noctem.
(Seize the night)

Invitation text:
We dare you to spend an evening at . . . your address, time, date, etc.

Greeting:
When the breath grows low, and the heart is chill,
The blood creeps ghost-like around it still . . .

Invitation text:
Please come creeping to our gathering at . . . etc.

Greeting:
Once upon a midnight dreary, while I pondered, weak and weary,
Over many a quaint and curious volume of forgotten lore—
While I nodded, nearly napping, suddenly there came a tapping,
As if some one gently rapping, rapping at my chamber door.
" 'Tis some visitor," I muttered, "tapping at my chamber door—"
—Edgar Allan Poe

Invitation text:
Could it be you and nothing more?
You are cordially invited to a Halloween party in our chamber at . . . etc.

Greeting:
Spiders crawl up the wall,
Cobwebs everywhere.
Dust and dirt are piled up high
On every crypt and chair.
Bats go winging overhead,
Round and round the room,
Come, my dear, oh do come in

And join me in my tomb.
—Margaret Keyes and Jeanne Youngson

Invitation text:
Won't you please join me this Halloween at . . . etc.

Greeting:
Double, double, toil and trouble;
Fire burn and cauldron bubble.
Fillet of a fenny snake
In the cauldron boil and bake.
—Shakespeare's *Macbeth*

Invitation text:
Won't you join our Hallowe'en feast on . . . etc.

Thirteen Party Decorating Ideas

Accidents, surprises, the threat of danger, and the unsettling feeling you're being watched—they're all elements of a good Halloween party. Take a tip from professional haunters and incorporate all five senses when you're planning. Shadowy lighting, unusual sounds and music, unexpected textures, and exotic, spicy tastes make a Halloween party cook.

Things That Go Bump, Bang, Clatter and Whoops: Rigging "Startles"
      —Courtesy of Ralph and Melissa Mitchell, southern Indiana

"Startles"—things that suddenly move, pop out in the dark, and otherwise frighten your guests—can be rigged on almost any door using a simple pulley system of fishing wire, string, and ceiling hooks. You can use this mechanism to animate Halloween props anywhere in the house. Melissa explains, "For example, if you anchor a line atop the bathroom door and string it to a hook in another room, say, above the couch—then, when the bathroom door opens, your spider will magically appear from behind the couch."

Start strings on the refrigerator door, front door, or any door that would normally open and close during the course of your party. On the other end, rig spiders, snakes, bats, or ghosts. Rig your closet door so that as the guest opens it, a coat sleeve rises up to salute her! Rig your shower curtain so that the moment a guest shuts the door the curtain pulls back to reveal a leering jack-o-lantern!

Rig your front door to surprise trick-or-treaters with a moving prop. Drawing by Denise Cohen.

Materials:
Any lightweight Halloween prop
Heavyweight fishing line
Carpet tack
3 small screw-in hooks

• Take a lightweight prop such as a bat, spider, or a small skeleton and tie it to a length of fishing line. The length you use will depend on the amount of movement you want.

• Hammer a carpet tack into the top left corner of the inside of the door (make sure it still closes).

• Nail or screw a small hook into the ceiling a few feet away from the door (Ralph and Melissa use small white hooks and leave them up all year—no one's ever noticed).

• Thread the fishing line through the hook and tie it to the carpet tack on your door.

• Place your prop on a table directly underneath the ceiling hook. Every time you open the front door the prop will lift off and dangle in the air!

Once you get the hang of this simple movement you can play around with more complex moves. By placing hooks either in front of or behind the door, you can create movement in different rooms from the same door. If the movement isn't what you wanted or doesn't travel far enough . . . move the hooks! *Hint*: Always lubricate the hooks. Bar soap will work. Try not to have the fishing line drag across doorframes or other rough surfaces because it will snap. If the door opens with a tug, your prop is too heavy. Choose a lighter prop or move the hook farther away to lighten the load. Done right, no one should notice the mechanism.

> "I took a spider, some fishing line and a piece of clear tape. I taped one end of the fishing line to the back of the door, up high. Then I ran the fishing line over a nail that's above the medicine cabinet, and tied it to the spider. When the door is open, the spider is out of sight below the sink. But close the door and the spider rises right into view as you head toward either the sink or the toilet. I tested it a couple of times, then left it. An hour later, my partner went into the bathroom and shrieked."

—Robyn Dochterman, Minneapolis, Minnesota

If you're thinking of haunting the bathroom, try this, courtesy of Chuck Rice, Campbell, California: remove the tops of three yellow Highlighter pens and tie them to the bottom of the tank of your toilet. Trade your bathroom light for a black light, and your toilet will give off an unearthly green glow with every flush!

Bats in the Lampshades

Materials:

Bat stickers or black posterboard

Thread

Around Halloween, lots of stores sell strips of bat-shaped stickers. You can decorate beverage glasses with these stickers along the outside rim, or arrange them flying in a gentle curve from base to lip. Stick them on the outside of a tall vase and display a single dead rose. Or stick them to the inside of your lampshades, and each time you turn on the lamp they'll show up in silhouette.

No bat stickers? Buy a sheet of black posterboard. Draw a bat on a piece of white paper—a three-inch wingspan works nicely—and use this pattern to trace several bats on the posterboard. Cut them out and tape each creature to a piece of thread. Tie a few threads to the inside of the lamp fixture and suspend the bats so that you can see their shapes silhouetted when the light is on. Tape some of the bat shapes directly to the shade; these will be the clearest. The ones closest to the bulb will spin slowly from the heat.

Creepy Drawers
Materials:
Craft moss or leaves
Leftover Halloween decorations
Cobwebs

Open a few drawers around the house and empty out the contents. Refill the drawers with moss or autumn leaves (find either of these at a craft store). Inside, arrange your Halloween paraphernalia: crows, skeletons, witches, gravestones, snakes, cats, bats, chains, old costume jewelry, skulls, or whatever you have left over from decorating. Cover the whole assemblage with cobwebs and light it with a strand of battery-powered holiday lights. Leave the drawers open for your guests to admire.

Glowing Ghosts
Materials:
Large white balloons
Two glowsticks (light sticks) for every balloon
Sheer fabric to cover each balloon "ghost" (old sheer curtains work beautifully)
String

These life-size ghosts will glow from the inside and sway ever so slowly when you suspend them in a dark hallway, window, or corner. Activate two glowsticks and push them into the balloon, then blow it up. Tie a piece of thin string to the knot. Poke a tiny hole in the center of the sheer fabric, thread the string through it, and drape the fabric over the balloon. Add more sheer fabric until you're happy with the look of the ghost. Tie the balloon ghost to a pushpin in the ceiling. He'll give off an unsettling glow as long as the glowstick package claims—usually around six hours.

The Cabinet of Dr. Caligari
Materials:
Empty jars, small boxes, cans and bottles
Self-stick labels

Stock one of the cabinets in your kitchen with an assortment of jars, bottles, cans, and boxes that you've "doctored" for the party and leave the cabinet open for guests to explore.

Collect containers over the weeks before Halloween. Fill the see-through jars with unlikely ingredients like olives or water chestnuts floating in colored liquid, or cooked pasta, raw liver, shrunken heads made of apples* or chestnuts suspended in corn syrup. Make a fake label for each container, using the most outrageous concoctions you can think of. Try a few from the famous *Macbeth* witch's brew for starters: fillet of fenny snake, eye of newt, wool of bat, tongue of dog, lizard's leg, tooth of wolf, or root of hemlock "digged i' the dark." Need more? Use items from the medieval recipe for witches' flying ointment: dead man's fingernails, blood of a thief, henbane, cinquefoil, belladonna, hemlock, and deadly nightshade. Customize for your friends and get creative (Tom's thumbs?). For a dramatic effect, illuminate the jars by aiming a strong flashlight at them from the side.

To make shrunken heads:

Peel a large apple. Carve a simple face with a sharp paring knife. Soak the apple in a mixture of three tablespoons baking soda and enough water to cover for twenty-four hours. Hang it on a knotted string to dry (if you dry it on a shelf, moisture will seep to the bottom and rot the apple) for two and a half weeks. It will shrivel to a quarter of its original size. Dip it in a sealer, such as polyurethane, to keep it mold-free.

Billowing Spook
—Courtesy of Janet Meyers
Materials:
1 pkg. cheesecloth
Acrylic matte gel (found at an art supply store)
Plastic skeleton mask
Bucket
Old paintbrush

Fold the cheesecloth in half lengthwise (it should be about ten feet long). Fill a large bucket halfway with water, and dilute enough acrylic matte gel to turn it the consistency of watery mayonnaise. Soak the folded cheesecloth in the gel mixture. Squeeze out excess and dry the cheesecloth flat, like a sweater. When it's completely dry, brush on a second coat of gel mixture with a cheap paintbrush and let it dry.

Billowing spook by Janet Meyers. Photo by Gary Duehr.

Cut the now-stiffened cheesecloth along the fold. Lay two pieces of stiffened fabric on top of each other and find the center point along one side. Glue (or stitch) the center points to the forehead of the skeleton mask so that the fabric falls down on either side like a bridal veil. Glue a loop to the top of the mask for hanging.

Hint: a little acrylic paint or food coloring in the gel mixture will give the cheesecloth color. Also, if you're going to use this for outside decoration, paint the cloth with several layers of gel mixture.

Half-Man in the Ceiling
—Courtesy of Ralph and Melissa Mitchell
Materials:
Old pants, shirt, and shoes
Long gloves
Wire coat hanger
Safety pins and pushpins
3 hooks

"Half man has been one of our best gags," says Melissa Mitchell, hostess of a greatly anticipated annual Halloween party. "We change his position in the house each year." Drawing by Denise Cohen.

Shape the hanger into a waist-size circle. Using this as a guide, place the hooks into the ceiling at three equidistant points on the circle (you do have to sacrifice three small holes in your ceiling, but you can use white on white). Cut off about eight inches of the bottom of the shirt and stitch a one-inch hem along the cut edge. Push the hanger through this hem and twist the edges together to form your dummy's waist. Hang this "waist" on the three hooks in the ceiling. Pin the bottom of the shirt fabric to the pants with safety pins. Attach the shoes to the ends of the pant legs with safety pins. Add hands by stuffing a long pair of gloves and use pushpins to attach them to the ceiling on either side of your guy.

Dummies make great Halloween props, no matter where they are. Pin an old pair of pants to some socks and shoes, stuff it all with newspaper and wedge him underneath your couch or leave him stuck in a window or drawer. Or try stuffing striped stockings to look like witch feet, and closing the oven door on them.

Smokin' Jack Centerpiece

Materials:
Jack-o-lantern
Cobwebs
Large bowl
Dry ice
Small black cloth
Halloween decorations
Holiday lights

Surround this swampy still life with candles, gourds, cobwebs, smaller carved pumpkins, crabapples, and autumn leaves.

Turn a large serving bowl upside down, and cover it with a black cloth to make a stand for your jack-o-lantern centerpiece. Carve a big pumpkin with an extra-large grimace and evil eyes. Light the pumpkin with battery-powered holiday lights and arrange another strand of lights among the bowls and food on your table. Place a fairly deep container inside the pumpkin—a clear glass vase is ideal—and scoop in six cups of dry ice pellets (see Decorating with Dry Ice). Just as your guests arrive, cover the ice pellets with warm water. The jack-o-lantern will gurgle and spew great clouds of fog for about fifteen minutes. You can keep the effect going if you add two cups of warm water to the vase every ten minutes and give it a stir. The pellets will probably dissolve after thirty minutes, but you can add more ice if you want to keep the fog going.

Hand in the Punch Bowl

Materials:

Rubber glove (latex disposable, or dishwashing glove turned inside out)

Elastic band

Food coloring

It's an oldie, but I've never seen it fail to get a reaction! Fill the glove with water, wrap a rubber band tightly around the end, and freeze it overnight. When it's time for your party, run the glove under hot water for a few moments, peel off the glove, and float the hand in the punchbowl. For a variation on this theme, use a few drops of food coloring in the water before you freeze it to make a green hand, or purple, or red. Or make two hands, right and left.

Fortunetelling Corner

Materials:

Small table covered with scarves or lace

Crystal ball

Pieces of velvet

Candles

Incense

Fortunetelling paraphernalia such as cards, runes, crystals, books on palmistry, etc.

Fortunetelling is as much a part of Halloween as pumpkins and ghosts, but we've lost much of this part of the holiday in its current incarnation. Bring it back. Darken a corner of a room in your home and arrange a few chairs and a small table there. Drape velvets on the chairs and cover the table with fringed scarves or old lace. Light as many candles as you can fit in the area. Burn incense. Don't have a crystal ball? Use a globe light fixture turned upside down and nestled in a silk scarf to hide the base.

If it's just plain entertainment you're after, then get a friend to play soothsayer. Have someone make up fortunes on the spot using cards, palms, or crystals. Alternatively, you can hire a real psychic to give readings at your party. Good psychics are insightful, and the experience of having a talented professional interpret tarot cards or runes or even your palm can be quite profound. It can also be expensive, but you really get what you pay for. Choose a psychic like you would a doctor; get personal recommendations. Incidentally, no psychic I've ever known will give you bad news. They'll describe your

A 1920s gypsy costume with vintage fortune-telling games and cards from the collection of Tina Reuwsatt. The crystal ball is made from a cracked glass globe tuned upside down, lit with a gold Christmas light bulb, and filled with crinkled iridescent cellophane paper. Photo by Tina Reuwsaat.

strengths, the challenges facing you, and what it is you must try to learn. The dark-eyed woman who shudders at the vision of your impending death exists only in the movies.

Decorating with Dry Ice

Dry ice creates fog, and there's nothing like it to spook up a party. But before you buy it, there are a few things you should know.

Dry ice is frozen carbon dioxide; it's not toxic. It doesn't melt, but rather evaporates directly into its gaseous form. However, dry ice is frozen at such a temperature (-109 degrees Fahrenheit) that it is too cold to touch or eat. When handling it, use gloves. Dry ice is available from most ice companies and is relatively inexpensive (somewhere around a dollar a pound). It comes in block form or pellets; pellets may be better for party use because they're more flexible.

You can store dry ice in an ice chest or Styrofoam cooler for about twenty-four hours with a towel thrown over it to keep in the gas (a freezer isn't cold enough). Never store dry ice in a closed container: it will explode.

That said, what can you do with dry ice?

Dry ice is kind of like fireworks—it's explosive at first, then fizzles and burns itself out. If you put even one pellet, for example, into a glass, it will create cascades of bubbling fog for about five minutes. So the objective is to use the ice at its most dramatic point.

Shovel six cups of dry ice pellets into a five-gallon bucket half-filled with warm water and create swirls of incredible fog that hug the floor of your entire living room (dry ice fog—which is mostly condensed water vapor—is heavier than air, so it falls, rather than rises). The effect only lasts about ten minutes, so choose carefully when to start. Add more warm water to keep it going. If you want to go with a block of ice, about twenty-five pounds will provide fog for two-to-three hours. Ask the iceman to slice it into five pieces; a five-pound block should fog a 10-ft. x 10-ft. room for fifteen minutes. After fifteen minutes, add more water to continue the effect. When the block is completely gone, add the next slab of ice and more water. Hot water produces more dramatic bubbling fog action.

For a cauldron-like effect, add two cups of dry ice pellets to your punch bowl just before you bring it out. The punch will bubble and smoke, sending clouds of fog slithering down the sides of the bowl and across the table. Again, the effect won't last more than about fifteen minutes (make it last longer by stirring the punch every time you pass by), but you can sustain the novelty by keeping a cooler of dry ice pellets nearby and adding some when you think of it. Although the pellets are harmless to the punch, aside from injecting a little carbonation, have someone responsible do the pouring. Renegade chips of floating dry ice are easy to spot: they look like solid white pieces of smoking candle wax (but should not be eaten).

To serve fog-bound hors d'oeuvres, put a handful of pellets in a small bowl. Place the bowl in the center of your serving tray and arrange the food around it. Just before you serve, cover the pellets with warm water to release the fog.

Dry ice, by the way, is loud when it gets going, and makes a sound that's somewhere between frying and boiling. In other words, it's pretty hard to hide the source of the fog. *Note:* If you're planning on fogging up large areas, or need constant fog for several hours, think about investing in a fog machine. They're sold for personal use in novelty stores and Halloween catalogs, and are available in various sizes. They're not cheap, but if fog is something you'll be using year after year, it may be worth your while.

Lights Off

Light—or lack thereof—can add more eerie atmosphere to your party than just about anything else.

• Light the party with firelight: just candles and jack-o-lanterns.

• Replace the hallway, bathroom, or porch light with a purple- or red-colored bulb.

• Replace regular room lighting with a black light and many white objects will glow (read about black light in Chapter One).

• Shine a strong light, like a flood light, through a window from outside the house—clamp it to a ladder leaning next to a window to create eerie shadows indoors. Cover your furniture with white sheets to add more drama.

• String tiny holiday lights behind gauzy window curtains.

• Place a floodlight on the floor in a corner, pointing out and upwards towards the guests. Their movement through the room will create huge shadows on the walls. If the white light is too bright, cover the floodlight with colored lighting gel from a theatrical supply store.

Did You Hear That?

Don't omit any of the senses! There's a lot you can do with sound to entertain your guests and stage a party they'll remember.

• Use tape recorders to play tape loops of sounds from different parts of the house, like crickets in a bedroom or a thunderstorm in the coat closet, a dentist's drill in the cellar, a heartbeat under the couch, or a tiny voice calling "help me" in the toy chest. (Record the sound continuously on a short cassette tape and play it on a deck that has automatic reverse).

• Plug a tape recorder into an outlet strip controlled by a light switch so that a prerecorded sound comes on when guests flip the switch. Like Bach's *Toccata and Fugue in D Minor* (the *Phantom of the Opera* organ riff) attached to the bedroom light switch.

• Record someone reading a ghost story and have it playing in a darkened corner.

• Strew a dark hallway with dried autumn leaves—it's unsettling to

hear and feel crunchy vegetation under your feet when you're indoors.
   • Hang a dozen wind chimes in the trees or railings leading to your front door.

Halloween Theme Parties

Once you've had a truly successful Halloween party, your friends will expect you to outdo yourself next year. Then what? Think themes. A strong theme can focus your party and help you get even more creative. Party themes can be as singular as "Aliens" or "Mummies," or conceptual, like a "Come as You Were" party where everyone is invited to dress as their favorite dead person. They can be literature-based—such as an Edgar Allan Poe party. Or activity-based, like a pumpkin carving party or a story party, where guests share Halloween-related stories they've either found or written themselves.

And who says you have to host a Halloween party in the twenty-first century? Halloween has gone through several incarnations over the centuries, and there's no rule against rifling through the past to resuscitate a good idea. Have a truly old-fashioned Halloween party with atmosphere, games, decorations, and even food from another time and place. Coming up next: ideas and how-to's for three themed Halloween parties: Old World, Gothic, and Victorian.

An Old World Halloween Party

Come inside, it's the eve of All Hallow's. But leave the door unlatched behind you, for the dead are cold and hungry and need a place to rest. Here they come now—welcome, grandmother! Welcome! Have something to eat, we've left some food for you. And here's a chair by the fire. Sit! Come home to us tonight and whisper the secrets of the dead in our ears.

For the ancient Celts, life began in the quiet of the seed hidden under the frozen ground. Darkness was a beginning, not an end. Death was renewal. And Samhain—a time when the earth itself took on a death-like pallor—was the start of the new year. It was time to face yourself and others, atone for transgressions, pay debts, and clear the slates. It was time for truce between neighbors and among generations, time to open the door to strangers traveling the rutted roads outside. It was also time to ask the dead what they knew of the future in hopes that they'd show you a path. [2]

With an Old World party, you can unearth long lost Halloween rituals and games, and take your guests back hundreds of years to a time when you needed four essential elements to help you celebrate: food, fire, fortunetelling, and phantoms.

INVITATIONS

Snippets of Halloween folklore make evocative invitation greetings. There are plenty of poems, superstitions, and sayings that have been recorded in volumes you can find at your library (see Resources). They originate from many countries, but especially from the British Isles. Here are a handful of possible party invitation greetings drawn from old folkways:

Greeting:
If you hear footsteps following you on Halloween,
you must not look round,
for it is the dead who are following,
and you should not meet their glance.
—old Irish Halloween superstition

Invitation text:
Follow the footsteps to our Halloween gathering at . . . etc.

Greeting:
Go to the crossroads at Hallowe'en and listen
to hear the future whispered in the wind.
—Old Welsh saying

Invitation text:
Meet us for a Halloween party at the crossroads of . . . etc.

Greeting:
Halloween will come, will come.
Witchcraft will be set agoing,
Fairies will be at full speed,
Running in every pass.
Avoid the road children, children.
—Irish verse

Invitation text:
Won't you join the fairies and witches at . . . etc?

Greeting:
For on Hallowmas Even the

Nighthag will ride,
And all her nine-fold sweenin on by
her side
Whether the wind swing lovely or
loud,
Stealing through moonshine or
Swathed in a cloud.
—Sir Walter Scott

Invitation text:
Come steal a little moonshine with us on Hallowmas Even at . . . etc.

PARTY GAMES

The autumnal fire is still kindled in North Wales, being on the eve of
the first day of November, and is attended by many ceremonies; such
as running through the fire and smoke, each casting a stone into the
fire, and all running off at the conclusion to escape from the black
short tailed sow; then supping upon parsnips, nuts and apples; catch-
ing at an apple suspended by a string, with the mouth alone, and the
same by an apple in a tub of water; each throwing a nut into the fire.
—Recorded in John Brand's *Popular Antiquities of Great Britain,* Vol. I,
1873

Fortunetelling with Food and Water

Leaving food for the dead on the eve of All Hallow's was both a
social and a spiritual offering. Its social function was to redistribute
the wealth for one night—in some areas, affluent families cooked a
feast and left it for the "spirits" (the town's poor) to eat while the
family was at church. The spiritual element was symbolic: food was
cooked for the ancestors to make sure that the living remembered
the dead. Younger people hoped against hope that the kindness
would then be repaid and the dead would pass on secrets from the
mysterious otherworld. You can invoke these centuries-old traditions
to plan activities for your party.

The Halloween Dumb Supper

Dumb cakes and dumb suppers most likely grew out of this idea of
feeding the dead. The cooking was done in complete silence, and,
often, backwards. If it worked, folks said, spirits would come to the
supper table. For at least two centuries, women on both sides of the
Atlantic tried Halloween dumb suppers with varying success.

Here's how to do it: sometime before midnight on Halloween, set a table for you, your guests, and a spirit. You must not speak during the entire process. Then, cook a meal—preferably something traditional for Halloween—and set it on plates. Serve each plate walking backwards, sit down, and, without talking, eat. A spirit should appear at midnight and take a place at the table. Some say this will be the spirit of your one true love.

Halloween Dumb Cake

Place a tin of flour and a small bowl of salt on a table. Have each guest take a handful of flour and place it on a sheet of wax paper. Each person then sprinkles the flour with as much salt as she can hold between her finger and thumb. Stir the flour and salt together, and hide a wedding ring in the mixture. Sprinkle it with a few drops of water and mix again. Heap the "dough" into a small bowl and pack it down hard. Turn the bowl upside down and unmold the dough carefully so that it retains its round shape. Have each person slice a piece of the "cake." The guest who gets the piece with the ring will marry next. To alter this game, use a charm that has special meaning, such as a coin for a new job, or a piece of eggshell for a baby.

Ducking for Apples

The apple is Old World Halloween's most potent symbol. It represents life-within-death, the essential drama of Halloween. At the year's end, death rules: leaves fall from trees, animals burrow, and the earth lies frozen and lifeless. But the decay that encrusts the earth protects and fertilizes the new life lying dormant within. Cut an apple in half sideways and you reveal a magical pentacle, the sign of Kore, imprisoned in Hades each winter waiting to be reborn come spring.

Almost as old as Halloween itself, ducking for apples may have once symbolized a journey through water to Avalon, or Apple-land, the mythical Celtic paradise. The apple was the talisman that admitted a favored mortal to the otherworld and gave power to foretell the future. According to Scottish historian F. Marion McNeill, apple ducking in old Scotland was done with a master of ceremonies who used a porridge stick (the equivalent of a Druid wand) to keep the apples moving. If you caught the apple, you won the ability to see into the future.

Fill a tub or bucket, the biggest you can find (I used a child's swimming pool once), with water. Stock it with apples and let several guests at a time try to grab an apple with their teeth. In the nineteenth-century, they said whoever snagged the first apple would marry first. Alternatively, the first name you heard spoken aloud after you had snagged your apple would be the name of your future spouse. In another variation, charms were pushed into the apples before they were set floating. He or she who snagged the apple with a coin would grow wealthy; a ring, be married; and a button, never marry.

Although I like second sight as a prize, especially on Halloween night, you can choose new meanings for your charms or prizes to modernize the game and make it more appropriate for your guests.

Alphabet Apple Peels

On Halloween in the nineteenth century, girls in the American South put trays of corn meal next to their beds in hopes that ghosts would write the initials of their secret lovers in it. Sometimes they'd wake to find messages: cryptic symbols engineered by worms who'd wiggled through the grain at night leaving trails taken to be letters.

You can adapt this game using an apple, as many other girls did, both in Europe and America. Give each guest an apple and a small paring knife. Have them peel the apple in one long strip, being very careful not to break it as it spirals off the fruit. One at a time, each person stands absolutely still, then throws the apple peel over his left shoulder. According to superstition, it will land in the initial of your future mate.

The Face in the Mirror

The games our great-great-grandmothers played came down through the generations, and although the medium may have differed—flour-and-salt dough, cornmeal, apple parings—the question has remained the same for centuries: who loves me secretly?

This divination also attempts to answer that question. But this one must be done alone. Set aside a room at your party where guests can be completely isolated for a few moments—a basement, maybe, or extra bedroom. Set a chair directly in front of a mirror. Put one candle, unlit, next to the mirror and turn off all the lights. The room must be pitch black.

Give your guest an apple and a box of matches. Tell him to enter the room alone, sit in front of the mirror, light the candle, and concentrate on his image in the glass. Slowly, very slowly, he should eat the apple, all the while looking into the mirror and repeating these words:

"Who my true love is to be

Come and look in this glass with me."

Tell him that if he does this, he'll see a reflection of his future love standing behind him.

There's another version of this game, also involving a dark room and matches, and done completely alone. Give your guest a box of matches and tell him to walk down the cellar stairs backwards, very slowly. Tell him when he reaches the very bottom step, if he strikes the match and spins around, he'll glimpse the shadow of his love. If your guests are at all imaginative and the least bit spooked, they're apt to see all manner of weird things.

The Game of the Three Bowls

"In order on the clean hearthstaue,
The luggies three are ranged;
And ev'ry time great care is ta'en,
To see them duly changed . . . "
—Robert Burns, "Hallowe'en" (1785)

Use three bowls. Put clean water in one, muddy in another, and leave the third empty. Blindfold a person, spin her around, lead her to the bowls and have her dip a hand in one. If she chooses the clean bowl, it means her future spouse will be someone who has not been married before; if she chooses the bowl filled with muddy water, a widower; and if she chooses the empty bowl, no marriage at all. Change the bowls' positions each time. And vary the meanings however you see fit.

In early twentieth-century Ireland, the game was played with four bowls: a ring (marriage), rosary beads (you'll become a nun), nothing (never marry) or clay (death). Cheery, eh? Victorians played the game with symbols such as earth (sudden or violent death), water (emigration or shipwreck), or a ring (a wedding). I've seen it played with flower petals (success), stones (strength) and peanuts (the number of nuts inside the shell signifies the number of children you'll have).

Playing With Fire

For the ancients, the body-to-soul transformation at the heart of Samhain manifested itself in fire. Just as death transforms the body into spirit, fire transforms peat and wood into spirals of smoke ghosting up to the heavens. A symbolic representation of the afterlife was mythologically important on Samhain; after all, the earth had just died. People needed to be reminded that she would renew herself and reawaken come spring. They looked to their October 31 bonfires for hope and guidance: hope that the fire would fuel the sun, whose light grew fainter by the day, and guidance from spirits of ancestors who crowded close to the living for warmth during this important seasonal festival.

Each family took a piece of the "new fire" (communal Samhain fire) and lit their own fire with it to express community and mark the beginning of a new year. Hearth fires were kept burning on this night so that ancestral spirits could find their way home. Here in America, they echo in Halloween candles, jack-o-lanterns, strings of holiday lights, and, should you be so lucky to have one, a fire in the fireplace.

Snapdragon

Here's a game based on the heroic paradigm that you must go through fire to find truth. Snapdragon is traditionally an after-dinner game.

Create one-sentence fortunes on slips of paper. Wrap the paper tightly in tin foil. Pour half a pint of brandy into a shallow dish and scatter the fortunes in the brandy. Add figs, raisins, almonds, and dried fruits. Light the brandy, and when it burns with a steady, low flame, turn out all the lights, and sprinkle salt in the dish. The flames will sputter, crackle, and turn varying shades of green, orange, and blue. Guests try to "snap" fortunes and treats from the dish with their fingers. Adults only, please!

Snap-Apple

Trial by fire and the apple-as-reward are Halloween themes that play themselves out in many games and tests. This one was so popular that Halloween used to be known as Snap-Apple Night in parts of Great Britain. The game originally required apples and lit candles. We'll play it with apples and a small bag of flour.

Suspend a stick, about four feet long, from a ceiling or archway in your home. Your nose should be the same height as the stick. Spear an apple with one end and tie a small cheesecloth bag filled with flour to the other end. Play with the balance until the stick stays horizontal, supporting both the flour and the apple (add a few bolts to the flour side for ballast if necessary). Give the stick a spin. The object is to bite the apple without getting whacked by the flour. One person plays at a time.

Burning Chestnuts

These glowing nuts are emblems true
Of what in human life we view;
The ill-match'd couple fret and fume,
And thus in strife themselves consume;
Or from each other wildly start,
And with a noise forever part.
But see the happy, happy pair,
Of genuine love and truth sincere;
With mutual fondness while they burn,
Still to each other kindly turn;
And as the vital sparks decay,
Together gently sink away:
Till life's fierce ordeal being past,
Their mingled ashes rest at last.
—Charles Graydon, "On Nuts Burning, Hallows Eve" (1801)

Have your guests gather around your fireplace (a barbecue grill works just as nicely). Pass around a bowl of chestnuts and let each person choose two nuts and name them for themselves and a lover, real or potential. Each player puts the nuts next to each other in the hot embers or coals. Now watch. The poem above gives a key for what the popping and burning predicts in terms of their relationship.

A Gothic Halloween Party

Contemporary Goths will be the first to tell you Goth is not a religion or a cult, but a lifestyle based on an appreciation for the darker side of life and art, a sensibility that attracts morbid dreamers who prefer blood-red roses and vampiric decadence to daisies and the Gap. Rather than wander into the realm of what is or isn't Goth, let's take the other gothic as inspiration. Gothic as in the architecture of the Middle Ages—cathedrals and buttresses—and gothic as in gothic fiction, the romantic, darkly lyrical stories, novels and poems that were the first to plumb the hideousness that hides in human consciousness.

INVITATIONS

Party invitations set the mood and verses from any of the more moribund poets—Baudelaire, Rimbaud, Blake, Poe, Aiken—would serve. Here is a handful for starters:

Greeting:

    I alone hold the key to this
    Savage side show.
    —Arthur Rimbaud

Invitation text:

    Step inside, won't you please? Date, time . . . etc.

Greeting:

    The skies they were ashen and sober;
    The leaves they were withering and sere—

Details like this rat and skull, or ghoulish photos framed as if they were family, add lots of atmosphere to a party. Photo by Tina Reuwsaat.

It was night in the lonesome October
—Edgar Allan Poe, "Ulalume: A Ballad"

Invitation text:

The best party night of the year.
Please join us on . . . etc.

Greeting:

She thinks of bones
And grinning skulls and corruptible death
Wrapped in his shroud; and now fancies she hears
Deeps sighs and sees pale, sickly ghosts gliding
—William Blake, "Fair Elenor"

Invitation text:

Must be Halloween . . . Please come to a party on . . . etc.

Greeting:

Her mouth is sinister and red
As blood in moonlight is
—Conrad Aiken, "The Vampire 1914"

Invitation text:

Join us for a moonlit frolic at . . . etc.

Greeting:

Something wicked this way comes . . .
—William Shakespeare, *Macbeth*

Invitation text:

. . . to a Halloween party at . . . etc.

Greeting:

A thousand shapes are at your side,
A thousand by your bed abide,
A thousand, hellish demon sprites
That bend ye to their foul delights.
—Arthur Cleveland Coxe, "Halloween A Romaunt"

Invitation text:

Come join the demons in their foul delights at . . . etc.

DECORATIONS

Rent your favorite vampire movie and check out the sets as inspiration for decorating. Gothic *was* setting. It was all gloomy forests, leaking cellars, secret passages, tomb-like dungeons, lightning, thunder, fog, and moonlight.

Buy a block of dry ice and create a ground-hugging mist to rival the omnipresent fog of Collinswood. Light the party using only clusters of votives to give a cathedral-type atmosphere. Use a contemporary gothic band, Gregorian chants, or movie soundtrack CD as background music. Add a medieval touch by draping lengths of dark, richly colored fabric over your smaller tables and filling your party rooms with all the throw pillows you can find. Throw in a few skulls and gargoyles bought from Halloween stores.

Decorate your rooms with clusters of lilies, bouquets of dead roses, or flowers you choose from the deep purple or wine-red blooms available at your florists' shop (you probably won't find black plants—they're extremely rare). If you're ordering flowers, ask for Queen of the Night tulips (they're a deep velvety maroon); Black Beauty lilies (dark blackish-red); or even Fire King lilies (a brilliant blood-red). For a more Victorian gothic floral bouquet, arrange sprigs of pointy purple delphinium in a black vase. Larkspur and lycianthus together will give you a softer-looking bouquet. Bright red roses turn the color of old blood when dried, and make great gothic decorations. To dry roses:

• Remove the bottom leaves from roses that still have their color and their petals.

• Tie two or three of the flowers together with string and hang them upside down out of direct sunlight.

• Wait two weeks.

• Untie them and coat each rose with hair spray.

• Arrange in vases throughout your rooms.

READINGS FOR A GOTHIC HALLOWEEN

The gothic novel was spawned in reaction to the science and logic of the Enlightenment. By the nineteenth century, Mary Shelley had given us *Frankenstein* (1818) and Bram Stoker, *Dracula* (1897), inspiring generations of horror writers. What better entertainment for a Halloween night than to read aloud something that raises the hair on the back of your neck?

You can ask all your guests to come prepared to read from their favorite gothic writers (limit the lengths to around ten minutes so that everyone gets a chance) and have a candlelit story session. Or find one friend who's an excellent reader and have guests gather for the story. Suggestions follow for ten short classics—each takes fifteen minutes or less to read aloud—from best-loved masters of dark fiction, followed by a few poems and poets sure to curl your toes.

Edgar Allan Poe, "The Black Cat"

We almost understand the step-by-step progression that compels Poe's drunken madman to bury an ax in his wife's head. A cat's oppressive affection incites the crime and seals the fate of the murderer as he tries desperately to entomb the evidence in loose brick and mortar in his cellar. The cat, of course, has the last word.

Edgar Allan Poe, "The Cask of Amontillado"

The story follows the naive and vain Fortunato as he's led deeper and deeper into the catacombs by a vengeful narrator under the guise of tasting the greatly prized wine of the title. As the catacombs grow narrower and the ceilings get lower you can't help but feel your lungs tighten and your nostrils sting from nitre [nitrogen] in the stone.

Ambrose Bierce, "The Damned Thing"

Bierce sets about making us see something that most characters in the story don't believe exists. Like a cadaverous bird circling closer and closer to its subject, he takes us from the coroner's inquiry room through the dead man's story to the impossible events of one afternoon in the woods.

Ambrose Bierce, "The Boarded Window"

This is a tight puzzle of a story with an unforgettable final image. The only window in old Murlock's isolated cabin has always been boarded up. Of course, it was once open, but that was when Murlock's wife was alive, before she got the fever, before she died, and before Murlock dropped into a deep, exhausted sleep as he was preparing her body for burial.

W.W. Jacobs, "The Monkey's Paw"

Suggested most often by the ghost story aficionados I queried, "The Monkey's Paw" is the classic tale of a man granted three wishes. Although he's been warned repeatedly not to use the mummified paw to wish upon, he does. Nothing good comes of it; each wish produces something more awful than the one before.

H.P. Lovecraft, "The Outsider"

Often called the twentieth-century Poe, Lovecraft was the child of psychotic parents who grew up to write what he called "cosmic horror." His stories often conjure an ancient evil, long thought extinct, which exists in the gray area between horror and science fiction. In this one, the protagonist seemingly crawls up the steep walls of a tower towards a dim and distant source of light. In the last few sentences, a sudden shift in perspective reveals his cruel circumstance.

Guy de Maupassant, "The Hand"

The writer had a very dark side. Maupassant cut his own throat and died nineteen months later, insane. The solitary Sir John Rowel moves into a Corsican town and instantly, rumors fly. The local magistrate, curious about the truth, befriends him and is jolted by something he finds chained to the wall in Rowel's drawing room: a black, withered human hand. Like the magistrate, Maupassant lays only the facts of the matter clearly before the reader, leaving your imagination to fill in the blanks.

H.G. Wells, "The Flowering of the Strange Orchid"

Winter Wedderburn is an orchid collector whose exciting, most recent prize is an unusual bulb found in a dead man's satchel. Wedderburn nurtures the plant, whose leech-like suckers and blood-red sap he has never seen before. Turns out there's a bit of the vampire in this plant, and possibly—readers will have to decide—in old Wedderburn himself.

Robert Louis Stevenson, "The Body Snatcher"

One of Stevenson's shorter stories recounts the tale of a pair of students and the cadavers they supply to a prominent British medical school. All does not go well, and the more naive character of the two, Fettes, begins to recognize some of the bodies as friends.

Patrick McGrath, "The Smell"

A cloyingly sweet smell maddens a control-freak husband and father; the odor grows, as do the imagined transgressions of his family. McGrath takes us inside the head of a madman who begins searching for the source of the sickly stench, and ends wedged in a chimney suffocating in his own imagination.

Poetry

Looking at Death is dying—
Just let go the breath,
And not the pillow at your cheek
So slumbereth.

Others can wrestle, yours is done,
And so of woe bleak dreaded, come—
It sets the fright at liberty,
And terror's free—
Gay, ghastly holiday!
—Emily Dickinson

Dark poetry can be found in most periods, but became really popular with some of the great Romantic poets. Many of them penned vampire poems. In fact, Samuel Taylor Coleridge's "Christabel" is said to be the first in English (written 1797-1800), although it never mentions the word vampire. Other good candidates for gothic Halloween reading are Keats' "La Belle Dame Sans Merci," Baudelaire's "The Vampire," Conrad Aiken's "La Belle Morte," and "The Vampire 1914." To find others, explore the collected works of artists such as Arthur Rimbaud (*A Season in Hell*), Charles Baudelaire (*Flowers of Evil*), and of course, Poe. [3]

A Very Victorian Halloween

Oh it was hard to yield my breath;
'Twas hard to breathe anew;
It was hard to come to life again,
And Earth once more to view!
—Arthur Cleveland Coxe, "Halloween A Romaunt"

The Victorians—the name conjures images of corsets, bustiers, parlor talk, and high tea, a time when piano legs were modestly draped, but bodices brazenly ripped open in cheap romance novels. When it comes to Halloween, Americans in the Victorian era did as much to nationalize the celebration as the thousands of Irish and Scots streaming across the Atlantic. The Victorian era (Victoria ruled England from 1837-1901) was the heyday of American publications such as *Godey's Lady's Book* and *Harper's Bazar*. Every October, ladies' magazines ran articles, poetry, and how-to items about Halloween that taught people the history and rituals of celebration. Victorian editors went digging back through the history books to find quaint old customs that would add a more pastoral, personal perspective. Some things they made popular anew; others they simply invented.

This need to connect with the past dovetailed with a revival of spiritualism in the States beginning around 1850, during which people flocked to clairvoyants to communicate with loved ones. Toss in a late nineteenth-century economic boom (for some, anyway), and Victorian Halloween parties became especially memorable.

INVITATIONS

People once sent greeting cards at Halloween with sprightly sayings and pretty drawings of cats, witches and little pumpkin-headed children. These vintage verses, along with Victorian-era poetry make perfect party invitations. Sample texts follow:

Greeting:
'Tis the night—the night
Of the grave's delight,
And the warlocks are at their play!
Ye think that without,
The wild winds shout,
But no, it is they—it is they!

Invitation text:
Please join us at the witching hour of . . . etc.

Greeting:
The witch cat wears its mystic ring,
The black bat spreads its gruesome wing,
Hobgoblins weirdly chant and sing

Invitation text:
'Tis Halloween.
Please come to a party at . . . etc.

Greeting:
Puck the sprite
Weaves tonight
Cobwebs bright.

Invitation text:
What a night!
Come to our Halloween party on . . . etc.

Greeting:
Tis Halloween!
And I must
stay and howl
my little life away!

Invitation text:
Won't you come howl along with us, etc?

FORTUNES AND FAVORS

If you have a sit-down dinner at your Halloween party, make sure the guests find a fortune at their place. Using old-fashioned pen and ink, copy a fortune onto a piece of antique-colored paper for each guest. Try the Victorian-style fortunes below, or make up your own. For an authentic touch, you can burn the edges of the paper carefully over a candle flame (have water nearby just in case). Roll the paper into a scroll and tie with a piece of raffia or fancy ribbon.

Whosoever is to your left
when comes to love is very deft

The handsome person on your right
would really rather kiss than fight

Look towards the door, who next comes through
has very important news for you

Close your eyes and count to three
The name you hear said next is (s)he
Who's always loved you secretly.

Victorian party hostesses often gave their guests favors, such as gilded wishbones and tiny pillboxes with "dream pills" inside to take home as a souvenir. In keeping with this tradition, give each guest a Bonnach Salainn (a salty Scottish oatcake made only for Halloween, see Recipes), wrapped in pretty paper and tied with a ribbon. But here's the catch: they must eat it in silence, just before bed. If they neither speak nor take a drink after they eat it, their true love will bring them a drink of water in their dreams.

DECORATIONS

"Autumn leaves should be gathered while still brilliant with autumn hues, and, after being brushed over with linseed oil, ironed with a warm iron, then put away until needed."

—*Godey's Lady's Book,* 1887

The Victorians found many ways to bring the outdoors inside at their Halloween parties. But if you can't find the time to oil and iron your leaves, fear not. You can do other things inspired by the spirit of nineteenth-century decorating. If you're lucky enough to have autumn leaves outside your door, collect some and arrange them on your food table. Decorate any tabletop with strewn leaves and place a jack-o-lantern in their midst. Then, fill the room with flowers. Marigolds and chrysanthemums are both fall blooms; they also carry the symbolism of death, always a plus. Make a vase out of a pumpkin (carve a pumpkin and place a real vase inside so that it's concealed) and fill it with big bunches of these flowers. Or, set groups of potted mums in the corners of your room.

Decorate your table with food, in Victorian fashion, that's color-coordinated. Cover the center of the table with bright red crabapples (available at the supermarket only at this time of year!). Place colorful bowls filled to the brim with every yellow, red, and orange food you can think of: bunches of fat red grapes, piles of apples, sweet oranges.

> We transformed our front room into a Victorian parlor. We hung blue velvet curtains from the windows and doors, made shrines, and placed old renderings of London on the walls. We arranged tattered Victorian couches and chairs before a fire and put out a small table with Tarot, crystal balls, magical artifacts and candles. French wines were served along with cheeses and chocolates, arranged on old family silver.
> —Victorian Halloween party in Santa Barbara, California

It is best to illuminate your entire party with firelight. Light as many candles as you can and place them throughout the house (but always err on the side of safety—don't place candles near curtains or fabric). Add jack-o-lanterns: three on a tabletop, one in a window, one in a hanging planter, one in an empty birdcage, more of them decorating bookshelves, running up the stairs, a cluster of them in a corner (arrange them in different heights by using an upside-down flower pots to elevate some).

A dramatic effect can be achieved by using a three-step ladder or plant stand. Cover the steps with black cloth and carve a pumpkin or two for each step. Wind tiny orange or white lights around the pumpkins and keep the rooms lights low.

If you do need to add light here and there, the next best thing to a candle is a decorated lampshade:

• Draw a witch, cat, moon, or star shape on a piece of black posterboard. Be as elaborate as you like!

• Cut out the shapes; trace the ones you like best to make more.

• Arrange the shapes on the inside of your lampshade and attach them to the shade using small, rolled up pieces of tape.

• Turn on the light to see the silhouetted scene come to life.

Vintage pumpkins arranged on a plant stand from the collection of Tina Reuwsaat. Photo by Tina Reuwsaat.

STOLEN KISSES: GAMES FOR VICTORIAN HALLOWEEN PARTIES

We opened all our house—as we knew the cellar would be as interesting to Uncle John as the attic would be to Great-Aunt Martha. We had jack-o-lanterns on the gateposts, and in the spooky corners of the cellar, and in the attic. All the young people were given cards, much like dance-cards, with spaces for engagements in regular order: "nine o'clock, Mr. B—, cellar stairs; half past nine, Mr. C—, library davenport; ten o'clock Mr. D—, kitchen-table; and so on. This arrangement of conversational "dates" kept the young people scrambling all over the house, upstairs and down, and there was no possibility of stagnation! At half after eleven, we all met in the big living-room and ranged ourselves around the great fireplace . . . we told ghost stories, and roasted chestnuts, and popped corn, and counted apple seeds until well after the charmed hour of midnight!

—*The Delineator,* October 1911

Victorian Halloween parties were really for young, single adults. Married people were rarely invited, as the main entertainment consisted of flirting games. Ladies were shown off to their advantage in firelight; men could demonstrate their bravery during Halloween fortunetelling forays into dimly lit rooms and gardens. At its dark little core, Victorian Halloween celebrations were about who was going to end up with who.

Like the tunnel of love only a few decades away, the purpose of most Victorian party games was to create opportunities for touching—they were excuses to interlace fingers, brush lips, gather close together in the dark, or bump blindfolded into each other's arms. Desire and superstition were stirred together to tantalize.

Sound intriguing?

Let's play.

Snap-Apple, Victorian Style

Hang a dozen apples from a doorway at head-height. Divide your guests into couples: one couple plays at a time. Tie each player's hands behind their back, and place players opposite each other with the apple hanging in between. Each tries to snag the fruit with his teeth; the winner is the one first to get the apple eaten (it's almost impossible to do this without brushing lips). Want to make it easier? Substitute doughnuts.

Matchmaking with Apples

Use half the number of apples as you have guests. Tie two six-foot lengths of ribbon to each apple; one red, one yellow. Place apples in one large basket on a table with the ribbons twisted together, then splayed out on the table. The women each choose a red ribbon and the men a yellow (or just divide your guests in half regardless of gender). At a signal, everyone follows their ribbon until each finds his or her mate, attached to the same apple. The apple is then cut in half: each person chooses a half and counts the seeds to find out what will happen between them:

One—I love thee
Two—You love me
Three—Wedded we will be
Four—You love me dearly
Five—You love me nearly
Six—A friend forever
Seven—We must sever

Eight—We met too late
Nine—Why hesitate
Ten—You are my chosen mate
Of course, you can make up your own verse or predictions!

Prophesying

Once girls did this with melted lead; melted wax drops from a candle will do just as well. You'll need a wide bowl filled with cold water, a few fat candles, and an imaginative "seer."

Each guest lights a candle and lets it burn until a small pool of melted wax surrounds the wick. Then quickly, with one movement, dump the wax into the water and blow out the candle. The seer interprets the guests' fate from the shape of the hardened wax. Is it the shape of a bird of some kind? Maybe there's travel ahead, or freedom from a hated job. Flowers? A wedding. . . a bountiful garden. . . fruition of efforts—the seer decides.

Blow Out the Candle

The best Halloween fortunetelling has to do with obscured sight. People must do their divining in the dark, in reflections, in shadows, or backwards. It adds to the mystery and the fun.

Light a candle and place it in the center of the room. Blindfold one player, and spin them around several times. The object is to blow out the candle, which is usually harder than it seems, and much more fun for those watching than whomever's doing the puffing. The number of puffs it takes to blow out the candle is the number of months before the player finds a soul mate.

Moon in the Mirror

Here's an outdoor variation of the Old World mirror and flame game that can be played by more than one. Send one of your guests outside in the moonlight with only a mirror. Tell him to walk backwards around the entire house, concentrating on the mirror and repeating this rhyme (write it for them on an index card):

Round and round, O stars so fair!

Ye travel and search out everywhere;

I pray you, sweet stars, now show to me

This night who my future husband (wife) shall be.

Tell him when he gets halfway around, he must stand very still and stare at the moon's reflection in the mirror until something happens. Of course you, as host, send at least two people out at the same time, but in opposite directions so that they're sure to bump into each other in the dark.

Shadow Games

Hang a white bedsheet or tablecloth from the ceiling or in a wide doorframe. Place a bright lamp on a table about five feet behind the "shadow screen." Turn out all the other lights nearby.

One person sits in front of the screen—this is the player. All the others wait hidden behind the screen. One at a time, each person takes a pose midway between the lamp and the screen. The goal is for the player to guess the identity of the poser. The poser's goal is to disguise themselves as much as possible. Props, prothestics, and all manner of deceit is okay in this game.

HOW TO STAGE YOUR OWN SEANCE

In the first half of the twentieth-century in Great Britain, a Scot named Helen Duncan supplemented her income as a part-time worker in a bleach factory by holding seances for her neighbors. Wearing a voluminous black dress, Helen sat on a wooden chair at the front of the audience. All those gathered would join in a hymn and a prayer, and then she would enclose herself in a makeshift cabinet constructed of black cloth. The only illumination in the room was a single red light.

After several minutes, as the audience peered through the dimness, a narrow white ribbon about eighteen inches wide would slide out from under the curtain and rise to a height of perhaps four feet. It would then "reveal" itself to be the spirit of someone recently dead, as identified by an audience member (While no one knows precisely how Mrs. Duncan worked her illusion, most imagine it involved "invisible" threads and bleached linen fabric. Some swear it was ectoplasm to this day, and in fact, there was a movement to exonerate Mrs. Duncan launched in Great Britain on the one hundredth anniversary of her birth.). It was only a matter of time before the inevitable happened. An audience member identified one of the apparitions as her husband—a soldier away at war—and by coincidence, unbeknownst to his wife, the man had died that day. The news spread: Helen Duncan gets her information straight from the spirit world!

Seances (a French word meaning "meeting") have been used to communicate with the spirit world for decades, and for a myriad of purposes from crime solving to finding lost objects to building roads.

According to the *New York Times,* in the late 1970s, Iceland's Public Roads Administration conducted a seance to negotiate with some angry elves who objected to the construction blasting. A truce was reached: the highway department would forego the demolition and the elves would behave themselves.

So—do they work? It depends on who you ask. Anyone who willingly attends a seance has, somewhere in the back of their mind, a faint spark of hope that something otherworldly will really happen.

Your entire seance room should be dark. The only light source should be located on the center of your seance table. You can have a candle, a small red bulb in a table lamp (or the dimmest possible white bulb, around 15 watts), or a glow stick under a translucent, but not clear, bowl. If you use a candle, you can doctor it to go out unexpectedly by cutting the candle in half, snipping out a piece of the wick, then melting it back together. You'll need a round table large enough to seat everyone, and a chair for each participant. Drape the table with a long cloth, or several overlapping cloths, reaching to the floor.

Play a subliminal soundtrack to add more atmosphere. At the Voodoo Museum in New Orleans, one room has the faint sound of a heartbeat-like drumming emanating from the baseboards. The effect is very creepy. Used subtly, this sort of sound can be unsettling. Various classical pieces could also be good mood setters, but when the time comes to conjure, turn your stereo off or you may never hear the messages from beyond. Final note with respect to sound: turn your phone off.

It will help induce the right frame of mind in your audience if you perform any of the following rituals before beginning:

• After all your participants are seated, walk around behind the chairs, sprinkling salt to form a "protective" circle that encloses the table.

• Crush fresh rosemary or other pungent herb or spice between your fingers over the light source in the center of the table. Explain that the pleasant fragrance will attract friendly human spirits.

Now for the manifestations: these are your actual tricks. A second person in on these is a great asset. They can play the part of the spirits, while you remain completely guiltless. A partner hidden at the far side of the room can:

• Create poltergeist manifestations by throwing small objects at a prearranged time.

• Manipulate a string or thread to set a chair or lamp sliding across the floor.

• Supply the knocks or ringing bells that the spirits will use to communicate.

• Flick light switches.

Remember, less is better than more. The first time a hairbrush flies across the room is shocking. By the fourth time, it can be downright silly. Plan your effects carefully with your partner, and keep them infrequent and simple.

Will your spirit communicate via ghostly knocks (one for yes, two for no)? Your partner can make the knocks from anywhere outside the room. If she's upstairs, she can make the knocks on the window of your seance room by lowering a bolt, tied to black string or fishing line, out a window. Use a baby monitor so your partner can listen in and know when to rap.

If you don't have a partner, you can fasten a cardboard box to the underside of the table with some duct tape. Tapping it with the toe of your shoe will create a hollow sound, and since it is up off the floor, you won't risk having someone else's foot bang into it. You can also have the seance table appear to move on its own.

After your rituals, seat yourself at the table and slip the toe of your foot under the nearest table leg. If you wait a sufficient amount of time (several minutes at least), you'll get a strong response with the slightest shift of the table. Deny that it happened. Insist you felt nothing. After another moment, do it again. How do you get your foot under the table leg? Have one table leg slightly shorter than the rest, and arrange the table so that this leg is next to your seat. You might prop it with something small that you can easily shoved out of the way with your toe.

Alternately, and depending on the weight of your table, you can move the table yourself by attaching rulers to your arms and hiding them under long sleeves. When the time comes to put your hands on the table, slip the rulers underneath and put your hands firmly on top. You will be able to rock, or even lift your side of the table.

Once your seance is underway, timing is your final important element. Never rush. A person who just sat down is in a very different frame of mind after sitting for ten minutes with his fingertips resting on the tabletop.

When your seance is over and all spirits have departed, escort your guests from the room before turning on the lights.

And remember—it's only a game, right?

CHAPTER FIVE

Halloween Music and Movies

A Guide To Great Halloween Sound And Video

Halloween Music

Around Halloween you can pick up a party tape of Halloween favorites just about anywhere. But choose carefully. You don't want the creepy "Tubular Bells" from *The Exorcist* playing at your party if people are looking to dance. On the other hand, you don't want the "Monster Mash" ruining the concentration of your psychic. The titles that follow are suggestions to get you started; they're all available at major on-line book and music stores. Most should be available at your local record store year-round, and if not, can be special-ordered.

COMPILATIONS:

Elvira Presents Haunted Hits CD
(1993, also available on cassette)
Includes pop classics like "The Monster Mash" (Bobby "Boris" Picket and the Crypt Kickers) and "Ghostbusters" (Ray Parker, Jr.), as well as "I Was a Teenage Werewolf" (the Cramps) and "Welcome to my Nightmare" (Alice Cooper). The cassette version has more off-beat tunes like Screamin' Jay Hawkins' "Little Demon," The Tubes' "Attack of the Fifty-Foot Woman," and "Attack of the Killer Tomatoes" by Lee Lewis.

New Wave Halloween: Just Can't Get Enough CD
(1998, also available on cassette)
This album includes fifteen tracks by the B-52s, Ministry, Roky

Erickson, Sonic Youth, Oingo Boingo, the Ramones, Dave Edmunds, plus the theme from *The Munsters* and "Time Warp" from *The Rocky Horror Picture Show*. As you can imagine, it's danceable and noisy with a few moody pieces thrown in. If you like this kind of music, the 1998 *Halloween Hootenanny* CD may also be a good bet—it's got music from Zacherle, Rob Zombie, Reverend Horton Heat, Satan's Pilgrims and many others of that ilk.

MUSIC FOR ATMOSPHERE
(also good for background during trick-or-treating hours)

Midnight Syndicate *Realm of Shadows* CD
(2000)
Call it gothic mood music: sinister and foreboding, a creepy soundscape for a night with no moon. Dark orchestrations and some vocals (mostly narration) follow a mythic story line with tracks like "Into the Abyss," "The Summoning," and "Witching Hour."

Dead Can Dance *Aion* CD
(1990)
Anything by Dead Can Dance would probably make good Halloween background music. Call it ethereal, liturgical, even Goth/folk. This CD sounds like it's been around for centuries, full of chanting, drumming, ballads, even bagpipes; it evokes everything from medieval cathedrals to keening banshees.

Music from the Haunted Mansion CD
A CD of tracks used in Disney's Haunted Mansion, fans claim the soundtrack—like the house itself—is simply terrific. Order from 1-800-362-4533. Disney delivers in four to six weeks.

Danny Elfman *Music for a Darkened Theatre—Film and Television Music Vol. 2* CD
(1996, two-CD set)
A mock-creepy, clever, eclectic set of film scores focused around the movies Elfman made with Tim Burton, such as *Edward Scissorhands, To Die For,* and *Batman Returns.*

Philip Glass *Dracula* CD
(1999)
The contemporary (and excellent) Kronos Quartet recorded this Philip Glass soundtrack, composed for the reissue of the 1931

Dracula movie directed by Tod Browning. Twenty-six tracks for fans of new music.

Elliot Goldenthal *Interview with a Vampire: Original Motion Picture Soundtrack* CD
(1994, also available on cassette)
A chilling counterpart to the film's visuals, this has both classical-type arrangements as well as a version of *Sympathy for the Devil* by Guns n' Roses. Tracks follow the nuances of the movie and include cuts like "Lestat's Tarantella," "Madeleine's Lament," "Armand's Seduction," and "Louis' Revenge."

Angelo Badalementi *Twin Peaks: Fire Walk With Me* CD
(1992, also available on cassette)
This is just what you'd imagine for a David Lynch movie—sexy, menacing and visceral. Badalementi uses some excellent jazz players on the sultry tracks, and Julee Cruise sings "Questions in a World of Blue." You can listen to this, use it as background mood music, and even dance to it.

Also good is *Twin Peaks the Series* CD (1990). If you were one of the millions who sat glued to the TV every week trying to figure out who killed Laura Palmer, you'll recognize every piece. If not, suffice it to say that this music's surreal and hypnotic and makes for great party atmosphere. It's not just creepy, either—there's a romantic side.

Alan Parsons Project *Tales of Mystery & Imagination* CD
(1987; original release, 1976)
Parsons used the writings of Edgar Allan Poe as a basis for this album, created in the '70s but revamped and modernized for its 1987 release. Half the CD is tense, orchestral-style music; the other half, songs. Tracks include "The Raven," "The Telltale Heart," and "The Cask of Amontillado." Orson Welles does some recitation.

SOUND EFFECTS

Halloween Sound Effects CD (Laserlight)
(1999)
Good for dubbing precise sounds for any startle-type scares at your party. The CD includes sixty effects including "Dentist Drill of Death," "Crazy Group Laugh," "Door Creaks," "Thrown Off a Cliff," and "Help Me."

Scary Sound Effects: Nightmarish Noise For Halloween CD
(1994, also available on cassette)
Similar to the above, and includes "Wolfman Growls," "Voodoo
Chant," "Little Girl Walking," "We're Digging Up Your Treats," and
"The Theremin Orchestra" among its forty-one cuts (the theremin
makes that wavering, high-pitched whistle you hear in *The Day the
Earth Stood Still*).

CLASSICAL MUSIC CHOICES FOR HALLOWEEN
—Compiled by Jackson Braider, WGBH Radio, Boston, Massachusetts
Ideal background music for the most elegant of parties. Make
your own compilation from these favorites:

Charles Gounod *Funeral March for a Marionette*
Also known as the theme from the Alfred Hitchcock TV show.

J.S. Bach *Toccata and Fugue in D Minor, BWV 565: Toccata*
This is the organ piece made famous by *Phantom of the Opera*.

Maurice Ravel *Gaspard de la nuit*
A ghostly tale told musically, this piano piece is lovely and foreboding, full of lush cascades of notes that suddenly go silent.

Frederic Chopin *Funeral March from Sonata in B-flat Minor, Op. 35*
If death had a signature piece, this is it, the dum-dum-dedum
dum-dedum-dedum-dedum played at every cartoon funeral.

Modest Mussorgsky *Night on Bald Mountain*
You may remember it as the tormented souls scene from Disney's
Fantasia.

Camille Saint-Saens *The Sorcerer's Apprentice*
Also from *Fantasia*, in this scene Mickey bewitches the brooms to
help him mop the floor.

Edvard Grieg *In the Hall of the Mountain King* (from *Peer Gynt* Suite
No. 1, Opus 46)
You hear this anytime elves go into a mountainside. It begins
sneaky and slowly escalates into a maelstrom of wailing violins.

Hector Berlioz *Symphonie fantastique*
A longer work, this piece includes movements such as *March to
the Scaffold* and *Dream of the Witches' Sabbath*.

Anton in Dvorvák: *The Noonday Witch* and *The Water Goblin*
Symphonic poems based on two Bohemian folk tales.

Richard Wagner: *Ride of the Valkyries*
This is the inspiration for the "kill the wabbit" theme from Bugs
Bunny cartoons.

These classical works don't exist on a single CD—you need to find
them through each composer. But here's one CD that will give you
a leg up:
Fright Night—Music That Goes Bump in the Night CD
(1989)
This compilation includes *Night on Bald Mountain, Marche funèbre
d'une marionette,* and *Ride of the Valkyries* (performed by the
Philadelphia Orchestra, Eugene Ormandy conducting); *In the Hall of
the Mountain King* (Philharmonia Orchestra, Andrew Davis conducting); *Toccata and Fugue in D Minor* (performed by E. Power Biggs);
The Sorcerer's Apprentice, (ORTF National Orchestra, Lorin Maazel
conducting); and *Symphonie fantastique* (only the fourth movement,
"March to the Scaffold").

Halloween Videos

For instant spark, play a movie in the background of your
Halloween party or in the front window as guests or trick or treaters
come to the door. Here are titles to consider, arranged by categories:
Monsters, Dracula, Haunted Houses, Classics, Kids, Camp, and the
Ten Scariest Movies of All Time. If the movie has been rated, the
rating is included. Most are available in video rental stores; some you
may need to special order.

Monsters

Cortlandt Hull runs the Witch's Dungeon Horror Museum in
Bristol, Connecticut, the country's longest running museum of fantasy and horror films. The museum houses authentic, life-size recreations of memorable movie monsters depicted in scenes from vintage spine-tinglers such as *The Fly* and *Frankenstein.*

"My first experience with classic horror came at the age of seven,"
says Hull. "I begged my parents to allow me to stay up past eleven
o'clock to see *The Mummy* with Boris Karloff on TV. After that night,
I was hooked."

His favorite horror classics of all time?

"It's a difficult task to narrow this down. But there is a quality most horror/fantasy classics have in common—each viewing is like renewing an old friendship. As Bugs Bunny once said, 'Monsters are such interesting people.'"

Here are Hull's top five:

1. The Phantom of the Opera (1925)

Directed by Rupert Julian, starring Lon Chaney, Sr., Mary Philbin

"Lon Chaney, Sr. was known as the Man of a Thousand Faces," says Hull, "but his most famous was that of Erik, the Phantom. When Mary Philbin snatched the mask from Chaney's face and revealed the skull-like visage underneath, audiences often fainted. The visual style and Chaney's performance were definite inspirations for the Andrew Lloyd Webber musical."

2. Dracula (1931)

Directed by Tod Browning, starring Bela Lugosi, Helen Chandler, Dwight Frye, and David Manners

"Just as Boris Karloff is the definitive Frankenstein Monster, Bela Lugosi will always be Dracula. Director Tod Browning had intended Lon Chaney, Sr. for the Count, since Chaney had previously created a vampire in Browning's *London After Midnight*. But shortly before Dracula began production, Chaney died. Although Lugosi had performed the role over one thousand times on the stage, he had to fight to win the part."

Hull adds one caveat: "The opening scenes in Transylvania are dripping with atmosphere. But once the story moves to England, the cinematography becomes far less imaginative. It is solely Lugosi's hypnotic performance and the support of Dwight Frye as Renfield that lift the film to classic status."

3. The Bride of Frankenstein (1935)

Directed by James Whale, starring Boris Karloff, Elsa Lanchester, Colin Clive

Hull's in-a-nutshell review of this classic: "Director James Whale surpassed his original *Frankenstein* in this sequel. The most visually beautiful of the series, it's got great gothic style. Whale's idea of having the Monster speak provoked a disagreement with Boris Karloff, but it gave more depth to the creature."

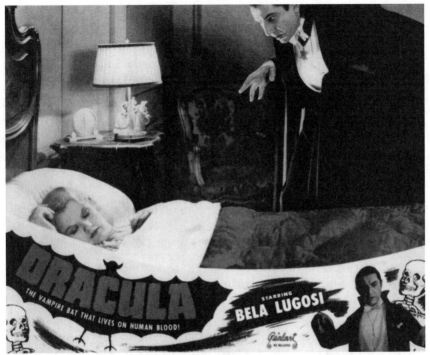

Bela Lugosi, as the famous Count Dracula in the 1931 classic, about to nibble on Helen Chandler. Photo courtesy of the Witch's Dungeon Collection.

4. The Werewolf of London (1935)

Directed by Stuart Walker, starring Henry Hull, Warner Oland

Henry Hull becomes a werewolf after a trip to Tibet, where he is bitten by another lycanthrope, Warner Oland (best known as Charlie Chan). Says Cortland of his great uncle, "Henry Hull did not agree with makeup designer Jack Pierce's early concept of the werewolf; he claimed it did not agree with the script, where the werewolf is recognized by his wife. Hull convinced Universal Studios the make-up should be modified. Pierce later applied his original design to Lon Chaney, Jr. in a 1941 film, *The Wolf Man.*"

5. The Abominable Dr. Phibes (1971)

Directed by Robert Fuest, starring Vincent Price, Joseph Cotten

Through the "ten curses of the Pharaohs" Dr. Phibes seeks vengeance against those responsible for his wife's death. "Dr. Anton Phibes is one of Vincent Price's most memorable portrayals in the horror realm," says Hull. "Price had the unique ability to frighten audiences, but with a wink. The tongue-in-cheek style of the film gives viewers both a chill and a smile, and it makes sense that the production team for *Phibes* had previously worked on the British TV series *The Avengers*. Set in the art deco period of the late 1920s, the *Phibes* film also possesses a striking visual character."

DRACULA

A snake's small eye blinks dull and shy;
And the lady's eyes they shrunk in her head,
Each shrunk up to a serpent's eye,
And with somewhat of malice, and more of dread,
One moment—and the sight was fled!
—Samuel Taylor Coleridge, "Christabel"

Professor Elizabeth Miller is a scholar of vampires. As an English professor, she bumped into John Polidori's *The Vampyre* (1819), the first piece of vampire fiction in English literature. Miller was hooked. She has spent years researching Dracula literature and Romanian history, which she has used to write many articles and books.

Dr. Jeanne Keyes Youngson, author and founder of The Vampire Empire, is a lifelong cinema fan and award-winning filmmaker. Employed at the Museum of Modern Art (NYC) in the mid-1950's, she was able to view rare black and white horror movies, and has since penned biographies of horror film stars such as Dwight Frye, George Zucco, and Peter Lorre.

Who better than these two to recommend Dracula movies?

Note: This list is by no means complete! If you go looking for one of these movies, remember the date and director. There are more than six hundred vampire movies, and many have similar titles.

Nosferatu (1922)

Directed by Fredrick W. Murnau, starring Max Schreck, Alexander Granach, and Greta Schroeder

"To me personally," Dr. Youngson says, "Schreck is and always will be, the ultimate and definitive Nasferatu." Adds Miller: "Yes, Schreck was his real name, coincidental though it may be ("Schreck" is German for "terror")! Even if you don't like silent films, you should see this one. The use of shadows for effect has never been better! You'll recognize some elements borrowed by Francis Ford Coppola for *Bram Stoker's Dracula*."

Abbot and Costello Meet Frankenstein (1948)

Directed by Charles T. Barton, starring Bud Abbott and Lou Costello

For those fans of old slapstick, both Miller and Youngson include this classic among their favorites: "In spite of its title, this is as much a Dracula movie as a Frankenstein one," says Miller. "A good spoof, guaranteed to raise a few laughs. The warehouse scenes are hilarious, though the comedy does wear a bit thin in the latter part of the movie." Youngson comments, "It's sad to see Lugosi as a stooge. But the movie's got Lon Chaney, Jr. as the Wolfman, Glenn Strange as Frankie's monster, and at the end, the unmistakable voice of Vincent Price as the Invisible Man."

Love At First Bite (1979)

Directed by Stan Dragoti, starring George Hamilton and Susan St. James, rated PG

In this vamp comedy, the Count is driven from his Transylvanian castle and moves to New York. Says Dr. Youngson: "A sophisticated spoof with an intelligent and hilarious script, nearly every scene is sheer comic delight, and the actors are attractive and competent. One has the feeling that everyone associated with the movie, especially the actors, had a wonderful time during the shoot. Sure wish they'd made a sequel." Miller recommends this as the best of the Dracula comedies.

Nosferatu, The Vampyre (1979)

Directed by Werner Herzog, starring Klaus Kinski and Isabelle Adjani, rated PG

A remake of the 1922 film, Youngson loves Kinski in this: "I always thought Kinski was one of the world's great actors and did a good job with this role. See it, if only for the rat scene. The original 1922 *Nosferatu* makeup was used in both this movie and *Salem's Lot*." Miller agrees about Kinski: "The movie's slow, in a powerful way, and wonderfully haunting. Klaus Kinski gives an unforgettable performance as the vampire who is 'conned' by a woman into staying up until sunrise."

Bram Stoker's Dracula (1992)

Directed by Francis Ford Coppola, starring Winona Ryder and Gary Oldman, rated R

"Coppola's rendering of the Dracula story is one of my favorites," Miller admits. "I know that many do not agree with me on this. I know the script takes liberties with Stoker's novel (don't they all?)

and maybe it should not have been titled *Bram Stoker's Dracula*. But as a movie, it's great! It combines the text, a bit of history (albeit distorted in a typically post-modern fashion) and influences of earlier Dracula movies with superb costumes and a marvelous soundtrack."

OLD FASHIONED FRIGHTS FROM
THE CLASSICS SECTION

For the next several categories, I took the advice of self-described film addicts, independent filmmakers, major metropolitan newspaper film critics, and last but not least, video store clerks. Here are their most-cited favorite Halloween movies.

Frankenstein (1931)
Directed by James Whale, starring Boris Karloff and Colin Clive

Although this movie launched the career of Boris Karloff, his name does not appear in the opening credits! The plot is as you'd expect: Dr. Frankenstein creates a naive, but murderous creature who breaks free and terrorizes the Bavarian countryside. Shot entirely on a soundstage, this is truly a nostalgia film, but it still has plenty of chills and good performances.

Cat People (1942)
Directed by Jacques Tourneur, starring Simone Simon and Kent Smith

A young Serbian woman is afraid to consummate her marriage because she believes she'll transform into a vicious cat creature. Most of the terror is left to the imagination: knowing, cat-like glances cast across a restaurant, shadows on a wall, growling echoing off the cement walls of a swimming pool as a woman bathes alone . . . very eerie.

Psycho (1960)
Directed by Alfred Hitchcock, starring Anthony Perkins and Janet Leigh, rated R

Psycho broke the dam for the flood of graphic horror films of the '70s, '80s, and '90s. It was the first to show a woman in her underwear, the first to film a toilet flush, the first to kill off its star early in the plot. The beautiful Marion Crane, who's just embezzled forty thousand dollars, stops at an isolated inn and meets the shy, odd proprietor, Norman. In the most famous shower scene in movie history, we see the action in flashes of image: the glint of a knife, blood eddying down the drain. Tense and suspenseful, *Psycho* features an especially unsettling performance by Perkins.

Night of the Living Dead (1968)

Directed by George A. Romero, starring Duane Jones, and Judith O'Dea

The quintessential zombie movie: the main characters are trapped in a house, unable to escape because they're surrounded by flesh-eating zombies. More creepy than gory, it was considered a groundbreaker for its time. Some view it as political, with the zombies vs. humans drama as a stand-in for racial tension in the late '60s.

FAVORITE HAUNTED HOUSE MOVIES

The Uninvited (1944)

Directed by Lewis Allen, starring Ray Milland and Ruth Hussey

The terror in this film comes as much from what you don't see as what you do. A music critic/composer and his sister buy a cliff-side haunted mansion, knowing that it's supposed to be haunted. It is. Known as one of the subtlest of the haunted house films, this is a thriller in which one of the scariest things is a fragrance.

House on Haunted Hill (1958)

Directed by William Castle, starring Vincent Price and Carol Ohmart

A rich couple throws a party in a reportedly haunted house, offering their guests ten thousand dollars apiece if they stay the night and live to tell about it. In this very tense film, it's hard to know who's dead or alive, what's real and what's not.

The Innocents (1961)

Directed by Jack Clayton, starring Deborah Kerr, Martin Stephens, and Pamela Franklin

In this adaptation of Henry James' *Turn of the Screw,* a Victorian-era spinster governess is hired to care for two children possessed by the spirits of dead servants The movie exudes gothic spookiness. Truman Capote co-wrote the screenplay.

The Haunting (1963)

Directed by Robert Wise, starring Richard Johnson, Claire Bloom, Russ Tamblyn, and Julie Harris, rated G

Some critics believe this to be one of the most frightening films ever made. Based on Shirley Jackson's 1959 novel *The Haunting of*

Hill House, a parapsychologist, two psychic women, and a young man gather in a large house that's reputed to be haunted. The film is without gimmicks or gore, it simply lets your imagination do the job.

The Shining (1980)

Directed by Stanley Kubrick, starring Jack Nicholson and Shelly Duval, rated R

A writer, his wife, and young son move into a remote Colorado hotel where the previous caretaker murdered his family. The place is haunted and dad loses his mind; history tries to repeat itself. The "shining" refers to the psychic gift possessed by the boy that blasts blood-drenched images into his head as warnings. Photographed in gorgeous saturated colors, this film has a synthesized score based partially on music by Bartok.

FAVORITE HALLOWEEN MOVIES FOR KIDS

Topper (1937)

Directed by Norman Z. McLeod, starring Constance Bennett, Cary Grant

Based on a novel by Thorne Smith, two young playful ghosts, visible only to Cosmo Topper, wreak havoc on his life.

It's the Great Pumpkin, Charlie Brown (1986)

Director: Bill Melendez, rated G

Everyone dons their costumes to celebrate Halloween except for the ever-hopeful Linus, who sits in the pumpkin patch all night long waiting . . . and waiting . . . for the Great Pumpkin to come with presents for all the good boys and girls.

Beetlejuice (1988)

Directed by Tim Burton, starring Michael Keaton, Alec Baldwin, rated PG

A pair of "newlydeads" enlist the services of a "bio-exorcist" to get some humans out of their (former) house. Objects have lives of their own and the sets are a weird cross between a cartoon and a surrealist painting.

CAMP, SPOOF, AND MUSICALS FOR HALLOPHILES

Little Shop of Horrors (1960)

Directed by Roger Corman, starring Jonathan Haze, Jackie Joseph

Here's a low-budget black comedy/fantasy about a bloodthirsty man-eating plant. Horticultural hobbyist Seymour breeds a blood-drinking plant he names Audrey II. The plant soon needs more blood than Seymour can provide, so he commits murder to feed her.

A young Jack Nicholson plays one of the several wacky characters.

The Rocky Horror Picture Show (1975)

Directed by Jim Sharman, starring Tim Curry, Susan Sarandon, rated R

"Damn it, Janet . . . " This cult classic pits a square young couple against eccentric transvestite aliens. The now-famous *Time Warp* song came from this movie, as did the notion that earth could be conquered by aliens in garter belts.

Lair of the White Worm (1988)

Directed by Ken Russell, starring Amanda Donohoe, Hugh Grant, rated R

The action kicks off when a Scottish archeologist finds a prehistoric skull, but the main event is neighbor Lady Sylvia and her secret—she keeps the Lair of the Worm, a Loch Ness-like Monster that feeds on virgins and has been trapped underground for centuries. This tongue-in-cheek horror farce about vampire snake-people is based on a post-*Dracula* Bram Stoker story.

Plan 9 from Outer Space (1956)

Directed by Edward D. Wood, Jr. , starring Gregory Walcott, Mona McKinnon

Bela Lugosi's last film, an aliens-try-to-take-over-earth movie, is famously cheesy, and has a cult following *because* of its wooden acting, awful dialogue and cheap production values (like spaceship models hanging from visible strings).

TEN SCARIEST MOVIES OF ALL TIME

Reel.com is a national movie sales web business launched by a group of film addicts in California. Here are their all-time top ten selections for Halloween horror; for sheer terror, any one of these would make a memorable Halloween rental:

1. *Don't Look Now* (1973)
2. *Rosemary's Baby* (1968)
3. *Suspiria* (1977)
4. *Halloween* (1978)
5. *Alien* (1979)
6. *The Hills Have Eyes* (1977)
7. *The Exorcist* (1973)
8. *The Hitcher* (1986)
9. *The Evil Dead* (1982)
10. *The Tenant* (1976)

CHAPTER SIX

Recipes for Halloween

Beyond Blood Punch And Peeled Grapes

Till buttered so'ns wi'
fragrant lunt [steam]
Set a' their gabs a-sterrin', [mouths watering]
Syne wi'a social glass
o' strunt [liquor]
They parted aff carerrin'
Fu' blythe that night
—Robert Burns "Halloween" (1785), translated by Ralph and
Adelin Linton

Maybe it's the first slap of late October frost that makes me dream
of hot apple dumplings steaming up the kitchen window; Halloween
and good food have gone hand in hand for hundreds of years.
Although many traditional dishes have been lost to us here in the
States, new ones are being created in restaurants we instinctively seek
out in late October for their mulled wines and tangy gingerbread.

What follows is a list of party recipes from the past as well as the
present: some a few centuries old, some from contemporary cooks
who have discovered wonderful new ways to celebrate the foods and
spices of Halloween.

Pumpkin Seeds

Sweet Pumpkin Seeds
1-2 cups raw pumpkin seeds
2 tbs. melted butter

¼ cup brown sugar
1 tsp. cinnamon
½ tsp. allspice
½ tsp. nutmeg

In a small bowl, toss raw seeds with melted butter, brown sugar, and spices. Spread them out on a baking sheet and roast at 350 degrees for 20 minutes.

Hot seeds

1-2 cups raw pumpkin seeds
2-3 tsp. vegetable oil
¼ tsp. chili powder
pinch of cayenne pepper
¼ tsp. salt

Spread seeds out on a baking sheet. Drizzle with vegetable oil and sprinkle them with chili powder, cayenne pepper, and salt. Bake 20 minutes at 350 degrees.

Rock & Roll Chef's Pumpkin Seeds

1-2 cups pumpkin seeds
2-3 tsp. vegetable oil
salt (or soy sauce) to taste

In a bowl, add cooking oil to coat seeds. If using soy sauce, add. Bake at 250 degrees for 30 minutes or until brown. Cool. Add salt, if using.

Soups and Salads

Sherried Pumpkin Soup with Candied Apple

—Courtesy of Michael Gagne, Chef-Owner of the Robinhood Free Meetinghouse, Georgetown, Maine

(serves six)
¼ cup diced onions
¼ cup diced carrots
¼ cup diced leeks
¼ cup diced celery
¼ tsp. minced garlic
2 tbs. clarified butter (melted butter with the solids skimmed off the top)
1 cup sherry
4 cups pumpkin, roasted and peeled

¼ cup rice

4 cups chicken stock

½ cup cream

salt and pepper to taste

pumpkin seeds (roasted and husked, available in health food stores)

1 Granny Smith apple, julienned

2 tbs. turbinado sugar (this is coarse, unrefined sugar—substitute brown sugar if you can't find turbinado)

1. Sauté all vegetables in clarified butter until tender.

2. Add one cup sherry and simmer until reduced by half.

3. Add chicken stock, rice, pumpkin, salt, and pepper.

4. Cook until rice is exploded (very overcooked).

5. Blend or process, then run through a sieve.

6. Add cream and reheat.

7. Saute julienned apples in butter and sugar until caramelized.

8. Garnish soup with pumpkin seeds and caramelized apples.

Pumpkin and Tomato Soup   —Courtesy of the Rock & Roll Chef

(serves eight)

3 tbs. olive oil

1 large onion, diced

28 oz. canned tomatoes (with juice)

4 cups pumpkin puree (canned)

3-4 cups chicken (or vegetable) stock

1 tbs. brown sugar

Salt

White pepper

1. Put a sauté pan or heavy pot (large enough to hold all ingredients) over medium-high heat, add olive oil. Add onions, sauté, and stir until translucent—not brown!

2. Put pumpkin, tomatoes and juice, brown sugar and sautéed onions in a food processor. Puree to medium-smooth consistency.

3. Return processed ingredients to pan.

4. Add stock to pan, stir. Add salt and pepper to taste.

5. When soup comes to boil, turn off heat.

Cut a medium-size lid in a pumpkin and clean out the seeds and strings. Pour the finished soup into the hollowed pumpkin and serve immediately. Garnish with roasted pumpkin seeds, a dollop of sour cream, or both.

Curried Pumpkin Soup   —Courtesy of Sally Wright
(serves four)
4 tbs. sweet butter
2 cups chopped yellow onions
5 tsp. curry powder
1 medium-size sugar pumpkin (about 3-5 pounds), baked
2 apples, peeled and cored
3 cups chicken stock
1 cup apple juice
Salt and pepper to taste

1. Melt butter in a pot. Add onions and curry powder, and cook, covered, over low heat until onions are tender (about 10 minutes).

2. Peel pumpkin, scrape out seeds, and chop rind into small pieces.

3. When onions are tender, pour in stock, add pumpkin and apples, and bring to a boil. Reduce heat and simmer partially covered, until pumpkin and apples are tender (about 25 minutes).

4. Pour the soup through a strainer, but keep the liquid.

5. Put the solid pumpkin mixture into a processor or blender, add 1 cup reserved liquid, and blend until smooth.

6. Return pureed soup to the pot and add apple juice and remaining reserved liquid until the soup is the consistency you prefer.

7. Season with salt and pepper and serve immediately.

Chef John Wright's Pumpkin Bisque
—Courtesy of Sue and Harris Zuckerman, Red Clover Inn, Mendon, Vermont
(serves six)
1 medium onion, chopped
2 stalks celery, chopped
3 cloves garlic, chopped
4 cups light vegetable stock (or light chicken stock, or water)
2 tomatoes, chopped
2 bay leaves
$\frac{1}{2}$ tsp. nutmeg
2 cups pumpkin puree
1 cup heavy cream
Salt and pepper to taste

1.Sauté onions, celery, and garlic in butter.
2.Add stock, tomatoes, bay leaves, and nutmeg.

3.Cook until vegetables are very soft.

4.Strain vegetables and reserve liquid.

5.Puree vegetables with some liquid and strain through a sieve.

6.Combine liquid, pureed vegetables, and pumpkin; heat.

7.Add cream and season with salt and pepper.

Halloween Fruit Salad

(serves twelve)

12 oranges

3 bananas, cut up

4 apples, cut up

3 pears, cut up

1.Cut off the tops and bottoms of 12 large oranges. Hollow them out, being careful not to break the skin (use a small serrated grapefruit spoon).

2.Carve a face in each orange.

3.Mix the fruit, including the oranges cut into sections, and pour into a bowl. Place the bowl on the platter and arrange the jack-o-lantern oranges around it. Put a tea light in each carved orange.

4.Light the miniature jack-o-lanterns when your guests arrive.

Hint: Keep the carved-out oranges and let them dry out on a shelf. When they become rock hard, dip each one in polyurethane to seal it against mold and hang it on a string to dry. These tiny jack-o-lanterns will last for years, and make unique napkin rings or ornaments on Halloween wreaths.

Breads, Oatcakes and Bannochs

Spicy Pumpkin Bread

—Courtesy of the Isaiah Hall B&B Inn, Dennis, Massachusetts

1 cup packed brown sugar

$1/3$ cup shortening

1 cup canned pumpkin

$1/4$ cup milk

2 cups flour

2 eggs

2 tsp. baking powder

$1/2$ tsp. salt

$1/4$ tsp. baking soda

1 tsp. cloves

$1/2$ cup walnuts, chopped

$\frac{1}{2}$ cup raisins

1. Preheat oven to 350 degrees. Grease a loaf pan.
2. Cream together brown sugar and shortening.
3. Beat in eggs.
4. Add canned pumpkin and milk; mix well.
5. In a separate bowl, mix together flour, baking powder, salt, baking soda and cloves.
6. Add flour mixture to pumpkin mixture and mix.
7. Stir in nuts and raisins.
8. Place batter into prepared pan, and bake for 55 minutes, or until a knife comes out clean. Cool ten minutes, remove from pan, and cool on rack. May be frozen.

Hancock Shaker Village Pumpkin Loaves with Orange Butter
—Courtesy of the Black Swan Inn, Tilton, New Hampshire
(makes three small loaves)
2 cups sugar
1 cup melted butter
3 eggs
2 cups canned heated pumpkin
2 cups sifted flour (1/2 white and 1/2 wheat, or all white)
$\frac{1}{2}$ tsp. salt
$\frac{1}{2}$ tsp. double acting baking powder
1 tsp. baking soda
1 tsp. ground cloves
1 tsp. cinnamon
1 tsp. nutmeg
$\frac{1}{2}$ cup chopped pecans or walnuts
$\frac{1}{2}$ cup golden raisins

1. In a medium-size bowl, beat sugar, butter, and pumpkin to blend.
2. Beat in eggs, one at a time and continue beating until blended.
3. In a separate bowl, sift together flour, salt, baking powder, baking soda, the spices, nuts, and raisins.
4. Beat the dry mixture into the pumpkin mixture.
5. Divide batter into three small greased loaf pans.
6. Bake at 325 degrees for 60 minutes, or until a toothpick inserted in the middle comes out clean.
7. Cool in pans for 10 minutes. Remove and cool on wire racks.

Orange Butter:
1-lb. tub sweet whipped butter
$\frac{1}{2}$ jar orange marmalade
1. Beat together ingredients and serve with pumpkin bread.

*Bonnach Samhthain/Bonnach Salainn** (Scottish Hallowmas Bannock-traditionally baked for the first day of winter, November 1)

—From *The Scot's Kitchen*, by F. Marion McNeill
(Makes one large pancake; adjust up for each person)
1 cup oatmeal
Pinch baking soda
Pinch salt
1 tsp. melted butter or bacon fat
Water to moisten
1. Mix all ingredients to make a stiff dough.
2. Rub flour on a board. Form dough into a ball, rubbing with flour, knead.
3. Roll out to $\frac{1}{8}$" thickness. Give a final rub with flour and trim to a circle.
4. Mark a crosshatch pattern on the top with a knife (don't cut all the way through).
5. Flip the pancake onto a hot, buttered griddle, smooth side up.
6. Cook until brown, then flip and grill the other side slightly.
7. Serve hot.
*Bonnach Salainn (salt bannoch) was the kind eaten in the Highlands at Hallowe'en to induce dreams that would foretell the future. Use the recipe above, but add lots of extra salt. No water could be drunk, nor any words spoken after it was eaten, or the charm would not work.

Pan de los Muertos (Mexican Bread of the Dead)

This bread is formed into a round shape and decorated with a skull and crossbones on top. Sometimes it's shaped like a person or an animal, and the decoration can vary region by region. The bread is used in Days of the Dead celebrations throughout Mexico.
Bread:
2 cups flour
2 tsp. baking powder
2 tbs. sugar
$\frac{1}{4}$ tsp. salt

1 egg
⅔ cup milk
¼ cup vegetable oil
10 drops anise extract
Topping:
1 tbs. flour
1 tsp. ground cinnamon
1 tbs. melted butter
Tube of icing
1. Preheat oven to 400 degrees. Grease a cookie sheet.
2. Mix all bread ingredients until smooth.
3. Mold dough into a round shape (skull), or into smaller round shapes for animals, faces, or angels. Place dough on cookie sheet.
4. Mix topping ingredients together: flour, cinnamon, and melted butter.
5. Brush topping on dough.
6. Bake for 20-25 minutes. Cool.
7. Draw skull shapes with tube icing or decorate with eyes, noses, etc.

Main Dishes

Pumpkin Kibbee
—Courtesy of Ruth Faris
(Serves six to eight)
1 fairly large-size sugar pumpkin, baked, peeled and seeded; need about 4 cups pulp
1 cup cracked bulgur wheat
4 medium onions, chopped
1 cup slivered or shredded almonds
Whole wheat flour (optional)
2 tbs. cooking oil (for sautéing)
Salt, pepper, allspice ,and cinnamon to taste
1. Soak bulgur wheat for half an hour. Preheat oven to 350 degrees.
2. Mash the cooked pumpkin pulp and add two chopped onions, raw.
3. Squeeze all water from the bulgur wheat and add it to the pumpkin mixture.
4. Add salt, pepper, allspice, and cinnamon to taste. Mix thoroughly.
5. For a smoother texture, add ½ cup wheat flour.
6. Sauté remaining chopped onion in oil.

7. Add ¾ cup nuts, more spices (salt, pepper, allspice, cinnamon) to taste.

8. Put half of the pumpkin mixture in a casserole pan and cover with a layer of sautéed onions, nuts, then top with remaining pumpkin mixture.

9. Sprinkle a thin layer of nuts on top.

10. Make slices through kibbee in triangles, as if you were slicing a pie.

11. Bake at 350 degrees for 45 minutes.

Kibbee can be frozen either before or after cooking.

Pork Chops and Pumpkin Butter
(Serves six)
6 thick pork chops
Pureed pulp from one medium-size sugar pumpkin
½ cup packed dark brown sugar
¾ tsp. cinnamon
¼ tsp. nutmeg
1 tsp. freshly grated ginger
2 tbs. freshly squeezed lemon juice
Salt and pepper

1. Cook pureed pumpkin over a medium-low heat, stirring often, until very thick (about 25 minutes).

2. Add brown sugar, cinnamon, nutmeg, ginger, and lemon juice; cook until sugar dissolves (about 5 minutes).

3. Put aside to cool.

4. Salt and pepper chops, then broil under high heat for 4-5 minutes per side (if using thermometer, pull chops out at 140 degrees).

5. Let chops sit for a few minutes to absorb juices.

6. Reheat pumpkin butter in oven about 10 minutes. Spoon a generous amount to the side of each chop and serve.

Bríd's Colcannon
—Courtesy of Bríd Coogan

This dish is a traditional Halloween supper in Ireland. It's meatless to honor the fasting day that precedes All Saints' Day, an official feast day in the Catholic church calendar.

(Serves six)
6 potatoes
1 bunch curly kale
½ onion, chopped fine

6 tbs. butter

½ to 1 cup milk

Salt and pepper

1. Boil potatoes with a pinch of salt.

2. In a separate pot, boil or steam a bunch of curly kale.

3. Mash the potatoes and mix in butter and enough milk to make a smooth consistency (don't whip them, they'll get gluey).

4. Add chopped onion, mix.

5. Chop the cooked kale as finely as you can and mix it into the potatoes.

6. Add plenty of salt and pepper.

7. Scoop the colcannon, hot, onto each plate.

8. Wrap a quarter in foil and hide it in each serving as a Halloween treat for kids.

Variation: use white cabbage instead of kale, and green onions instead of white. Boil the onions in ½ cup of milk until soft, then add them to the mashed potatoes. Serve with lots of butter.

Irish Champ (*like Colcannon, but with leeks*)

(Serves six)

6 potatoes

1 bunch of leeks, washed well

6 tbs. butter

½ cup milk

Salt and pepper

1. Peel and boil the potatoes.

2. In a separate pot, boil leeks until very tender (about the same amount of time it takes to boil the potatoes).

3. Mash the potatoes with milk and butter.

4. Chop the leeks.

5. Mix the potatoes and leeks together and turn the mixture out into a big bowl.

6. Add lots of salt and pepper.

7. Wrap a coin, a thimble, and a ring in foil and bury them in the champ. The coin means wealth; the thimble, hard work; the ring, marriage.

8. To serve traditionally, spoon a helping of champ on each plate. Dig a big hole in the middle and fill it with melted butter. You dip your spoon in the champ, and then the butter each time you take a bite.

Boxty Pancakes (*traditional Irish Halloween supper*)
—County Cavan recipe from *Irish Country Recipes*
(Serves six)
3 raw potatoes
3 boiled potatoes, smashed
2 cups flour
2 tsp. salt
1½ cups buttermilk
1 tsp. baking powder
1. Peel raw potatoes, grate, and wring liquid out into a bowl. Reserve liquid.
2. Mix raw potatoes and boiled potatoes in a large bowl.
3. Watch the reserved liquid: after a few minutes the starch will sink and solidify. Pour off the water and scrape the starch on top of the potatoes.
4. Mix well. Sift together flour, salt, and baking soda, and add to the potatoes. Mix.
5. Add enough buttermilk to make a batter you can drop from a spoon.
6. Beat the batter, then let it rest a few minutes.
7. Grease a frying pan and put it on medium heat.
8. Drop batter into the pan in spoonfuls. When it browns underneath, turn it and brown the other side.
9. Butter the boxty and serve it hot, spinkled with sugar.

Potato Pudding for Halloeve
—County Londonderry recipe from *Irish Country Recipes*
Makes a fragrant side dish or delicious buffet choice.
(Serves six)
6 potatoes
1 cup flour
½ cup milk
¼ tsp. caraway seeds
½ tsp. cinnamon
¼ tsp. ground ginger
¼ tsp. ground cloves
½ tsp. sugar
½ tsp. salt
1. Cook and mash potatoes well, leaving no lumps.
2. Mix in flour, seeds, salt, spices, and sugar.
3. Roll ¼ of the dough out on a floured board.

4 .Butter and flour a baking dish, then put the first layer in the bottom.

5. Roll three more layers, adding each layer to the dish.

6. Bake in a 350-degree oven for one hour, pour milk over the pudding, and bake 30 minutes more.

7. Wrap a ring in waxed paper and hide it in the pudding just before you serve as a treat.

Drinks

Spiked Halloween Punch

    3 qts. apple cider
    2 cups rum
    1 apple, any kind
    2 tbs. lemon juice
    30 cloves
    1 lemon, sliced
    4 cinnamon sticks
    2 tbs. brown sugar
    1 tbs. finely grated orange peel to garnish

1. Core and slice an apple into rings. Sprinkle with lemon juice to prevent browning. Stud each ring with 5 cloves. Place in a punch-bowl and set aside.

2. In a large pot on the stove, mix all other ingredients (except orange peel).

3. Simmer 5 minutes. Cool slightly.

4. Pour over apple rings.

5. Add grated orange peel to garnish.

6. Serve warm or cold.

Blood-Red Cocktails

    1¼ oz. vodka
    ¾ oz. Chambord
    Splash of cranberry juice
    Ice

1.Mix all ingredients together in a shaker with ice.

2.Strain into a glass.

Spicy Bloody Mary

    46 oz. can tomato juice
    4 oz. lemon juice

2 tbs. Worcestershire sauce
Salt
Fresh pepper
Generous dash of horseradish
1½ oz. vodka per serving
Ice
10 thin slices of lemon to garnish
1. Mix all ingredients except vodka, ice, and lemon slices, and chill.
2. For each drink, pour ice into glass, add vodka, then tomato juice mixture.
3. Garnish with lemon slice.

Halloween Schnapps
1 bottle Apple Schnapps
1 bottle Cinnamon Schnapps
Red Hot sauce
1. Mix equal amounts Apple Schnapps and Cinnamon Schnapps in shot glasses.
2. Add a drop of Red Hot sauce to each one.

Desserts

Halloween Jell-O
Go classic: buy brain, hand, or heart molds, and make icky Jell-O body parts to your heart's content. Aficionados swear by watermelon or peach-flavored gelatin mixed with fat-free evaporated skimmed milk for the perfect flesh color (you stir in the milk after you've added the hot and cold water to the gelatin powder). If you'd like to try your hand at food-as-art, here's how to make a Jell-O graveyard.

Jell-O Graveyard
(Party-size)   —Courtesy of Stuart Schneider
If you can make Jell-O, you can make this sculpture. But make it at least one day ahead of your party because the longer it sets, the better it looks.
1 package black cherry Jell-O
4 packages orange Jell-O
1 package plain gelatin
12" x 18" glass baking pan
Few drops of red and blue food coloring

1. Make a package of black cherry Jell-O. Add a few drops of blue and red food coloring to it to make it darker, and add one package of plain gelatin for stiffness. Pour a ½" layer into any shallow baking pan and refrigerate to harden.

2. Make three packages of orange Jell-O in one big batch. Pour a ½" layer of the orange Jell-O into a glass baking pan. Let it harden in the refrigerator (you now have two pans of Jell-O hardening: one dark cherry and one orange).

3. Unmold the dark cherry Jell-O onto a sheet of wax paper. To unmold, place the dish in a sink of hot water, but don't let the water get into the Jell-O. The bottom will loosen up and you can slide it out of the dish onto the paper.

4. Using a sharp knife, carve trees, tombstones, bats, ghosts, and whatever else you want out of the dark cherry Jell-O. Cut the foreground items—things like the tree and tombstone—out of the thickest part of the Jell-O, and carve the shapes that go in the background—bats, ghosts—out of thinner slivers.

5. Arrange all your dark shapes on top of the hardened orange Jell-O to create the scene.

6. Now mix up your last package of orange Jell-O and let it cool, but not solidify. Pour a very thin layer on top of the dark pieces in the dish. This is done to glue them in place. If you just pour in all the Jell-O, the dark pieces will float and ruin the artwork.

7. Put the sculpture in the fridge. Once the thin layer of orange

Jell-O graveyard sculpture created by Halloween author Stuart Schneider.

Jell-O "glue" has set, pour in the rest of the orange to finish the dish. Refrigerate overnight.

8. Twenty-four hours later, the Jell-O sculpture will be finished. The thinnest pieces will be just a shadow of the their original color, and the thickest ones will retain their dark color. Serve from the pan.

Granny Smith Apple Turnovers
—Courtesy of pastry chef Daniel Morley
(makes eight turnovers)
store-bought puff pastry for 8 turnovers
4 Granny Smith apples, peeled and diced into 1/4" chunks
¾ cup turbinado sugar (raw, unrefined sugar)
⅓ cup cake or cookie crumbs, very finely ground
½ cup chopped dried apricots
finely grated rind of ½ lemon
¾ tsp. lemon juice
½ cup chopped walnuts, toasted
6 tbs. orange or apple juice
1 egg white
¼ tsp. ground cinnamon
¼ tsp. salt
½ tsp. vanilla extract
Preheat oven to 400 degrees

1. Mix all filling ingredients (everything but the pastry squares and egg white) together in a bowl. Save a bit of the turbinado sugar for the end.

2. Place eight squares of pastry dough on a buttered and floured cookie sheet and brush each square with egg white.

3. Spoon an equal amount of filling on the center of each square. Then fold one corner of each pastry square over the filling to the opposite corner.

4. Press the edges together with the tines of a fork to seal them.

5. Brush the tops of the turnovers with egg white and sprinkle with turbinado sugar.

6. Bake in a 400-degree oven for ten minutes, then rotate sheet pan, and lower temperature to 350 degrees. Bake about ten minutes more until golden brown.

7. Serve with vanilla ice cream or fresh vanilla-flavored whipped cream.

Baked Apple Dumplings   —From *The Good Wife's Cook Book,* 1911
   (Makes four dumplings)
   4 cups flour
   3 tbs. shortening
   2 cups whole milk
   1 tsp. baking soda dissolved in hot water
   2 tsp. cream of tartar
   1 tsp. salt
   4 apples
   Butter to grease pan
   3 egg whites, beaten
   1. Sift flour with tartar and chop in shortening.
   2. Add baking soda and mix together.
   3. Add milk and mix into a paste.
   4. Roll out to ¼" thickness and cut into 8" x 8" squares.
   5. Put one apple, pared and cored, in the center of each square.
Bring the corners of the square to meet and pinch them together.
   6. Bake in a buttered pan, pinched side down. Bake 1¼ hours,
until pastry is brown. Remove from oven.
   7. Brush with beaten egg whites and bake 2-3 minutes more.
   8. Serve hot, with vanilla ice cream.

Pumpkin Chocolate Cheesecake
   —Courtesy of the Smith family at The Vermont Inn, Killington,
Vermont
   Two 16 oz. pkgs. cream cheese
   1 ⅓ cup sugar
   ½ tsp. cinnamon
   ½ tsp. ginger
   ¼ tsp. cloves
   1 cup pumpkin puree
   10 eggs
   1 cup heavy cream
   6 oz. semisweet chocolate
   Crust:
   1½ cups graham crumbs
   6 tbs. brown sugar
   6 tbs. melted butter
   1. Whip cream cheese and add pumpkin, sugar, and spices.
   2. Add eggs one at a time.
   3. Add first ½ cup of heavy cream.

4. Bring second ½ cup of heavy cream to a boil, and pour over chocolate to melt it. Swirl chocolate and cream into mix of ingredients above.

5. Mix graham crumbs, brown sugar and melted butter together to make crust.

6. Butter 10" pie pan and press in crust.

7. Pour mixture into pan and bake at 275 degrees for 60 minutes.

8. Cool, then chill for two hours.

To Add a Spider Web Design Topping:

Draw concentric circles onto the top of the chilled pie with a tube of black decorating gel. Drag a knife from the inner circle to the outermost five times (as if you were slicing a pie into five equal pieces) to make a spider web design.

Rock 'N Roll Chef Marty Larkin's Halloween Pumpkin Cookies
(makes two dozen)
16-oz. can of pumpkin
1½ cups butter
4 cups white flour
2 cups brown sugar
2 cups quick oats
1 cup raisins
2 tsp. baking soda
1 cup chopped nuts (or roasted pumpkin seeds)
2 tsp. ground cinnamon
1 tsp. vanilla
1 egg
1 tsp. salt

1. Preheat oven to 325 degrees.

2. Cream pumpkin, egg, butter, vanilla, sugar until fluffy.

3. Slowly add remaining ingredients, mixing all the while.

4. Drop teaspoon-sized pieces of dough on greased cookie sheets. Leave room between the cookies for them to expand.

5. Bake 20-25 minutes, or until golden brown.

6. Cool and serve.

Pumpkin Dessert Dip with Ginger Snaps
2 cups powdered sugar
8-oz. whipped cream cheese
15-oz. pumpkin puree
½ tsp. cinnamon
½ tsp. nutmeg
½ tsp. ginger

1. Mix all ingredients well and chill for one hour.

2. Spoon into hollowed-out pumpkin shell.

3. Serve with gingersnaps for dipping.

Pumpkin Flan

(serves six)

1 cup pureed pumpkin

5 large eggs, beaten

$1\frac{1}{4}$ cup sugar

$\frac{1}{2}$ tsp. salt

1 tsp. cinnamon

$\frac{1}{2}$ tsp. cloves

$\frac{1}{2}$ tsp. nutmeg

$1\frac{1}{2}$ cups evaporated milk

$\frac{1}{3}$ cup water

1. Preheat oven to 350 degrees.

2. Melt $\frac{1}{2}$ cup sugar over medium heat until it turns liquid. Do not brown. Pour into a six-cup soufflé dish and set aside.

3. Mix all ingredients thoroughly. Pour into soufflé dish on top of melted sugar.

4. Set dish into a pan of hot water that comes halfway up the side of the dish and bake for one hour and twenty minutes. Cool and refrigerate.

5. When ready to serve, run a knife blade around the inside of the dish and invert onto a flat plate (to invert, hold a serving plate firmly centered over the soufflé dish and turn quickly upside down).

Pumpkin Ginger Cake

$1\frac{1}{2}$ cups all-purpose flour

1 tsp. baking powder

2 tsp. ginger

$\frac{1}{2}$ tsp. salt

1 stick unsalted butter

$\frac{1}{2}$ cup dark brown sugar

2 eggs

2 tbs. dark molasses

2 tbs. ginger marmalade

1 cup canned or homemade pumpkin puree

1 tbs. confectioner's sugar

1. Preheat oven to 325 degrees.

2. Grease an 8" cake pan with oil.

3. Fit a circle of wax paper into the bottom of the pan.

4. Sift together flour, baking powder, ginger, and salt. Set aside.

5. Cream the butter and dark brown sugar together.

6. Beat in the eggs.

7. Add molasses, ginger marmalade, and pumpkin.

8. Add the flour and spice mixture and blend thoroughly.

9. Spread evenly in the prepared pan and bake for 60 minutes (it is done if a toothpick inserted into the center comes out clean).

10. Cool ten minutes.

11. Remove the cake and peel off the wax paper.

12. Sift confectioner's sugar over the top while the cake is still warm.

13. Serve with whipped cream.

Pumpkin Pies

American colonists made "a pudding baked in a crust" with spices from the very first supply shipments from England, and we've been baking pumpkin pies ever since. Various pies over time included ingredients as intriguing as rosewater, listed in Amelia Simmons' pumpkin pie recipe in *American Cookery* in (1796), and brandy, used in Mary Randolph's pie in *The Virginia Housewife*, 1824.

To make the perfect pumpkin pie, bake the crust first (because the filling is custard-y, the crust gets soggy if it's not pre-baked). And don't use a knife to test for done-ness because once a cut is made, it will widen. Try instead to look for signs that the pie is done: the surface will have a dull, uniform sheen and, if shaken gently, the filling will move slightly but not be liquid in the center. If the pie cracks at the edges, it's done. The pie is best if eaten the day it's baked, and ideally, when it's warm and the crust still crisp.

Joan's Super Pumpkin Pie

(This pie has a splash of liquor that makes it sing. The final stages need some coddling, but the pie is worth it.)

$^3/_4$ cup brown sugar

$^1/_2$ tsp. salt

$^1/_2$ tsp. cinnamon

$^1/_2$ tsp. ginger

$^1/_4$ tsp. ground cloves

$^1/_4$ tsp. nutmeg

2 cups canned pumpkin

1¼ cups evaporated milk

¼ cup bourbon or any kind of whiskey

2 tbs. molasses

3 eggs, slightly beaten

Pre-made pie shell

Topping:

⅔ cup brown sugar

3 tbs. melted butter

1 tbs. heavy cream (or evaporated milk)

Pinch of salt

Pecans to garnish

1. Pre-bake the pie shell: brush the bottom and sides of the pie shell with egg white and line the edges of the crust with foil. Put ½ cup rice in the shell to weight it down and bake at 425 degrees for ten minutes, then 350 degrees for the next ten minutes. Set aside while you make the filling.

2. Mix all the spices and brown sugar with the pumpkin.

3. Beat in cream, bourbon, molasses, and eggs.

4. Brush the bottom and sides of your pie shell with egg white. Pour the filling into the crust. Bake ten minutes at 450 degrees, then reduce the heat to 325 degrees, and bake 30-40 minutes longer.

Topping:

1. Mix together sugar, butter, cream, and salt, and pour the topping on the pie.

2. Arrange pecans as a garnish.

3. Put the pie under the broiler until the surface bubbles (a few minutes). This is when you have to watch carefully. If you don't catch the bubbling, the surface of this beautiful pie will burn. Serve immediately.

Wilson Farm's Dessert in a Pumpkin Shell

—Courtesy of Lynn Wilson

Native Americans used the pumpkin for medicinal purposes, wove strips of dried pumpkin into mats, and roasted them to eat. But it was the colonists who invented pumpkin pie by slicing off the top, removing the seeds and pulp, filling the inside with milk, spices and honey, and baking it in hot ashes. Sound good? Here's a modern adaptation of pie-in-the-pumpkin:

(Serves six to eight)

1 sugar pumpkin (3-5 lbs.)

1 tbs. butter

1 tbs. brown sugar

$^{1}/_{4}$ teaspoon cinnamon

1 box gingerbread mix, made up into batter following package instructions

1. Preheat oven to 350 degrees.

2. Cut off the top of the pumpkin straight across, then clean the pumpkin out thoroughly.

3. Put butter, brown sugar, and cinnamon in the shell and bake for 20-30 minutes. Brush the butter and sugar around the inside of the shell several times while it heats.

4. When the pumpkin shell is hot, brush the butter and sugar around the inside once more and pour out the remaining syrup and juices.

5. Add the batter, filling the pumpkin two-thirds full to allow room for expansion.

6. Bake until done. Allow more time than the filling recipe usually takes. For instance, a gingerbread mix that calls for 30 minutes baking time will take 45 minutes to an hour in the pumpkin.

7. Cool slightly.

8. Decorate the top with whipped cream and cut the pumpkin into wedges; serve with ice cream beside each wedge.

Soulmas Cake

—From "Saints and Soul-caking," Maggie Black, *History Today*, November 1981

Soul cakes were little cakes or breads baked by homeowners and given away to 'soulers,' (sometimes poor people, sometimes children) who would say a prayer for the dead in exchange for the cake. Catholic, rather than Celtic (although they overlap in some countries), variations of soul cakes were baked in countries as far-flung as England, Italy, Spain or Poland, wherever the Church brought its tradition of honoring all dead souls on November 2.

1 stick butter

1 cup dark molasses

$3^{1}/_{2}$ cups oatmeal

$2^{1}/_{2}$ cups flour

$^{2}/_{3}$ cup packed dark brown sugar

1 tsp. ground ginger

$^{1}/_{2}$ tsp. salt

$^{1}/_{2}$ tsp. cream of tartar

1 tsp. baking soda

$^{1}/_{4}$ cup milk

1. Preheat the oven to 325 degrees. Grease an 8" square pan.

2. Put butter and molasses in a heavy saucepan and heat gently; stir together, then put aside.

3.In a mixing bowl, mix together oatmeal, flour, brown sugar, ginger, salt, and tartar.

4.In a small bowl, stir the baking soda into the milk until it's dissolved.

5.Pour the butter and molasses mixture into the dry mixture, stir slightly, then add the milk. Stir thoroughly.

6.Turn into pan and bake for one hour, or until a toothpick inserted in the middle comes out clean. Cool in the pan.

7.Cut into bars or squares. Serve with butter (this dense, delicious cake will keep for weeks in a cool place).

Irish Barn Brack (Halloween fruit cake)

"We knew Halloween was coming when mom would put up jars of tea and fruit on the windowsill to age properly for the barn brack," says my friend, Bríd, from Dublin. All the kids in the family looked forward to this traditional Irish Halloween fruitcake because there would be a trinket*—a ring or coin—buried in the cake for each child in the family.

4 cups flour

¾ cup sugar

2¾ cups dried mixed fruit (apricots, figs, dates, raisins, and cherries)

1 tsp. baking powder

1 egg

1 tsp. of mixed spice: two parts cinnamon to one part ginger and one part cloves

1 cup of Irish tea

1. Soak the dried fruit in the tea overnight.

2. The next day, add the sugar and egg to the fruit mix.

3. Sift in the other dry ingredients. Mix gently. Do not over-knead the dough or the fruit will break up.

4. Wrap your trinkets in foil and stir them gently into the dough.

5. Bake in an 8" round pan at 350 degrees for a little over an hour, until a toothpick stuck in the center comes out clean. Turn out and cool on a wire rack. Serve with butter.

*Traditional charms are a ring (marriage); button (bachelorhood); thimble (spinsterhood); coin (wealth); wishbone (heart's desire); horseshoe (good luck); and swastika (for its original meaning of happiness—this charm dates from before World War II!).

Day of the Dead Sugar Skulls

Every autumn the monarch butterflies return to the sheltering fir trees in Mexico for the winter. Mexicans like to think the butterflies bear the spirits of their dead loved ones, and celebrate their homecoming. This is a joyful time, because, they say, the path back to the living world must not be made slippery with tears. Decorated sugar skulls are given to children, often with the child's name inscribed across the bony forehead.

Hint: The only place I've been able to find meringue powder is on the Internet (see Resources), so unless you have a Mexican bakery nearby, you may need to order it online. The same is true with the skull molds.

(Makes 20 medium skulls)

Skull molds

¼ cup meringue powder (this is what makes the sugar hard—it's a combination of egg whites, starch, and other miscellaneous edible ingredients)

5-lb. bag of granulated sugar

10 tsp. water

Large bowl

Small squares of cardboard to set skulls on to dry

Note: You can't make sugar skulls on a rainy or humid day—they won't release from the molds.

1. Mix water, meringue powder, and sugar until sugar is moistened. It is ready when you squeeze the sugar mixture in your hand and your fingerprints remain. If it doesn't hold together, add more water. Stir the mixture frequently as you're making skulls, because the water will sink to the bottom. If the mix gets dry as you're working, spritz with water.

2. Pack sugar mixture firmly into mold.

3. Scrape the back of the mold flat with a piece of cardboard or a ruler.

4. Invert the mold onto a stiff piece of cardboard and lift it off carefully (if the sugar shape doesn't come out of the mold easily, it's too wet—remix and try again with more sugar).

5. Air dry skull on cardboard for eight hours.

6. Decorate dry skull with tube icing (or the rock-hard icing you use for gingerbread houses) and/or beads, colorful foil, paper, feathers, or anything bright you can think of. Glue decorations to skull with icing.

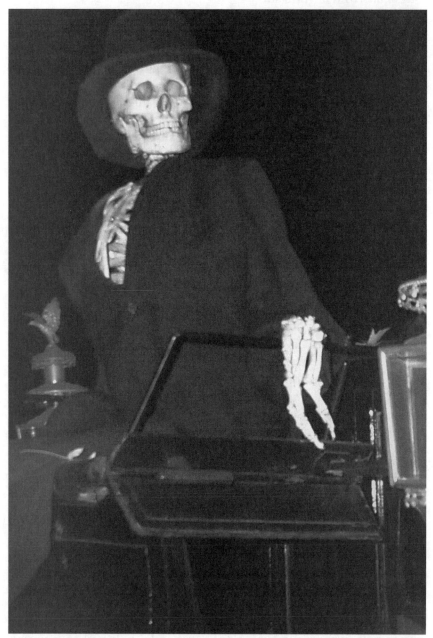

Nineteenth-century horse-drawn hearse from the collection of Tina and Tim Reuwsaat.

CHAPTER SEVEN

Haunted Expeditions

Where To Go And What To Do On Halloween

Long story short: there's no lack of things to do at Halloween. Haunted houses, tours, costume parties, parades, horror flick fests, even Boo at the Zoo nights have become annual events in most cities.

Want to try something a little different? You can suss out a haunting with real ghost hunters or visit hundreds-years-old cemeteries (with or without ghosts—your choice). Or you can take in the Mattel-originated Dream. Halloween fundraiser in Santa Monica that auctions off treasures like a custom-made Cher doll in a Bill Mackie outfit. How about a ride on a ghost train? Or a tour through Queen Mary's haunt, "Shipwreck?" Maybe you'd like to drop into a haunted theater, haunted farm, haunted mansion or even haunted winery ("25 rooms of horror and fun in a 120 year-old winery"). You can go to a "dance with the devil under the pale moonlight" barn dance (no experience necessary). Or do an annual 5K Halloween walk, check out the Halloween Swimwear Party at the city pool, or walk in the woods past costumed animals enacting environmental skits. No? OK, how about a concert of ghostly music or a Gothic Funeral Party? No? Then go for broke: take a tour to Transylvania with a stop at Vlad the Impaler's castle.

How to choose?

I offer you this: an American Halloween sampler. But be warned, it's by no means complete! For every haunted house, pumpkin festival or ghost tour listed, there are thousands more; for every graveyard, haunted B&B or parade, countless others. This is a peek at the breadth of what's happening on Halloween, and a few of the folks who are making it happen. My hope is that you can find something intriguing, point your car, and find even more great things to do along the way.

Key to ticket prices:
($)   under $15
($$) $16 to $30
($$$)   over $30

Citywide Halloween Celebrations

SALEM HAUNTED HAPPENINGS

Downtown Salem, Massachusetts. Produced by the Salem Halloween Committee, P.O. Box 8139, Salem, MA 01970-8139. Twenty minutes north of Boston by MBTA commuter train, thirty minutes by car. Info line: 978-744-0013. Halloween Committee: 978-744-0004. Many events are free.

Salem has become the Mecca for Hallophiles, the motherlode, and the touchstone for all things Halloween. A Massachusetts city with a rich maritime history (the infamous witches were from nearby Danvers, once called Salem Village, but the innocent folks were tried and hanged in Salem), Salem gives itself over completely to Halloween come October. It's the only place in the New World made famous by witchcraft, and has been a magnet for neopagans and witch-history buffs since the sixties; the town currently claims around two thousand practicing witches. If you want to be at the vortex of Halloween, Salem is where you should go. Preferably at night.

Begun as a two-hour festival on a Saturday in October 1980, Salem Haunted Happenings is now a twenty-four-day family Halloween celebration kicked off the second week of October with the Salem Haunted Happenings costume parade. A grand promenade with a hometown feel, the parade includes hundreds of schoolchildren and costumed marching bands alongside novelties such as the infamous East Beverly Lawn Chair Drill Team and the Official Witches of Salem. There's an opening night ceremony and a Boston-to-Salem Fright Train. From then on, the sky's the limit: make a wand, ask a witch a question, get fitted for custom fangs, enter a costume contest, channel a past life.

What happens on the streets of Salem is a people watcher's dream, especially if you're there at night; and the closer to Halloween itself, the better for gawking. All in all, a half-million people come through

Salem Haunted Happenings, according to an estimate by Salem Halloween Committee Executive Director Henry Witham.

Find the city's Downtown Command Center (ask anyone) and pick up a program guide—you'll also find them in stores or at kiosks throughout the city, or you can get one in advance through the mail. Events change slightly year to year, but there are some activities you can always expect to find, such as:

• Candlelit walking tours (they last about an hour) that are informative and fun, and usually hosted by experienced Salem historians. ($)

• Haunted houses such as Boris Karloff's Witch Mansion, Terror on the Wharf, Museum of Myths and Monsters, and Dracula's Castle. Check for new ones in the program guide. ($)

• Witch history museums aplenty. These attractions are set up largely for a year-round tourist trade; at Halloween, they add staff and a few extra touches. What's confusing is that all the attractions are similarly named, and their descriptions and entrance fees equally similar. So here goes: the Salem Wax Museum of Witches and Seafarers has a few rooms full of life-size dioramas populated by vintage London-made wax figures. Downstairs, a hands-on area lets kids experience a simulated seventeenth-century jail cell, make gravestone rubbings, and do other history-related activities. Across the street is the Salem Witch Village, where a practicing witch recites historical information as she leads you through dark corridors painted with scenes that open onto life-size dioramas. The Salem Witch Museum has a thirty-minute, audio-visual treatment of the 1692 witch trials, and a room dedicated to contemporary witchcraft, but no real people. The Witch Dungeon Museum offers a live re-enactment of Sara Goode's trial by two young actresses, who then lead you through the diorama portion of the museum. The Witch History Museum tells the story with a brief, one-actor performance, then a guided tour past scenes brought to life through animatronics and recorded voices. ($)

Salem Haunted Happenings also traditionally hosts a dance party, costume contest, Eerie Events (costumed actors telling ghost stories in the Peabody Essex Museum's Historic Houses) and Kids Day. The Annual Halloween Costume Ball happens at the Hawthorne Hotel each year (very elegant and often sold out; buy tickets in advance if you want to go, 978-744-4080). ($$$) In addition to official entertainment, many of Salem's occult businesses post their own schedule of events for the month; these can be as entertaining as the bigger events.

SALEM'S HISTORIC SITES

Very little survives of the Salem from the time of the witchcraft trials. The locations of the graves of the executed aren't known, for example, and neither is the site of Gallows Hill, where they were hanged. There are, however, several places to visit that highlight Salem's past, and it would be a shame to get all the way to Salem and not spend time investigating the city's history.

The Peabody Essex Museum's Phillips Library on Essex Street houses the Witchcraft Papers, actual handwritten trial documents. Some are out on display, protected from light by individual curtains; you raise each one to see the original pages. The Witch House (310 Essex Street), also known as Judge Corwin's House, belonged to one of the witch trial judges, and exemplifies seventeenth-century architecture and lifestyle. The House of the Seven Gables (54 Turner Street) was Nathaniel Hawthorne's inspiration for the novel of the same name. Hawthorne was the great-great-grandson of another trial justice, Judge Hawthorne. All historical attractions, ($).

Don't skip the graveyards: the Olde Burying Point Cemetery (Essex Street, next to the Salem Wax Museum) is final home to Justice Hawthorne, Chief Justice Benjamin Lynde, Jr. (presiding judge at the Boston Massacre trial), and many other historical figures. Next door to Olde Burying Point is my favorite Salem attraction: the Witch Trial Memorial. A small park surrounded by twenty stone benches, one for each person killed, the space invokes a meditative state. Protests of innocence from trial testimony are carved into the paving stones. The memorial was dedicated by Nobel Laureate Elie Wiesel in 1992, marking the tercentennial anniversary of the Salem witch hysteria. The graveyard and memorial are free.

Hint: Getting to Salem can be tough. Traffic gets snarled on the only two-lane highway that winds into town, so Salem Haunted Happenings runs shuttle buses from the nearby North Shore Mall parking lot and Salem State College (among others). Commuter trains from Boston run regularly through Salem, and the train station is a short walk from the festivities. In fact, Salem's downtown area is completely walkable: it's compact and flat, anchored by a beautiful town green surrounded by historic houses and period gaslight lamps.

The East Beverly Lawn Chair Drill Team make an annual appearance at the Salem Haunted Happenings parade.

Everyone wears a costume in Salem at Halloween, even the Fire Department. Photos by Gary Duehr.

SLEEPY HOLLOW/TARRYTOWN, NEW YORK

Legend Weekend, 914-631-8200, ext. 618. The weekend closest to Halloween. ($)

Twenty-eight miles north of New York City on the Hudson River lies the gateway to the Catskills where Washington Irving's "The Legend of Sleepy Hollow" was set. There are still places in Sleepy Hollow, known as North Tarrytown until 1996, which are described in Irving's 1819 tale about schoolmaster Ichabod Crane. For example, there is the Old Dutch Church, built in 1685, with three centuries of church memorabilia on display in the balcony; the bridge over the Pocantico River; and the brook where British spy John Andre was captured. The graveyard of the Old Dutch church holds the remains of Eleanor Van Tassel Brush, said to have been Irving's inspiration for the character of Katrina Van Tassel. Irving himself is buried in the adjacent cemetery.

Irving's short story is a blueprint for Halloween in the early years of our nation, built as it is upon tales of hauntings told around a fire, a dark night, a demon, and a smashed pumpkin. It stands to reason that Tarrytown and Sleepy Hollow offer something a little special on Legend Weekend, when Halloween events occur at many of the area's historic attractions.

Old Dutch Church

Route 9, Sleepy Hollow. 8 P.M. Friday and Saturday of Legend Weekend. 914-631-1123 after Labor Day. ($)

The Church sponsors a candlelit reading of "The Legend of Sleepy Hollow." Tickets are available only in advance from the Reformed Church offices, 42 North Broadway in Tarrytown. There are also free walking tours of the Dutch Church burial grounds from 10 AM - 4 PM.

Sunnyside

Route 9, Tarrytown. 10AM-5PM Saturday and Sunday.

The historically stunning set of buildings known as Sunnyside was Washington Irving's riverside home. Costumed guides lead you though the woods that surround the nineteenth-century estate, spinning spooky tales. Many other family friendly events are scheduled year to year, and have included shadow puppet shows and readings of Irving's stories.

Philipsburg Manor

Route 9, Sleepy Hollow. 6 PM- 9 PM Friday and Saturday (reservations suggested).

An eighteenth-century working farm, Philipsburg Manor hosts an annual ride of the Headless Horseman himself. Amidst ghouls, witches and other characters from Hudson Valley folklore, the horseman gallops across the grounds illuminated by hundreds of candlelit lanterns. The Manor is also open during the day for tours and demonstrations.

Lyndhurst

635 South Broadway, Tarrytown. 914-631-4481. 4 PM- 7 PM Sunday.

A gothic revival mansion built by former New York City Mayor William Paulding plays host to fictitious residents involved in mysterious activities on Legend Weekend.

Side trip: Frankenstein's Fortress, Creamery Road in Stanfordville, New York. 914-868-7804. Open weekends in October. ($)

Drive about sixty miles from Tarrytown up the beautiful Taconic State Parkway, and you'll find Frankenstein's Fortress. Staffed mostly by kids, the Fortress is filled with the eccentric creations of Peter Wing. "There are no generic scares in this haunt," says Wing, "There's something totally different at every turn." Take, for example, the rusty old toilet Wing built a while back. It was on rollers and a track, and the kids hiding behind it had a stick and lever. When people came by, the toilet rolled out, the lid flew open (it had *teeth*) and people screamed. Wing adds scenes to the Fortress each year, like the old train station and vintage train he's got in store for the next show. "It'll be full of dead divas and Marlene Dietrich singing 'I'm in Love Again,'" promises Wing.

HALLOWEEN IN NEW ORLEANS

The city's primary party allegiance goes to Mardi Gras, but come October, Halloween lights up this city like flashpaper. The setting is near-perfect: once a malarial swamp infested with snakes and alligators, not to mention pirates, prostitutes, and thieves, New Orleans now fans the flames of a vibrant voodoo and vampire culture. These things make for a Halloween that is truly unique to this city that buries its dead above ground and claims to have more real haunts than any other. Tales of murder, fire, and unexplainable blood-drained dead bodies waft in amongst the horse-drawn carriages and sputtering gas lamps that dot the French Quarter. And the city's love of masquerade is legendary. Says resident storyteller and history-lover Mary Millan, "I used to live in New York, and at Halloween parties maybe one out of four people would dress up. Here, one hundred percent of the people dress up, and they have four more costumes back in the closet."

Although many residents will carve a pumpkin and trick-or-treat, more and more cluster to the Quarter for Halloween, where they can listen to voodoo music, take in a costume ball, Goth bar, or tour the above-ground "cities of the dead." Like Salem, it's entertaining to just walk around. Halloween is at its most extreme on Bourbon Street, where the non-stop partying is legendary. As Mardi Gras is to Lent, so is Halloween to All Saints' Day: the people of New Orleans know how to let off steam before the serious stuff starts. Listed below, just a few of the things you can do there.

Hint: Reserve your room far in advance. October is a big convention month for New Orleans, and with all the Halloween activity piled on top, finding a place to stay at the last minute can be nearly impossible.

The New Orleans Historic Voodoo Museum's Halloween Voodoo Ritual

724 Rue Dumaine, New Orleans, Louisiana 70116. 504-523-7685. Halloween night, 8 PM. ($)

The museum's a jumble of tiny rooms stuffed full of alligator skulls, blowfish heads, human bones, gris-gris bags, altars, a portrait gallery, and one live and very large snake (don't skip the video on voodoo history and practice in the back room—it's really good). On Halloween night every year since 1972, hundreds of participants gather at the museum to honor ancestors through an ancient voodoo ritual. Everyone is led to a sacred tree and altar where a voodoo queen presides over drumming, chanting, and, very likely, snake dancing. If you've brought an offering—flowers, fruit, honey, rum, candles, pumpkins, and champagne are suggested—this is where you leave it. On some Halloweens, weddings and initiations are woven into the ceremony, and, depending on how many people there are, you may get a chance to ask the priests and priestesses for messages from your ancestors.

French Quarter Halloween Walking Tours

Both day and nighttime tours are popular in New Orleans, and around Halloween many companies beef up their nighttime spooky tour business. Anything that gets you beyond Bourbon Street and into the back alleys and cemeteries of New Orleans' French Quarter is well worth doing. There are dark treasures tucked into corners that you'll only find on foot. ($-$$)

Magic Walking Tours (504-588-9693) and Historic New Orleans

Walking Tours (504-947-2120) get high ratings for being entertaining as well as for providing well-documented ghosts and hauntings. Haunted History Tours' Halloween "Ghost and Vampire Expedition" (504-861-2727) is high camp and great fun. It snakes through back alleys past sites of graphic vampire-like killings, and includes a stop in a "haunted" bar. Bloody Mary's Tours (504-486-2080), connected to the Voodoo Museum, offers both "Voodoo Cemetery Tour of St. Louis #1" and a special Halloween "best of" vampire/voodoo tour.

Speaking of St. Louis #1, New Orleans' historic cemeteries are spectacular, free, and open to the public. Most residents are interred above-ground in architecturally gorgeous mausoleums, tombs, and vaults set in street-like rows, giving rise to the description "cities of the dead." One year and a day after entombment, families can instruct a caretaker to gather up the jewelry and bones, and add them to a cache in the tomb so the space can be reused. In this fashion, each tomb can house many remains. Locals warn tourists not to visit cemeteries alone or at night—heed their advice.

Annual Gathering of the Coven

Hosted by Anne Rice's Vampire Lestat Fan Club at the State Palace Theater on Canal Street. Recorded info: 504-897-3983. Usually the Friday closest to Halloween at 6:30 PM.

Tickets go on sale in August or September through Ticketmaster, 504-522-5555. Sells out quickly. ($$-$$$)

Vampires. The word "upir" first appeared in 1047 in reference to a Russian prince; he was a "Upir Lichy" or wicked vampire. A fistful of notable vampiric murderers dot the last four hundred years. Vlad the Impaler, of course, was the fifteenth-century feudal baron known for impaling his victims on stakes; Elizabeth Bathory, on the other hand, was arrested in 1610 for the vampiric murders of several hundred whose blood she used for bath water. Eighteenth-century Serbian Peter Plogojowitz reportedly appeared to various townspeople after his death, and so was disinterred and allegedly found to be breathing slightly. [1]

In 1976, Anne Rice published *Interview with a Vampire,* joining a legion of writers drawn to vampirism that includes Goethe ("Bride of Corinth"), Alexey Tolstoy ("Upyr"), and Alexandre Dumas (*Le Vampire*) to name a few. Rice's novels gave birth to the vampire Lestat, and to a new generation of vampire-philes who congregate annually in New Orleans at the Gathering of the Coven. The party features live concerts and movie screenings, and is held in a huge function room that's very, very crowded.

Here you'll be among Anne Rice's biggest fans—legendary in loyalty and dress—a group of men and women mostly in their twenties and thirties, who keep up with Rice on the Internet and use the gathering as a kind of reunion. If you go, what you wear for a costume is critical. Read *Interview with a Vampire* and you'll know what to do. And, yes, Rice usually appears.

House of Shock Horror Show

4951 River Road, Jefferson, Louisiana (on River Road underneath the Huey P. Long Bridge on the East Bank). 504-734-SHOC. Open every weekend in October and every night the week before Halloween. Beer sold on premises. Not recommended for children. ($)

Founded in 1993 by Phil Anselmo, vocalist for the band Pantera, and his friends from the local rock community, this attraction started as a "Horror Club" with a membership that had parties around the year and decorated a float each Mardi Gras. The club's first two Halloween haunts were in a backyard, but when lines started forming around the block, the group found a warehouse space. Now they host upwards of thirty thousand people over fifteen nights. House of Shock performs with an army of two hundred die-hard volunteers willing to do anything for the art of the scare.

"House of Shock started because there was a lack of true horror," says Ross Karpelman, one of the four producers. "We thought there was too much comedy and special effects, like an MTV-view of what horror used to be up till the 1970s. House of Shock gets back to the terror and horror of '70s movies like *Deranged* and *Evil Dead.*"

Karpelman likes to call House of Shock a horror show and interactive haunted house, to tip off audience members—things *happen* to you here. "Most people don't expect what they get," says Karpelman. "So we try to prepare them."

Even before you go in, the pre-show raises the bar: you're instantly assaulted by distorted hard rock and a profane master of ceremonies. Sacrilegious, gory, and outrageous, House of Shock is an extreme experience that's not for everyone and makes no apologies.

Karpelman plays Lord Belial, who delivers a satanic sermon on an altar (complete with virgin) that rises twenty feet over the heads of the audience. Performers may jump out at you or swing from bungee cords attached to a twenty-five-foot ceiling. Inside the huge warehouse, you'll go through a cemetery, catacomb, and swamp, as well as an evil church and strobe-lit maze, to name just a few of the rooms. Outside, a movie theater plays short clips of gory, underground horror flicks.

Because the House's fictional theme of Satanism has made it constantly controversial (folks have claimed the House of Shock is a satanic recruiting station), they've occasionally had to fight to stay open.

Side trip with kids: Much of New Orleans' Halloween offerings are adult in nature and happen long after most kids' bedtimes. If you're looking for a good time for the whole family, try Sheriff Charles C. Foti's Haunted House in City Park. It's a whole Halloween-themed carnival with food, games, and two haunted houses—one for toddlers and another for bigger kids. A police car half-submerged in a swamp or an electrocution scene give you pause when you consider the creators of this particular haunt: convicted felons help build it top to bottom.

HALLOWEEN SAN FRANCISCO-STYLE

If you pass a man dressed as Marilyn or Barbra, or simply wearing a pair of black socks, period, you know you're getting close to San Francisco's impromptu Halloween party in the Castro. When you spot the Sisters of Perpetual Indulgence, a gaggle of tall drag queens dressed in gothic witch/nun outfits collecting money for charity, you know you're there.

It all started as a costume party for kids back in the 1940s when the Castro was a working class Irish neighborhood. Grandpa Ernie, owner of Cliff's Hardware Store, now Cliff's Variety, sponsored the party every year; Ernie eventually abandoned it in the late 1960s. An adult version of the party took over and quickly grew into one of the biggest, most outrageous costume showplaces in the country. People parade wildly creative, weird, or barely visible costumes through the tightly packed streets of the Castro while thousands of onlookers come to watch the show. Police barricade Castro Street early in the evening and keep closing streets as the crowd swells. Here you'll even see costumes drawn on with body paint. It's not a parade per se, just a sort of mingling, like Bourbon Street without the alcohol overload. And it's not an official event, it just happens and everyone knows about it. A neighborhood street party with no civic organizer, there are no entry fees and almost no violence or crime. In a case of too much of a good thing, by 1996 Halloween in the Castro became such an enormous draw that some organizations and merchants complained it was too crowded.

In stepped a consortium of non-profits and city associations to produce an official Halloween benefit, bringing Halloween to the Civic Center. The idea was to spread the holiday out, thin the crowds in the Castro, and at the same time raise money for anti-violence and AIDS groups. The party has had celebrity hosts, live bands, DJs, and food booths offering everything from margaritas and Vietnamese cuisine to chimichangas and pizza. There are tattooing stations, horror flicks, and of course, costumes. At the 1996 event, two hundred thousand spectators attempted the world's largest Macarena.

Although the Civic Center party started out with a bang, the crowds have largely drifted back to the Castro. Locals say that the Civic Center is where you'll find the out-of-towners (tourists and folks from the suburbs), and the Castro is where you'll find the locals. Take public transportation to either.

Halloween in the Castro

In the heart of the Castro neighborhood, Castro Street between Market and Nineteenth Streets. Halloween night. Free.

Halloween at the Civic Center

Van Ness, Grove, Hyde, Hayes, and McCallister Sreets near Market Street. 415-826-1401. Halloween night. Not recommended for children. ($)

Side trip with kids: The city's Fair Oaks Street neighborhood's annual Halloween children's party, while not an official San Francisco event, is a magnet for kids all over the city. From around 4:30 PM to 10:00 PM, the residents block off the street and turn it into a Halloween extravaganza where kids can bob for apples in between trick or treating. The people go out of their way to decorate, and they pride themselves on their homemade costumes and elaborately carved jack-o-lanterns. Just to give you an idea of what goes on, a favorite 1999 display was two houses, side by side, with the same haunted theme—they both featured mad scientists whose experiments had gotten mixed up. One home displayed monsters made of all limbs. Next door, creatures were all heads and torsos. In another display, two boys lowered buckets from a rooftop, supposedly filled with candy, but actually filled with a concoction made of frozen peas and Jell-O.

Halloween Theme Parks

In 1969, Disneyland in California opened its Haunted Mansion and raised the bar for the entire dark ride industry. The Haunted Mansion was the first (and some say still the best) high-budget haunt to apply state-of-the-art technology to the art of the scare.

It wasn't long before other large commercial ventures appeared: Knott's Scary Farm opened for the first time in 1973, followed by a whole series of independently-owned mid-sized haunts. Universal Studios in Florida started its "Halloween Horror Nights" in 1990 (Universal in Hollywood didn't open until 1996), and by 1991, Six Flags Corporation had opened spook houses at five of its eight parks (with the new Brutal Planet as Six Flag's latest attraction). In 1999, Williamsburg Busch Gardens launched its Howl-O-Scream, which pushed park attendance up by twenty percent in October. Even Sesame Place in Langhorne, Pennsylvania created "The Count's Spooktacular" to drum up business in October.

In a few short years, there was a new breed of Halloween event: large-scale, megabucks, October-only themed attractions—the big boys in the dark amusements industry. Let's take a look at two of them: Spooky World, which comes to life for the Halloween season then fades back into the woods in southeastern Massachusetts, and Knott's Scary Farm, the fall offering of Knott's Berry Farm, a year-round southern California family theme park.

Spooky World: America's Horror Theme Park

In the woods at Foxboro Stadium, 60 Washington Street, Foxboro, Massachusetts (thirty minutes from Boston and Providence). 978-838-0200. Open Friday through Sunday evenings in October. Handicapped parking and a specially adapted hayride wagon. Attractions are rated one to five skulls. Don't bring the young kids. ($$)

Spooky World began as the Fun Farm in Berlin, Massachusetts and closed down the freeway the first year it was open. Now, only nine years later, it occupies twenty acres behind the New England Patriots' football stadium in Foxboro. Unlike other theme parks that devote a section of their operation to Halloween, Spooky World creates a total Halloween environment only for October, like a Renaissance fair gone Goth.

There's a 3-D Disco, the Phantom Mine Shaft, and a killer clown-infested Cirque Macabre, not to mention the New Reaper's Hayride of Terror, a haunted hayride featuring chainsaw-lugging maniacs and zombies who rise from fog-infested graves. A Monster Midway encircles the park. There's also a superstore (severed fingers? you can never have too many), sideshows featuring snakes and deformed amphibians, the Hell House of Hollywood wax museum (Manson, Rev. Jim Jones and friends), horror industry celebrity appearances, and the American Horror Museum, where you'll see the original dress worn by Anthony Perkins in *Psycho*, Freddy Krueger's glove, and one of Jason's masks from *Friday the Thirteenth*.

Spooky World also has some controversial features. Animal activists have boycotted the park, alleging it abused the rats used in their "Animal Room" (Spooky World hired a veterinarian who certified that the rats were well taken care of). The park draws more than five thousand people a night. It tries to take the edge off of long lines by employing "walkabout" characters and pumping in lots of music.

Knott's Scary Farm

At Knott's Berry Farm, ten minutes from Disneyland at 8039 Beach Boulevard, Buena Park, California. 877-TKTS-2-DIE-4 or 877-858-9234. Open Friday and Saturday nights in October, some weekday evenings and Sundays. No costumes allowed. Not for children under thirteen. ($$-$$$)

Every October since 1973, Knott's Berry Farm has transformed itself into Knott's Scary Farm. According to park officials, more than five thousand gallons of fake blood, one million yards of cloth, and fifteen thousand gallons of black paint have gone by the boards in pursuit of the ultimate scare.

This is where you'll find Elvira, in the flesh, doing her own show. There are ride- and walk-through mazes the likes of vampire-infested Dominion of the Dead, and Alien Attack, where you walk across a floor made of bodies encased in blocks of ice (attractions can change year to year). There's also the Hanging, a macabre Friar's Roast on steroids where actors, stunt people, and comedians ruthlessly murder pop icons of the past year (1999 saw the deaths of the Spice Girls, Austin Powers, and the producers of *The Blair Witch Project*). More than one thousand monsters, ghouls, and gruesome beasts lurk in the fog at Knott's. Patrons report large crowds and long lines for some of the rides and attractions (the security check at the gate makes for a wait), but the lines move quickly. Horror fans find enough at Knott's to keep them coming year after year. You just have to know what you're getting into: this is a huge, crowded theme park with lots to do, but some waiting around to do it. The season kicks off with a not-to-be-missed hearse procession.

Knott's Berry Farm also runs daytime Camp Spooky for children eleven and under that bears no similarity at all to its older brother.

Hint: Friday nights may be less crowded than Saturdays. If you go to the Early Bird Dinner on a preview weekend, it's slightly less expensive, and you get to enter the park early for a head start on lines.

Parades

You can tell by the costumes exactly where you are: if you see puppets more than twenty feet high or a hyperactive gang of pit bulls, you're in New York City. A ten-foot-tall headdress? Key West. Coolers, a giant pair of flip-flops, a set of six pineapples, and a snorkeler with a fish tank on his head? That's got to be Lahaina, on the island of Maui, where people come from all over the world to do Halloween Hawaiian-style. From the oldest, continuous parade (Anoka, Minnesota) to the largest (Greenwich Village), the fanciest (Key

The Giant Luna Moths were created by master puppet designer Alex Kahn of Superior Concept Monsters especially for the parade's twenty-fifth anniversary. Photo by Larry Nussbaum.

West and West Hollywood) to the longest (Toms River, New Jersey), Halloween parades are a good time for everyone. Most parades will let you join in, which poses this difficult choice: which is more fun— to watch, or to be watched?

Village Halloween Parade, Greenwich Village, New York City

Greenwich Village up Sixth Avenue from Spring Street to Twenty-second Street.

7 PM Halloween night. Free. If you want to participate, gather on Sixth Avenue south of Spring Street down to Broome Street between 6 PM and 7 PM; no registration or fee required.

> "The Halloween Parade is a parade about spirit—and I mean that in the spiritual sense. I think it's because of the times we live in and the nature of the parade itself—and because Halloween is a night of freedom and creativity. More people need what the parade has to offer— a joyous get-together of diversity in harmony. The spirit of the event is palpable."   —Jeanne Fleming, Artistic Director of the parade

This is the nation's largest, one-day public Halloween event. Hailed by national and international press as the biggest and the best, and funded by the National Endowment for the Arts as an arts celebration, the Greenwich Village Halloween parade is the granddaddy of all large-scale theatrical events. Does it live up to its reputation? Yes.

The parade celebrated its twenty-fifth anniversary in 1998. Once a gaggle of theater artists parading mask-maker Ralph Lee's puppets through the streets and inviting spectators to join them, the parade now attracts an estimated crowd of two million spectators and forty thousand marchers (about as big as the St. Patrick's Day parade). It's even won an Obie. To honor the parade's role "in bringing the city together," former Mayor Dinkins declared October 24-31 to be "Halloweek" in New York City in perpetuity. There are events all week leading up to the parade.

What will you see? Puppets, to be sure, most likely including the Giant Luna Moths commissioned for the parade's twenty-fifth anniversary. Here's a statistic for you: it takes one thousand volunteers to carry the huge puppets built for this parade. You'll also hear music, every kind you can think of, from steel bands to the Gay and Lesbian Big Apple Corps, from rap, kazoo, samba, and voodoo to Ivy League college marching bands.

What won't you see? Much crime. There is less criminal activity in the Village on parade night than the rest of the year.

Fire Company No. 1 Halloween Parade, Toms River, New Jersey

Toms River, New Jersey, in Ocean County, one hour and twenty minutes south of New York City on the Atlantic Ocean. 732-244-7941. Halloween night, 7 PM. Free. The parade marches down Main Street (Route 166). If you want to join in, register at 9 AM on the morning of the parade at the firehouse in Toms River.

One of the country's earliest, and now the second largest in the nation, the Toms River parade was founded by fire fighters. Anyone can be in the parade, as long as you're "street legal and non-offensive," say organizers. But no politicking—no campaign signs, literature or candidate hand-shaking. If Ross Perot's people want to march, fine, but if they drive a bus plastered with slogans, the parade folks will (and did) cover it up with black crepe paper. If the governor wants to join in, great: you can spot her marching with the Boy Scouts.

Floats (including some from the Miss America pageant in nearby Ocean City), bands, entire schools of children, even babies in their red wagons done up as Red Baron fighter planes, march by the judges to vie for one of the one hundred twenty-five trophies Toms River gives out.

Hint: Come early, because people start filling up the curbside at two in the afternoon, and some set chairs out the night before. Expect the parade to run around three hours.

Fantasy Fest Parade, Key West, Florida

Contact Key West Visitor's Bureau, 402 Wall Street, Key West, Florida 33040. Call 1-800-LAST KEY. Last Saturday in October, 7 PM. Free.

The Key West Fantasy Fest, now more than twenty years old, is a ten-day festival culminating on Halloween. As in San Francisco, Key West's Halloween celebrations evolved from gay festivities, but here they're close enough to the Caribbean to feel the influence of steel drums and salt-rimmed margaritas: less fog, more skin. No crisp autumn leaves like New England, but no Puritans either. Everyone's welcome here, even the dog.

Fantasy Fest is a collection of parties, street fairs, masquerade balls and, of course, the Fantasy Fest Parade, which attracts a crowd of around seventy-five thousand to watch an opulent procession of floats, bands, dancing groups and costumed marchers. People wear Mardi Gras-like beads and most everyone's in costume; even homes and businesses are decorated. Costume contests are the heart of

One of the most popular Key West Halloween events is the Pet Masquerade and Parade, which attracts several thousand spectators; entry fees benefit Lower Keys Friends of the Animals. Photo courtesy of Stuart Newman and Associates.

the Fest: expect anything from headdress balls to toga parties, from "home-made" bikini shows to celebrity look-alike contests. The premiere costume competition is said to be the Pier House Resort and Caribbean Spa's "Pretenders in Paradise" Costume Competition, where international designers try to outdo each other. A wingspan of twenty-five feet here is nothing. Festival events range in price.

Hint: Take heed of the Fest's official rules: the city's open container law is suspended within designated festival areas (to allow public drinking), but no glass or cans are allowed. Although nudity is illegal and Key West Police publish warnings such as "body paint does not constitute clothing," there may be nudity nonetheless. The Fest provides several satellite parking lots with shuttle service to and from the main festival area and extra taxi and bus service. Kids are fine during the day (Kids Day is part of Fantasy Fest), but you might want to get a sitter and check out the nightlife without them.

Side trip: Key West Halloween Ghost Tours depart nightly at 8 PM rain or shine from the Holiday Inn La Concha Hotel (430 Duval

Street, Key West; 305-294-9255; reservations required). Find out which famous bar served as a graveyard and the city morgue, or if Count Carl von Cosel really did marry the reconstructed corpse of his girlfriend. Ghosts of cigar makers, pirates, voodoo practitioners, and even that of a tattered doll live on through these walking tours.

Grand Day Parade, Anoka, Minnesota

Anoka Halloween Inc., P.O. Box 385, Anoka, Minnesota. Twelve miles north of Minneapolis. Anoka Area Chamber of Commerce: 763-421-7130. Last Saturday in October. Free.

Anoka considers itself the site of the oldest, continuous Halloween celebration in the country (the Neeowollah—Halloween backwards—Festival in Independence, Kansas claims to have had the first city-wide Halloween celebration in 1918, but it has not been held every year; Anoka's has).

In 1920, George Green got frustrated with the soaped windows, missing gates and relocated outhouses of Halloween. He gathered Anoka's leaders together and proposed a radical idea: give the kids something else to do on that night, like a Halloween parade or costume contest, with free candy, lots of it. If we get them all together, he argued, we can keep an eye on them. It worked, and over the years, Anoka built itself up into the self-proclaimed Halloween Capital of the World.

Four generations later, Anoka's Halloween is not very different from what Mr. Green proposed. It's grown of course—the festivities now last two weeks and include more activities. There's the five-kilometer Gray Ghost Run (named for an elderly veterinarian who used to jog through a local cemetery), where, one year, a group tied themselves together and jogged as a centipede. And there's the annual Anoka Rotary Duck Drop, where folks "adopt" plastic ducks and drop them from the Main Street bridge into the Rum River (first duck over the finish line wins five hundred dollars).

But the Grand Day Parade's the thing. It's huge, attracting bands and beauty queens from all over the state. And there's a parade just for kids: the Big Parade of Little People, always held the Friday before the Grand Day Parade, when the town's elementary students march in costume.

Halloween Carnaval, West Hollywood, California

West Hollywood Chamber of Commerce, ½ Santa Monica Boulevard, West Hollywood, California 90046. The parade goes down Santa Monica Boulevard (La Cienega Boulevard to Doheny Drive). City of West Hollywood Halloween Hotline: 323-848-6547. Held the Saturday nearest Halloween, 7 PM. Free.

Organizers say their Halloween party rivals San Francisco's, perhaps not in numbers, but in glamour. It may have a leg-up on weather: it's always clear, sunny, and warm in West Hollywood. The city (openly gay, with a gay mayor) crowns a celebrity honorary mayor to preside over the festival, hires the entertainment, names a grand marshal, and sponsors costume contests. One mile of the four-lane Santa Monica Boulevard is closed completely to accommodate crowds of around three hundred thousand, and the prime spot for viewing is Santa Monica and La Cienega Boulevards. Arrive early to find parking.

Side trip: If you travel a few miles west to Santa Monica City, check out the homes on streets that run north of Wilshire Boulevard between Twenty-fourth and Twenty-eighth Streets. This wildly decorated area attracts trick-or-treaters from all over the country. Rumor has it that here, full-size chocolate bars are an understood part of the purchase and sale agreement for buying a house.

Haunted Trails and Hayrides

"What if no one comes?" worried Link Moser's mother, after the family put together their first haunted hayride. Link had read about a farmer in upstate New York who had started a successful Halloween hayride, and the Mosers just spent three weeks building scenes on their fifty-acre New Hampshire farm. It was 1994, and, unbeknownst to them, families all across the country were retrofitting their hay wagons and begging friends and relatives to chase audiences through the fields with chainsaws.

A few hundred miles away in Pennsylvania, Randy Bates was wrestling with a different problem: his haunted hayride business had been going for four years already, and he was trying to figure out how to handle the crowds.

"We started the hayride as a fun social event that would also make a few bucks for me and some of my friends," said Bates. "We had a haunted trail, lit with kerosene lamps and Coleman lanterns. The first year, we just about made expenses. Now, the profits help the family farm stay viable, raise funds for Boys Scouts and 4-H clubs, and help put our kids through school. Needless to say, it's become a huge part of our life."

And it's a big part of the lives of Nancy and Michael Jubie, who spend the better part of a year creating effects like collapsing barn roofs, phlegm-spewing devices, and giant praying mantises to thrill the throngs at their Ulster Park, New York Headless Horseman Hayride. This is no small undertaking. Many busy hayride businesses have watched their staffs grow from family and friends to upwards of one hundred employees. In Huntington, Vermont, four hundred volunteers help create, stage, and produce the Haunted Forest, a labor of love done to raise money for the Green Mountain Audubon Society Nature Center.

Although hayrides aren't nearly as numerous as haunted houses (they tend to be independently or family-run, many as seasonal extensions of the family farm), they're tremendously popular. The first year, the Mosers got five hundred people at their Windhill Farms Haunted Hayrides, and by now, their attendance has more than quadrupled. Just about everyone in northern Vermont knows about the Audubon Society event, and the Jubies have to recommend reservations because the crowds get so large. As for the Bates' Arasapha Farms and Bates Motel, by 1999, they were up to ninety-five employees; ten haywagons with high tech, digital sound systems; electrical and pneumatic automation; and huge crowds.

Haunted trails and hayrides have a lot going for them: Mother Nature provides a good part of the atmosphere, not to mention ten thousand years of genetic coding to give us the shivers when we're out in the middle of nowhere after dark. People just plain like to push the limits of what frightens them. "They arrive at our hayride fully prepared and eager to be scared," says Moser. "Perhaps facing the darkness and coming safely out the other end strengthens their own belief that good can triumph over evil."

Windhill Farm Haunted Halloween Hayrides

Windhill Farm, 7249 Pleasant Street, Loudon, New Hampshire. Call 603-267-6454. Open evenings in October. Concession proceeds benefit Greyhound adoption. ($)

Says Link: "We work hard to keep the ride changing from year to year: new scenes are added and old ones are redesigned. And we don't use a lot of blood and guts, but try to scare people based on the unknown instead."

Arasapha Farms Haunted Hayride and The Bates Motel

1835 N. Middletown Road, Gradysville, Pennsylvania on Route 352. Accessible from Philadelphia, Wilmington, and the

Lancaster/Harrisburg area. Call 610-459-0647. Open weekend evenings in October, every evening from mid-October through Halloween. Okay for kids—actors use discretion in dealing with young people. ($)

The scares come from everywhere: above, behind, in the air, from the ground; people on one side of the wagon see a different show from those on the other. The wagon goes at a steady, walkable speed and some of the characters will catch up with you. After the hayride, you can warm yourself by a fire and have hot chocolate before you check out the Bates Motel, a haunted house on the same site. Added perk: the exit door to the motel is placed so you can watch people come out screaming while you enjoy your refreshments.

Headless Horseman Hayrides and Haunted House

778 Broadway, Route 9W, Ulster Park, New York 12487. 914-339-BOOO. Open weekend evenings in October. Wagons leave every five minutes. Reservations strongly suggested. ($)

Ride through Michael and Nancy Jubie's forty-five-acre farm past orchards, ponds, fields, woods, an historic two hundred-year-old stone caretaker's house and, of course, a centuries-old graveyard. Shows change year to year but the fourteen-foot-tall, flame-shooting skeleton head under a thirty-foot waterfall is permanent. The wagon lets you out at a corn maze; you have to finish the trail on foot. There is also children's daytime entertainment (only certain dates, call for schedule).

Green Mountain Audubon Society's Annual Haunted Forest

Produced by the Green Mountain Audubon Society (GMAS), 255 Sherman Hollow Road, Huntington, Vermont 05462 (about thirty minutes from Burlington or Montpelier). Call 802-434-3068. Three evening performances (for ages eight and up) and one matinee (for younger kids) in late October. Tickets must be purchased in advance; they go on sale in mid-September at GMAS, and can sell out quickly. ($)

Black-caped guides lead groups of spectators through wooded trails lit by over two hundred and fifty jack-o-lanterns, past staged scenes that pop to life in the dark. The hike takes about an hour to finish, and usually includes a dance scene that varies year to year: once it was a score of skeletons dancing in a graveyard; another time, it was shadows on a scrim. The Vermont Chamber of Commerce lists the Haunted Forest as one of Vermont's top ten fall events.

Pumpkin Festivals and Contests

You can grow them, throw them, eat them, carve them, weigh them, decorate them, even carve marriage proposals in them. Halloween pumpkin festivals grew out of the tradition of fall harvest fests, and have become the ultimate October destination for thousands, coast to coast.

The Great Jack-o-Lantern Festival

Route 12, Carbuncle Park, Oxford, Massachusetts (call for details; the festival sometimes moves to locations other than Oxford). Call 508-987-5681. Open dusk to 10 PM, eight nights in mid-October. ($)

One October, when his kids were little, John Reckner took his family up to northern Vermont to see the covered bridges. The light grew dim, it got colder, and the family packed into the car to drive home. To their amazement, up on the side of a mountain, they saw five hundred pumpkins, carved and lit—a sight they'd never forget.

The Great Jack-o-Lantern Festival in Oxford, Massachusetts. Photo courtesy of John Reckner.

In 1985, Reckner began his jack-o-lantern festival in the craggy hills behind Oxford High School. Four thousand carved jack-o-lanterns dot the hillside, hang in the trees, nestle among the rocks, and sit on pedestals, while folks stroll along a trail to view them. Around two hundred of the pumpkins are big, 100-700 pounds, intricately carved with themes like Hollywood or the Sixties. But the pumpkins don't just sit there. Each grouping of pumpkins, or "skit" as Reckner calls it, has a soundtrack, and many have special effects: fog, a mirror ball, or strobe light. It is, quite simply, something you have to see.

Cincinnati-born Reckner went to art school, as did his wife and children. They collect design ideas and patterns for carving all year long. At harvest time, they buy the pumpkins and do the sketching. Once the carving madness begins, there's no rest until it's done: they can't start too soon before opening night or the pumpkins will rot before the festival's end. Some pumpkins go to local schools for kids to carve. The rest get turned over to "gutting marines" who clean out the pulp, and soak the pumpkins with a watered-down fungicide. Then, for a week straight, they carve. Or rather, engrave. The team of about ten art school graduates use flexible paring knives to skin off a thin layer of rind, making carvings that are extraordinarily fine and detailed. A candle inside illuminates the designs with a luxurious golden glow.

Reckner's favorite? The seven hundred-pound pumpkin engraved as the *Titanic* that was displayed half-sunk in the pond, while the movie soundtrack played in the background.

The Great Jack-o-Lantern Festival is one of two Halloween events nationwide to be selected by the Library of Congress as a local legacy for their Bicentennial celebration.

This was the other:

The Circleville Pumpkin Show, a.k.a. "The Greatest Free Show on Earth"
159 East Franklin Street, Circleville, Ohio 43113 (Columbus, Ohio is the closest major city). Call 470-474-7000. Always the third Wednesday through Saturday in October. Free.

This unique agricultural exhibit and street fair had its humble origins in 1903, when George R. Haswell, who was then mayor of Circleville, conceived the idea of holding a small exhibit in front of his store on West Main Street. Corn fodder and pumpkins (many of them cut into jack-o-lanterns) formed the principal decorations and were responsible for it being dubbed "the pumpkin show." The following year, neighborhood merchants joined Haswell, and from then on the exhibition grew steadily.

Witness feats like hog calling, egg tossing, big wheel races, pie-eating contests, and of course, a pumpkin toss. A huge event with a small-town feel, the Circleville Pumpkin Show is the sixth largest such festival in the U.S., with an annual attendance in four days and nights of over three hundred thousand people.

Downtown Keene, New Hampshire Pumpkin Festival

Produced by Center Stage Cheshire County, 39 Central Square, Suite 305, Keene, New Hampshire. Call 603-358-5344. Held annually on the Saturday before Halloween 10 AM-10 PM. Jack-o-lanterns are lit around 4 PM. If you go, bring a pumpkin to add to the display. Free.

This festival is nuts about numbers: it holds the world record, as of 1999, for number of carved pumpkins, and all the pumpkins, every last one of them, get counted each year. At the first festival in 1991, there were six hundred jack-o-lanterns. By 1998, a new record was set with 17,693 jack-o-lanterns. That year an impressive tower of pumpkins included a carved-out marriage proposal (she said yes). Everyone who helps carve, including around five thousand schoolchildren, artists, corporations and city workers to name a few, signs a Guinness log book to become an official part of the record-breaking attempt. The pumpkins are counted by a local certified accounting firm, and when the number is announced, the excitement is palpable.

Main Street is closed to traffic and kids can trick or treat in the stores. Besides pumpkin gazing, there's a Halloween parade, plenty of food, and a fireworks show at the end of the day. Shuttles run from company parking lots.

The World Championship Punkin Chunkin (near Millsboro, Delaware)

Located on county roads 305 and 306 in Sussex County, Delaware. Sponsored by the Punkin Chunkin Association, c/o B&B Mechanical, RD #4, Box 192-D, Georgetown, Delaware 19947. 302-856-1444. First Saturday after Halloween. Gates open at 8:00 AM, chunkin starts at 10 AM. ($)

So the challenge was made and the gauntlet was laid,
to build a machine to power a punkin through the air . . .
—1989 Ballad of Punkin Chunkin

Alternately referred to as Delaware's Homegrown Insanity or the World's Largest Tailgate Party, this is the first and the biggest of pumpkin hurling festivals. Kicked-off in 1986 in the southernmost county of Delaware, the contest reputedly began with a wager.

Half Moon Bay's mid-October Art & Pumpkin Festival (650-726-9652) happens the weekend following Columbus Day, 10 AM to 5 PM. Free. Half Moon Bay is twenty-five miles south of San Francisco and feels more like autumn than anyplace else in the area.

In November of that year, the contestants met on Thompson's farm outside Milton, Delaware with their inventions. Cobbled together from auto springs, garage doors, car frames and wooden poles, the first contraptions netted the inaugural record of one hundred seventy feet. Three years later the giant, centrifugal sling hurler appeared and set a six hundred-foot record. In 1994, the first heavy-duty air cannon quadrupled the record toss.

Second only to the yearly NASCAR races at Dover Downs, this is Delaware's biggest annual two-day event. Crowds of over twenty thousand stand behind fences (for safety due to occasional misfires) to watch machines named Old Glory, Bad to the Bone, and Punkinator launch ten-pound pumpkins to distances exceeding thirty-five hundred feet. There are only four rules:

1. Pumpkins must weigh between eight and ten pounds.
2. Pumpkins shall leave the machine intact.
3. No part of the machine shall cross the starting line.
4. No explosives allowed.

Chunkin Divisions include: Youth, Youth Unlimited, Human Powered, Catapult, Centrifugal, and Air Cannon. Youth Divisions use smaller pumpkins. Contact the Punkin Chunkin Association to enter.

OTHER PUMPKIN HURLING EVENTS

Punkin Chuckin' Contest, Morton, Illinois, off I-74.

For information, contact the Morton Chamber of Commerce: 1-888-765-6588. Third weekend in October, 2 PM until dark. ($)

Farms surrounding this small Illinois town claim to supply about 80% of the nation's canned pumpkin. Because Morton considers itself the "Pumpkin Capital of the World," the Chamber of Commerce thought it only fitting to send a pumpkin hurling team to Delaware. So was born the Mighty Aludium Q-36 Pumpkin Modulator, an 18-ton, 100-foot cannon made of 10-inch diameter plastic pipe powered by compressed air and mounted on an old cement mixer. Experienced chunkers sniffed at the new contraption. But the Q-36 Pumpkin Modulator blasted off and jaws dropped. It won the division title with a chuck of just over 2,700 feet, and went on to establish a 1998 Guinness Book record with a chuck of 4,491 feet. The Morton team brought more than bragging rights home to Morton. Since 1996, the town has produced its own pumpkin hurling festival, a full-out annual competition patterned after Delaware's.

Pumpkin chucking competitions have since been initiated in

Raleigh, North Carolina; Busti, New York; Canfield, Ohio; Lancaster, Pennsylvania; and York, Pennsylvania to name a few. Because of its mix of physics and fun, pumpkin hurling is becoming popular at public schools around the country, so check your local paper for a punkin' chunk near you.

Halloween Museums, Tours, & Novelties

Ever thought of spending Halloween behind bars? Underwater? Or on the same horsehair couch where Lizzie Borden gave her father 41 whacks with an ax? Offbeat establishments everywhere seem to be retooling their standard, if unusual, offerings to entice the more adventurous Halloween thrill-seekers. And why not? If ever there was a time to indulge in the oddball side of American culture, this is it.

Eastern State Penitentiary Halloween Tours

Twenty-second Street and Fairmount Avenue, Philadelphia, Pennsylvania, five blocks from the Philadelphia Museum of Art. Call 215-236-3300 (info); 215-336-2000 (tickets). Open last two weeks in October, nights and hours vary; "Slight Fright Family Nights" available. Reservations strongly recommended; tickets go on sale in early September. Kids under five not allowed on the site. All proceeds benefit historic preservation. ($-$$)

Just being inside an abandoned, one hundred and sixty-five-year-old prison at Halloween is enough to give anyone the creeps. The Halloween tour sends you through a dark maze of crumbling corridors past haunted scenes in and amongst rusted-out jail cells.

The penitentiary was designed to be frightening. Thirty-foot castle-like walls enclose eleven acres of cellblocks built in a unique wagon-wheel configuration that was eventually imitated by an estimated three hundred prisons worldwide. It was the most expensive building of its day.

Opened in 1829, the prison was inspired by Quaker beliefs in solitary reflection and penitence (hence the word penitentiary). It was the environment that caused crime, went the thinking, so criminals left in isolation would rehabilitate themselves. Cells were equipped with doors for food (no communal dining) and individual exercise yards. Inmates wore masks to keep them from communicating during rare trips outside their cells.

Halloween tours through the Eastern State Penitentiary raise money for historic preservation. Photo by Randall Wise, Eastern State Penitentiary Historic Site.

Once an innovative experiment, the system eventually broke down and was deemed cruel and wrong-headed. By 1925, the penitentiary, designed to hold two hundred and fifty inmates, held seventeen hundred. And some prisoners were more equal than others. Al Capone, held for eight months in 1929-30, had a skylight, paintings on the walls, and a radio.

The penitentiary was closed completely by 1971, its last residents a family of stray cats. Now declared a National Historic Landmark, the site is in the midst of restoration and houses a museum that visitors may see after the Halloween tour.

Side trip: Grisly Gothic Gables, a Philadelphia-area haunted house known for its detailed sets, is the brainchild of Allan Erush. Open weekends in October and Halloween week, evenings. ($) Contact: Skeletons in My Closet Productions, 112 E. Washington Lane, Philadelphia, PA, 19144.

The Witch's Dungeon Classic Movie Museum

New England's First Classic Movie Museum, 90 Battle Street, Bristol, Connecticut 06010. Call 860-583-8306. Open weekend evenings in October. Not recommended for children under six. ($)

Begun in 1966 as the cherished vision of a father and son, the museum is now the longest-running movie museum in the country. An unabashed love letter to the creatures that haunted our dreams as kids, the Witch's Dungeon features life-size recreations of the classic movie monsters played by Boris Karloff, Vincent Price, Bela Lugosi, and Lon Chaney, Sr. and Jr. in dioramas based on vintage cinema chillers. Special voice tracks by Vincent Price, June Foray, Mark Hamill and John Agar bring the scenes to life.

In October, horror movie notables make guest appearances, such as Dick Smith (makeup artist for *The Exorcist*) or Sarah Karloff (daughter of Boris). Museum owner Cortlandt Hull also runs a film series, "Horror at the Bijou," nearby during the Halloween season. Before each showing there's a talk about the actors and what went on behind the scenes in the night's feature film.

Hint: The Witch's Dungeon Classic Movie Museum has plans to expand and add original props, models, costumes, and rare posters, and to relocate into a gothic Victorian venue, open year-round. Call before you go for directions.

Halloween Tour of Poe's Grave

Westminster Burying Grounds and Catacombs, Baltimore,

Maryland. Call 410-706-7228. Tours leave 6 PM- 9 PM continuously on Halloween night. Appropriate for all ages. ($)

In 1849, Edgar Allen Poe was buried here in an unmarked grave. Years later, the site grew over with weeds, and word of this neglect reached Poe's beloved mother-in-law, Maria Clemm. She wrote Poe's cousin in Baltimore begging him to make it right, and cousin Neilson Poe tried. He had a headstone made up, but it was destroyed in a freak accident with a train.

With pennies from schoolchildren and gifts from friends, enough money was collected to commission a monument for Poe, which was dedicated in the front corner of the cemetery in 1875. His wife, mother-in-law, and presumably Poe himself, are all interred at the monument (there's a rumor that Poe's remains were never moved, and that he still lies in an unmarked grave at the rear of the church).

Since 1949, on the night of the anniversary of Poe's death, they say someone enters the cemetery and leaves a partial bottle of cognac and three roses on Poe's grave. The roses are likely for each of those buried below. The cognac . . . no one knows.

The Halloween tour takes you through the church, where you'll hear music played on its fully restored, hand-stenciled Johnson pipe organ, down through the catacombs under the church and out through the graveyard. Poe himself (usually portrayed by a local actor) performs here, as does "Frank the Body Snatcher, the University of Maryland's resident grave robber." There's classical music, popcorn, and cider to round out your visit.

Side trip: Kim's Krypt, 1202 Berkwood Road, Baltimore, Maryland. 410-391-7726. Open October 20-31, evenings. ($) Reputedly one of the more original haunted houses you'll find, Kim personally leads all the tours. Hearse rides while you wait, only one dollar.

Lizzie Borden Bed and Breakfast/Museum

92 Second Street, Fall River, Massachusetts 02721 (about twenty minutes from the start of Cape Cod). Martha McGinn and Simone J. Evans, owners. Call for rates, 508-675-7333. Yes, you can tour the actual house where the murders occurred. Or you can spend the night, but plan in advance; Halloween's booked pretty early.

Lizzie Borden allegedly killed her father, Andrew, and his second wife, Abby, on August 4, 1892. Although she was tried and acquitted, Lizzie was ostracized by her community—most of them thought she did it. Theories still abound; some think it was Bridget, the maid, while others believe it was a conspiracy. Some say she was covering for an illegitimate brother, though most still hold out for Lizzie. The crimes are still considered unsolved.

In August 1996, one hundred and four years to the day after the crimes, the present owners opened the house to the public and hosted a wedding. It's been a bed and breakfast ever since.

The B & B is a circa 1845 clapboard house furnished with late nineteenth-century period decor. Because it's also an open-to-the-public museum, guests have to leave their rooms between 11 AM and 3 PM in the summer and around Halloween so that tours can come through. You can take the tour and hear all the theories about who did it and why.

Or you stay overnight and reserve Lizzie's bedroom, which is a two-room suite she shared with her sister Emma. You can also book the murder room, the upstairs guestroom where Lizzie's step-mother's body was found. This room—Abby's room—is the one that's supposedly haunted, although co-owner Martha McGinn says that guests report ghostly activity throughout the house. In the par-lor of the B & B stands a replica of the black velvet horsehair couch on which Lizzie's father was killed. The original autopsies were done on the dining room table (the current dining room table, however, is not the original). The breakfasts served duplicate Mr. and Mrs. Borden's last: oatmeal, eggs, and johnnycakes; there's also a platter of freshly baked hatchet-shaped muffins, an invention of the owners.

Parallel universe: If you live closer to the Midwest than Cape Cod, visit Villisca, Iowa, a small town of thirteen hundred rocked by the unsolved ax murders of eight residents in 1912. Darwin and Martha Linn bought the home where the Moore family murders took place and offer tours along with stories of the strange events and colorful characters who made the crime so memorable. The home is pre-served as it was in 1912, down to kitchen appliances and Moore fam-ily photos on the walls.

Villisca is a little more than an hour from Des Moines. Tours of the house start from the Olson-Linn Museum in downtown Villisca. Call 712-826-2756 to inquire about tour hours.

Haunted New England Cemetery Tours

Part of the October-long Haunted Newport Halloween celebra-tion. Tours leave from the Gateway Visitor's Center, 23 America's Cup Avenue, Newport, Rhode Island. Haunted New England Cemetery Tours info line: 401-849-7416; reservations 401-845-9130.

Not recommended for children under eight. ($) Haunted Newport info: 401-849-8048. Appropriate for all ages. ($)

If Salem's too much for you, try a more laid back, simpler New England Halloween experience. You'll find a heavy emphasis on tours here, since Newport's famous mansions have made it a destination for the curious for generations. Newport is just getting its own Haunted Happenings going—1999 was the first year—and what a location! If you haven't been, just the mansions will bowl you over. The reportedly haunted ones are Belcourt Castle, the summer "cottage" of the heir to the American Rothschild fortune, which offers ghost tours; and real estate barons Mr. and Mrs. John Jacob Astor's Beechwood mansion, which hosts murder mysteries and an enactment of a Poe story. Come October, Newport is rife with ghostly mansion tours, psychics, and an annual costumed Ghoul's Ball.

If you think you might like the atmosphere of F. Scott Fitzgerald's gin-sipping upper-class in tandem with a little vampiric blood sucking, walk through Newport's Common Burying Ground with vampire scholar Christopher Rondina, and hear tales of the restless undead buried nearby. Learn about Mercy Brown, for example, whose body was exhumed to prove she was the vampire causing rampant illness; or about the Rhode Island town that forgot to relocate their dead when the Scituate Valley was flooded.

Side trip: Newport is about forty-five minutes from Providence, Rhode Island, host to WaterFire (downtown Providence; 401-272-3111; free), an event initiated in 1994 by visual artist Barnaby Evans. WaterFire is an art installation of one hundred flaming braziers floating in downtown Providence's river ways, set to a score of eclectic music. Technicians in gondolas pole down the river stoking the fires so they'll keep burning throughout the event, a truly otherworldly sight. You can take it in along sidewalks and bridges, in and amongst lots of other smiling folks. And although Halloween's not the only night they light the river on fire, it's certainly a great time to see it. WaterFire Halloween usually happens the Saturday prior to Halloween at sundown. Costumes are welcome.

Shipwreck at the Queen Mary
South end of the 710 Freeway, 1126 Queen Highway, Long Beach, California. Call 562-435-3511. Open weekend evenings in October, most nights the week before Halloween. No costumes allowed. Not recommended for children under 13. ($$)

Hitler offered two hundred and fifty thousand dollars to any submarine captain who sank the *Queen Mary* when she was employed as the "Grey Ghost," a troop ship in World War II. Halloween, 1967, she embarked on her last cruise from Great Britain to Long Beach. Now her decks are annually revamped as a haunted attraction after the regular ship tours close down for the day. It is worth noting that, according to some, the *Queen Mary* shelters a fair number of actual ghosts. Women in vintage bathing suits have been reported near the First Class Swimming Pool, and overnight guests have often said they felt a tugging at their bed blankets. "Shipwreck" is usually very crowded—expect a long wait to get in. The haunt is not included in the regular admission to the *Queen Mary*, and parking is extra, too.

Winchester Mystery House Halloween Flashlight Tour

Winchester Mansion, 525 South Winchester Boulevard, San Jose, California 95128. 408-247-2000. Tours given every Friday the thirteenth, several nights in October, and on Halloween night. ($$)

Sarah Winchester, heiress to the rifle fortune, employed workmen around the clock for thirty-eight years to construct the biggest, most architecturally maddening mansion in the world because spirits told her to do it.

The Winchester was the first repeating rifle, and Sarah, miserable from twenty million dollars of blood-tainted money her husband left her, was convinced that her building spree could wipe the money clean by providing shelter for the spirits of the gun's victims.

Workmen labored around the clock putting in Italian marble, ornate fireplaces and silver and bronze window inlays. The spirits eventually had over 150 rooms, 10,000 windows, 950 doors, and an isolated seance room with thirteen hooks for the ghosts to hang their coats on when they came to give Sarah instructions. Workmen built false roofs, staircases that didn't lead anywhere, and corridors that ended in blank walls. Chandeliers had 13 bulbs, ceilings had 13 panels. The heiress became reclusive, choosing only spirits for companions until her death in 1922.

The workmen finally stopped building.

The Halloween Flashlight Tour takes you on a guided one and a half-hour tour of the labyrinthine mansion at night. There's also trick-or-treating and entertainment outside in the garden for kids.

Haunted Houses

Post-war amusement parks featured the first dark rides, cheesy haunted houses you went through in a little car—remember? There

The 1999 cast of Castle Blood's Halloween Adventure Tours in Beallsville, Pennsylvania (724-632-3242; open the last three weekends in October), where guests must collect talismans as they go through the haunt. ($) Photo courtesy of Richard Dick.

were strips of cloth slapping across your face in the dark, sudden buzzers, quick corners, bright flashes of light, and split-second sightings of monsters made of fake fur and painted plaster.

"Haunted houses grew out of carnival attractions and the Tunnel of Love," according to Leonard Pickel, owner of Elm Street Hauntrepreneurs, consultants to the dark attraction industry. "They featured horrific scenes to make your honey shriek and grab a hold of you—or at least give her the opportunity if she wanted to."

Haunted houses first became popular at summer season amusement parks along the East Coast. In the early 1970s, the Junior Chamber of Commerce hit on the haunted-house-for-charity idea, printed up a manual, and distributed it to Jaycees nationwide. The idea spread quickly. Charity houses in the 1970s and 1980s were extremely profitable, so much so that the entertainment industry jumped in and carved out a large piece of the pie with larger, more expensive haunts. Today, industry folks estimate that there are between three and seven thousand commercial and non-profit haunted houses up and running, and, according to *Haunted Attraction Magazine,* attendance is currently growing at a rate of about thirty percent a year. Coast to coast, the haunted house hot spots are New England (high population density), the Midwest (the Jaycees led the way, and now nearly every town has at least one haunted house), Texas (one of the top three states for number of haunted houses), the Southeast (churches and farmers are the primary operators here), Florida (high tourist traffic) and California (ditto, as well as large population).[2]

In the early 1980s, independent haunted attraction producers sidled up next to corporate giants like Disney and Knott's. These houses were begun by young theater, film and art school grads looking for a creative way to earn their living.

Joe Jensen and Sharon Marzano were just such a pair.

"In 1975 I was sixteen. I was driving down a winding hill to the beach where I had been hired to be a lifeguard. Halfway down, Joe threw himself over the hood of my car. He was six years older than I, majoring in theater and practicing his stunt falls."

So began the team of Joe Jensen and Sharon Marzano, a haunt-building pair who produced plays together in college, then went on to create the Chicago area's longest-running haunt, Hades Haunted House (1978-1998).

It started out with a two thousand-square-foot haunted house that fit into three Ryder trucks and traveled throughout Illinois. "Joe dressed as a gatekeeper and stood outside holding a large pole," says Sharon. "Stacey stood above him on a six-foot platform in a wild costume made from a torn curtain. For eight hours a day, music blared, Joe moved like a robot and Stacey swirled overhead dancing and shrieking. Needless to say we drew quite a crowd."

Hades outgrew the Ryder trucks, moved into a tent, then outgrew that, and finally moved indoors to the Expo Center in Chicago, where by 1996, it was grossing one million dollars. The attraction's last year was 1998; Sharon and Joe moved their operation into cyberspace, launching an industry Internet business called hauntedamerica.com.

Over the more than twenty years they've been in the business, Sharon and Joe have had a chance to get to know plenty of attractions. Here's hauntedamerica.com's list of ten houses worth a visit, starting in the Northeast and traveling down the coast, then out through the Midwest, south to Texas, and points west. Attractions sometimes change their themes and offerings year to year, so call before you go to get the latest details.

Note: None of these close enough to where you live? Check out the Resources section for help finding a haunted house in your state.

Active Acres Haunted Farms: Midnight Productions Haunted House and Sleepy Hollow Hayride

881 Highland Road, Newtown, Pennsylvania (I-95 to exit 31/New Hope). 215-860-6855. Open weekends plus some weekdays in October, evenings. ($-$$)

Newton Gilchrest and Allen Doak came to the dark attraction business by way of the theater. Newt was an actor, and Allen built sets for movies and did some work for U2 and the Stones. In 1990, they settled in Pennsylvania and built their first haunted house. Ten years of haunting later, Allen and Newt built their own attraction on the Active Acres Haunted Farm site and produced a show called the Dredd Funeral Home, where ghosts materialize and coffins wait for each and every guest ("If someone is missing from your party, don't worry," says Gilchrest. "You will find them, just not where you want them."). The show changes year to year; patrons report that this is one of the most imaginative, creative haunts out there.

Frightland Haunted Scream Park

Route 13, Middletown, Delaware (one mile south of the St. George's Bridge). Call 302-378-VAMP. Open evenings from the first week in October, weekends, some weekdays around Halloween. ($)-($$) A portion of the proceeds benefit the Leukemia Society.

The haunters that run this dark park say that you are not going to grandmother's house on this trip through the woods. Offering four attractions, live entertainment, a carnival, and midway, Frightland was described by one reviewer as "the place to be for cars, chicks and creatures."

The park was born in the imagination of Aven Warren in tandem with Robert Dudzieck, George Long, and Phil Miller, and includes a hayride that's just as likely to steer past *Hellraiser*'s Cenobites as a skeleton answering nature's call on people's heads while whistling "Singing in the Rain." Also at Frightland is the haunted barn, a corn maze, and the classic Idalia Manor, with what patrons call the best black hole illusion ever—you have to crawl through it on all fours.

Dr. Evil's Haunted Houses

Created and produced by Leonard Pickel for Morris Costumes. Monroe Road, Charlotte, North Carolina. Call 704-333-4653. Thursday through Sunday every weekend in October, evenings. ($)

As an architecture student at Texas A & M, Leonard Pickel built his first haunted house in his dorm; life hasn't been the same since.

Hauntrepreneur Leonard Pickel, a.k.a. Dr. Mayhem, works on a patient in a scene from one of his haunted attractions. Photo courtesy of Leonard Pickel.

Pickel creates dark attractions where most of the terror comes from behind the audience, literally chasing them through the house.

"Scaring people is like telling a joke. It's all in the timing. You have to set them up for a scare," says Pickel. "They're not really afraid of the dark, they're afraid of what might be in the dark. You let them see a piece of the monster but not the whole creature standing there in the daylight. People's imaginations can create a creature that you could never afford to build."

Using state-of-the-art design, Pickel built two walk-through attractions featuring the ubiquitous Dr. Morpheous Mayhem and his ongoing study of people's reactions to fear. Scenarios include the Hall of Vampires, a gauntlet of arches, each hiding a giant, sleeping human bat; Philip's Attic, a cobwebbed maze of discarded creatures; the Arbor-eat-um, a Victorian greenhouse; and the Slabatory, where the evil doctor is working on his next experiment.

Netherworld

Georgia Antique Center, I-85 Access Road, 6624 Dawson, Norcross, Georgia. 404-608-2484. Open late September through Halloween. ($-$$)

As a child, Netherworld co-creator Ben Armstrong turned his Florida carport into a haunted house. Billy Messina caught the haunt-building bug in college when he worked on low budget Arnold Gargiulo films. The two hooked up to open Netherworld, a high-tech, intense and very creepy attraction. All their projects (Netherworld now has three attractions) are built like movie sets with one-of-a-kind props and masks.

Scenes vary, of course, but you can expect the likes of Netherworld Primeval, where mutated dinosaurs roam the planet; Netherworld 4D, an adventure in 3-D ChomaDepth Technology; and a very gory Netherworld Museum of Medieval Torture. Aroma generators are up next.

Hint to parents: The Museum of Medieval Torture is not recommended for children under seventeen. There's no age limit for the others, but be aware: they are very scary.

The Haunted Hydro Dark Attraction Park

1313 Tiffin Street, Fremont, Ohio 43420 (a suburb of Toledo). 1-877-GO-HYDRO or 419-334-7774. Open Thursday-Sunday in October plus Halloween, evenings; sneak previews the last weekend in September. Not recommended for children under ten. ($-$$)

"My wife and I owned a golf course/recreational complex. Golfing dies in the fall in Ohio, so we started a very small haunted house in our maintenance barn to generate some cash flow. Each year it continued to grow and we needed a much bigger building. There was this old abandoned hydro electrical plant adjacent to our property that we leased for the first year in 1993. One thing led to another. My wife and I always joke around that the epitaph we should put on our tombstones is: 'Made fun. Had none.'"
—"Crazy" Bob Turner, owner of the Haunted Hydro Dark Attraction Park

He's kidding. The Turners have turned their golf course into a twenty-five-acre Halloween park with enough dark attractions to please even the most needy scare-addicts. There's the Haunted Hydro itself, turned into a haunt each season. There's the Freakshow Mega Maze (a six thousand-square-foot maze with lights, beepers, buzzers, and freaks roaming around inside); Ghost Town Mini-Golf, thirteen-holes with a haunted theme that's played with glow-in-the-dark balls; and Crazy Bob's Toll Road of Terror, where you drive through in a golf cart. And there are psychics, a rock 'n roll show and celebrity appearances. You get tickets Chinese menu style (one of these, two of those), or buy a pass that lets you into everything. Each year new things are added and others re-tooled to keep them fresh.

Industrial Nightmare

835 Spring Street, Jeffersonville, Indiana. Infoline: Call 502-254-8333. Open evenings in October. Not recommended for children under ten. ($)

At the entryway of this gothic-industrial-themed attraction, gargoyles with five-foot wingspans greet patrons. Automatic doors open and shut to urge audiences towards disasters like the Toxic Pit, where a stack of fifty-five-gallon metal drums suddenly begins to topple, or across a bridge overlooking the basement with green "toxic waste" dripping into a pool below. Smoke-filled tunnels, realistic sound effects, screaming actors, and spiked walls lie ahead. For those who appreciate state-of-the-art technical wizardry, you'll find plenty of computer-controlled pneumatics and high-end digital soundtracks here.

Haunted Verdun Manor at Thrillvania

I-20 and Wilson Road in Terrell, Texas (25 miles east of Dallas). Call 214-559-5779. Open weekends from the end of September through Halloween. Not recommended for younger kids—very gory! ($-$$)

Haunted Verdun Manor is a werewolf-infested, two-story antebellum plantation mansion occupied by creatures and scenes from Wolf Studios. Each scene is detailed down to Arabic medical texts strewn about the laboratory, or an unfinished chess game in the dining room. Nearly every prop and mask is handcrafted and original, and the werewolf costumes are stunning.

Verdun Manor is one of four haunted attractions at Thrillvania, a forty-six-acre expanse of land that also houses Cassandra's Labyrinth of Terror, Sam Hain's Hayride and Doctor Phineas' Phantom Phrolics.

According to reports from folks who have visited Verdun, the wait in line is worth the price of admission. The line snakes through a bayou and graveyard packed with animatronics, so the longer you wait, the more you get to see. The mechanical action, live ghouls, and bursts of flames from the top of the house make the time shoot by.

Hangman's House of Horrors

2300 W. Freeway, Fort Worth, Texas 76102 (I-30 & Forest Park Boulevard). Info line: 817-336-HANG. Open every Friday and Saturday in October, daily the last week in October, evenings. Proceeds support local programs of the National Multiple Sclerosis Society. ($)

Hezekiah Jones, a.k.a. The Hangman, is the House's huge and hooded, very unnerving, central figure. The attraction, which strives to startle and disorient spectators rather than terrorize with graphic gore, has lots of good special effects, including a storm maze that showers victims with a light rain. High-wattage speakers create a pervasive low rumble and an unsteady vibration underfoot. While the theme and scenes change every year, past popular settings have included a school cafeteria (Café Hell-o), dentist's office, haunted rodeo, and a maze with over two hundred sheets that must be pulled out of the way to find multiple exits, only one of which is the real one.

For kids, there's a Pumpkin Patch Party held in the daytime in the week before Halloween, where lights are up and characters are friendly.

Dr. Blood's Screamscapes

2001 Irving Boulevard, Dallas, Texas, a half-mile west of Stemmons (I-35E), between Wycliff and Oaklawn near downtown Dallas. Call 214-744-6705. Open on and around the weekends in October. Not recommended for children under ten. ($)

"Listen to me! I am Dr. Blood, the Physician of Fright! Together with my team of Terror Technicians and Practitioners, I operate out of my secluded, subterranean Institute of Phobiatric Research. I use horror entertainment as my experiments and utilize Fearapy to study what frightens people . . . HA! HA! HA!"

So says the mirror-masked Dr. Blood as you begin your tour through Screamscapes, a pair of haunts named the Terrortorium (concentrating on Dr. Blood's experiments) and the Necrotorium, a tour through a gothic graveyard. The brain child of Gene and Betty Braden together with dark design firm Vorta, scenes include the likes of the Catacombs ("a hellish procession of monks haunting labyrinthine corridors of a subterranean sacred place"), Voodoo Island, Outer Spaces, Werewolf Realm, and Inferno.

Use your imagination. That's what Dr. Blood would want you to do.

Side trip: The Bradens operate a second attraction in Texas called Nightmare on Grayson, 201 East Grayson Street, across from the Pearl Brewery in San Antonio, Texas; 210-299-1555. Open on and around the weekends from late September through October. ($)

Rocky Point Haunted Houses

Locations in Salt Lake City, Utah and Ogden, Utah. Check local papers for phone numbers, hours, and directions since both haunts relocate each year to leased spaces. Open the last Friday in September through Halloween, closed Sundays and Mondays. Proceeds benefit local charities. ($)

Rocky Point, once an exclusive restaurant in Ogden, Utah, was built entirely by hand by Scott Crabtree and his family high atop the hill that inspired its name. Three years after it opened, the restaurant burned and the building sat vacant until Crabtree's son, Neil, created a "spook alley" at the site. Years later, another freak fire burned the building to the ground. Scott's daughter Cydney Neil took over the show, and today the Rocky Point Haunted Houses operate in two separate locations and have raised more than three hundred and fifty thousand dollars for charities since 1989.

Both shows adopt a completely new look each year. In celebration of their twentieth anniversary in 1999, they created Creepy Classics (all the classic horror monsters), Psycho Circus in 3D (painted by Disney artists), and Bat Caves, with sets and props from the movie *Bats*, among others.

The Rocky Point Haunted Houses are known for their elaborate set designs and attention to detail. Cydney and brother, Neil Crabtree, still produce and direct both shows.

(Possibly) Haunted Halloween Destinations

If you are one of the millions who confess to curiosity about spirits, entities, ghosts, and poltergeists, here's a listing of expeditions, cemeteries, and gravesites that just may be up your alley. If All Hallow's Eve is the night to honor the dead, these are the places you'd be most likely to bump into them.

GHOST HUNTING EXPEDITIONS
(NOT FOR THE NERVOUS)

According to some professional ghost hunters, ghosts are more likely to be found wherever people have died violently in fear and pain, since high levels of emotion and stress leave a psychic imprint that can endure for many years. Others believe that those violently torn from life are often confused and sometimes unaware they are dead. Therefore, the most ghostly places are those with the most colorful history, full of intrigue and unfinished business, and the sites of murder, suicide, war, or disease.

Troy Taylor, president of the American Ghost Society and author of *The Ghost Hunter's Handbook,* will tell you outright that he's never seen a ghost, but he's had some very weird experiences in many years of ghost hunting. Taylor recommends some of his favorite real haunts coast to coast, from Alcatraz (yes, still haunted) to Gettysburg (definitely still haunted).

The Bell Witch Cave

Adams, Tennessee: take exit I-24 near Clarksville, Tennessee, and follow Highway 76 to Adams. Turn right after the small Amoco station onto Eden Road and watch for the sign. 615-696-3055. Open seven days a week, May-November, 10 AM-6 PM. ($)

The Bells, a prosperous farm family from Tennessee, began noticing odd knocks, rapping and scratching noises in their home beginning in 1817. The phenomena escalated: something was pulling blankets off the beds and pinching, slapping, and sticking the family with pins. Finally, a voice materialized.

Taylor tells the story this way: "According to the annals of supernatural history, the spirit identified itself as Kate Batts, a neighbor with whom John Bell had bad business dealings over some purchased slaves. 'Kate,' as the local people began calling her, made daily appearances in the Bell home, wreaking havoc on everyone there. People soon learned of the spirit and she began to appear all over Roberston County."

The cave is located on the property once owned by the Bells, tucked into the side of a bluff near where the farm once stood, and close to the old family cemetery, where many of the Bells still rest.

According to Taylor, there's still a good deal of ghostly activity in and around the cave. "The steep incline over the Red River hides a narrow path that leads down to the cave. Strange figures have been reported here, and knocking sounds and poltergeist-like events still take place in the house built by former owner, Bill Edens," he says.

Taylor says that current owners Chris and Walter Kirby also report eerie events in the cave, such as strange apparitions and unexplained sounds.

Bachelor's Grove Cemetery

Midlothian, Illinois: take Cicero Avenue to the Midlothian Turnpike and go west to Rubio Woods. Park across the road from the trail entrance. The cemetery is patrolled by police and rangers, and closes at sundown. Free.

Taylor says, "There are more ghost stories and eerie legends told about this small, abandoned cemetery than any other place in the Chicago area." He knows of over one hundred documented reports taken at this site.

The haunted history of the place began in 1864 when it was a burial ground for a settlement of German immigrants who had helped build the Illinois-Michigan Canal and stayed to work on small farms. Since most of the men were unmarried, the place became known as Bachelor's Grove.

The cemetery is in terrible condition, desecrated by vandals and forgotten. Few of the graves are still standing, and some markers have been stolen and then returned, giving rise to legends that the gravestones move by themselves.

According to Taylor, the ghost lights in and around the cemetery "are well known to researchers. The strange lights on the trail are said to be red and move so fast that they leave a streak behind them in the air. The blue balls of light in the cemetery itself seem to have an intelligence, dancing just out of reach of those who pursue them."

Next to the cemetery is a swamp Chicago gangsters once used as a dumping place for bodies during Prohibition. It, too, has its share of paranormal activity, and even the turnpike nearby is said to be haunted.

Dudleytown, Connecticut

Dudleytown, located in Litchfield County in northwestern Connecticut, is now a private nature preserve of over eight hundred acres near the Housatonic River. Follow US Highway 7 to Cornwall Bridge and go east for two miles to Cornwall. Take Clark Entry Road from Cornwall to Dudleytown. Some walking is involved to get back to the actual site. Free.

Long before *The Blair Witch Project*, this spot in the quiet, northwest corner of Connecticut was known as a "dead zone," where people claim you can't hear any birds, rustling, or wildlife. A forty-minute hike into the woods will bring you to the site of a former colonial-era town where just cellar holes and stone fences remain. The local historical society believes people left Dudleytown because the land was too harsh for farming; others think the colonists were plagued by disease, madness, and suicide for a reason.

> "According to legends," says Taylor, "many of the people in this former town went, or were driven, insane by what they described as creatures and strange beings. The stories soon circulated that the area was cursed and many of the residents left the region. Eventually, the entire town was abandoned. Reports from investigators and curiosity-seekers today still hint at the idea that whatever it was that haunted Dudleytown is still there. There have been literally hundreds of reports of unexplained sounds, lights and apparitions in the woods around the ruins of the town."

Note: Also on Troy Taylor's list of favorite haunts in America are the Lemp Mansion (St. Louis, Missouri, a murder mystery theater restaurant and B & B), the Old Slave House (Equality, Illinois, currently closed to the public), Gettysburg National Battlefield (Gettysburg, Pennsylvania, tours available), Alcatraz (San Francisco Bay, tours available), Winchester Mansion (San Jose, California, tours available, but Taylor believes its paranormal activity has stopped), Myrtles Plantation (St. Francisville, Louisiana, tours and overnight accommodations available), and the Whaley House (San Diego, California, tours available).

Graveyards to Visit on Halloween

No one knows cemeteries like Scott Stanton, a.k.a. the Tombstone Tourist. He has traveled over a million miles to find the final resting places and shrines of the famous, infamous, and just plain notorious.

Here, then, are some of Scott's favorite folks to visit on Halloween (remember, most cemeteries close at dusk):

Machpelah Cemetery
82-30 Cypress Hills Street in Queens, New York. 718-366-5959. Open 9 AM-4 PM, Sunday through Friday. Free.

Harry Houdini could escape from anything—prisons, straight jackets, water torture cells—why not death? Here's how the story goes: prior to his last tour, Houdini made a pact with his wife Bess that whoever died first, the other would send back a secret ten-word message that only the two of them would know. On Halloween night, 1926, Houdini died from complications resulting from a burst appendix. Every year on the anniversary of his passing, Bess held a seance in hopes of making contact with her husband. She tried for ten years, then snuffed out the light beside his portrait in her home.

Since the 1940s, magicians have taken up the cause. Every year around Halloween, magicians from around the world pay tribute to the world's greatest illusionist by holding a candlelight procession through Machpelah Cemetery. The ceremony is private, and the date and time of the event changes every year to keep curious spectators away.

Houdini's in a twenty-four-grave family plot (he was the son of a rabbi from Appleton, Wisconsin) and has his given name on the stone: Ehrich Weiss.

October 31—Happy Birthday
Various locations, Los Angeles, California.

Why not surprise cultural icons born on Halloween? No presents required, but bring flowers! John Candy can be found in Holy Cross Cemetery (just above Fred MacMurry and across the hall from Spike Jones in the mausoleum). Michael Landon is resting at Hillside Memorial Park (just a stone's throw from Dinah Shore and Lorne Green, baseball great Hank Greenberg and Max Factor). Esther Williams is buried at Glendale Forest Lawn Cemetery (in the Garden of Acension along the walkway).

Side trip: In 1993, outside the Viper Room, 8852 Sunset Boulevard in Hollywood, River Phoenix suffered cardiac arrest around one o'clock AM on Halloween; efforts to resuscitate him failed. Although he was cremated and his ashes scattered over the family ranch in Florida, the front sidewalk of the Viper Room has become a shrine to the film star each Halloween. Fans scribble graffiti on the wall near where he collapsed, and flowers mark the spot where he died.

Bonaventure Cemetery

330 Bonaventure Road, Savannah, Georgia 31404. Call 912-651-6843. Open 8 AM-5 PM Monday through Friday. Free.

Says Stanton: "Now this is a cemetery. As you drive in and park near the entrance, you can't help but walk under the live oak and moss canopy that takes you to the river and the grave of songwriter Johnny Mercer in Section *H*. One section over is a bench marking the spot for novelist and poet Conrad Aiken, where legend has it that you can drink and never get drunk because the ghosts will steal the spirits from your drink before you have a chance to consume it." Two of the cemetery's more recent residents include Jim Williams and Danny Hansford—real-life characters from the best-seller *Midnight in the Garden of Good and Evil.*

GRAVEYARD GHOST HUNTING ON YOUR OWN

The passion for all things Halloween has kicked off a resurgence of interest in old graves. From Boston to Austin to Sacramento, people are being wait-listed to take a Halloween stroll through their local graveyard. Chances are that no matter where you live, there's an old cemetery nearby and a costumed character willing to lead you through it by lantern and spill a few scary tidbits along the way.

But maybe you want to do something different for Halloween, like investigate a local graveyard or old home on your own. There's quite a bit of information out there (see Resources), and the more your read, the more intriguing it all becomes. Needless to say, you're less likely to find ghosts if you don't believe they exist, so this section is for those of you who do. Here, from Dr. Dave Oester, co-founder of the International Ghost Hunters Society (a society of Ghost Researchers, Ghost Hunters, and Ghost Believers), is a short primer on searching for ghosts:

"Pick an old cemetery that allows you to enter after dark legally. Pick a date around the new or full moons to reap the benefit of geo-magnetic fields, and when the weather is good (mist, rain, snow, or fog can all show up in photos and be misleading). Bring friends.

"Arrive at the cemetery at dusk and walk around for fifteen minutes. Stop at various graves and think about who is buried there. In your mind, let the spirits know who you are and why you are in the cemetery. Think positive thoughts and do not bring along someone who is skeptical because their energy will dampen your results.

"Do not be afraid—we have never been threatened by ghosts while conducting investigations, and we have never encountered evil or demonic spirits in cemeteries. Try to feel the emotions present in the cemetery. Let the spirits know (through your thoughts) that you mean them no harm or disrespect. After fifteen minutes, begin taking photos of the tombstones or your friends (if you do catch something on film, you'll see it when you develop these shots). Use a flash and be sure your subject is within nine to twelve feet of the flash. Do not aim your camera at shiny or reflective surfaces to avoid lens flare. If your camera has a strap, remove it so it doesn't interfere with the photo. Any camera with a flash will work. We recommend Kodak Gold 400 or Kodak 800 Max color print film.

"Take along a tape recorder and let it record continuously while you are walking around shooting pictures. You might find some interesting sounds recorded. When you are done, thank the spirits for their contributions and depart. Normal investigation time at a cemetery is about thirty minutes after you begin taking photos."

CHAPTER EIGHT

Halloween Myths and Monsters

The Truth About Halloween

"I hate Halloween," exclaims an elderly caller on a radio talk show in Maryland. "They should get rid of it. Kids today are just destructive."

"Halloween glorifies Satan," warns a preacher on national cable television. "Kids shouldn't dress up as devils, period."

"I would never let my children go out trick-or-treating alone," confides a D.C.-area mom of her six-year-old and ten-year-old. "I'd never forgive myself if something happened."

People hurl invectives at Halloween like bullets. It's dangerous. Bang. It's satanic. Bang. It's commercial. Bang. It's too scary, too corrupted, too sanitized. Bang, bang, bang. But the holiday doesn't sink to its knees and die. It grows bigger and more pervasive, with eight out of ten adults currently celebrating it in some fashion.

When people rail against Halloween, they don't really mean Halloween itself—what they usually mean is getting rid of vandalism, begging, or scary costumes. The actual holiday serves a need so human, so indefinably essential that we'll probably still be celebrating when the ice cap melts and we're all trick-or-treating in powerboats.

You can tell how evocative Halloween is by looking at its detritus— the urban myths surrounding it—and the waves of anti-Halloween crusades that threaten to ban, change, contain, or otherwise control it. These are all signs that the holiday is a very powerful cultural event. If it didn't mean anything, if it didn't answer a need, if it wasn't of use to us, it would gradually fade away like May baskets and Sadie Hawkins Day.

But the more popular Halloween gets, the more we hear about

the negative side: poisoned treats, razor blades in apples, black cat kidnappings, and satanic rituals. How dangerous is Halloween? What's true, exaggerated, or just plain made up? Like shapes in a dark room, there are many stories associated with Halloween that dissolve when you look at the facts. Let's turn on the light and see what's a monster and what's simply a coat tree casting a shadow on the wall.

Halloween Myths: True or False?

Adults put razor blades in apples and give them out as treats. False.

You've read about this one in the papers. Somewhere there's a fiend who buries razor blades in the flesh of ripe apples and entices neighborhood kids to take a big bite and swallow. Every year we warn our kids to watch out for him, and every year newspapers publish Halloween safety tips that often include "check for tampered treats."

But this particular fiend doesn't exist. He never has. According to police reports and studies, not one child has been killed by a sadistic stranger lying in wait on Halloween with a deadly treat. The story of the razor blade in the apple is what sociologists call an urban legend, similar to the rat supposedly found in fast food fried chicken or the man who woke up with a pain in his back and discovered one of his kidneys missing. These are stories, told and retold, that could be true—it's possible that these sorts of things could happen—but they're too perfect. Their symbolism is too contrived; the plot too neat. They usually contain a warning against the dangers of urban life in the guise of a good story. Urban legends actually serve a purpose—they give our fear a symbolic form so we can express it.

The image of a razor blade in an apple fits the criteria for an urban legend beautifully. The metaphor is rich. The apple is a symbol of the afterlife, of old world Halloween. It's the fruit used to tempt the innocent (Adam and Eve, Snow White), but sliced through the middle by an ugly blade. The Halloween sadist, an otherwise productive member of society who turns into a psychopath just one night of the year, is pretty unlikely. This holiday has always been about death and fear: the tainted treat-toting psycho is but a new icon in the pantheon of Halloween spooks.

Then there's the practical side. First, how do you hide a razor blade in an apple without putting a telltale gash in the skin? Moreover, who among us would honestly root through Snickers bars and Butterfingers to sneak a bite of an apple on Halloween?

Joel Best, Chair of the Department of Sociology and Criminal

Justice at the University of Delaware, has studied the Halloween sadist phenomenon in depth. Together with Gerald Horiuchi, Best published a 1985 study that concluded the Halloween sadist was essentially a myth. Their often-cited article in *Social Problems* outlines the team's findings:

"A review of news stories about Halloween sadism from 1958 to 1983 suggests that the threat has been greatly exaggerated. Halloween sadism can be viewed as an urban legend, which emerged during the early 1970s to give expression to growing fears about the safety of children, the danger of crime, and other sources of social strain."

Best and Horiuchi drew several conclusions. First, they discovered no evidence of children being harmed by anonymous strangers. Best was able to track about eighty cases of sharp objects hidden in Halloween treats and discovered that almost all were hoaxes. There were only two deaths related to tampered treats, and both were poisonings. One child died after eating heroin found in his uncle's home (not hidden in his treats, as initially reported), and a second was poisoned by his father, who allegedly put cyanide in the child's candy to claim a large insurance payment. Best and Horiuchi found no justification for the claim that Halloween sadists are a threat to kids. They also found, interestingly, that of the cases reported, most were incidents perpetrated by the kids themselves to gain attention, or to get back at an annoying sibling. [1]

Still, stories of tampered treats spread throughout the 1970s and 1980s. Hospitals began offering X-ray screening of treats (although most eventually stopped, as they rarely found anything and X-rays cannot detect poison), and some towns banned trick-or-treating for a few years. However, most parents dealt with it on an individual basis. There was no nationwide movement created to deal with the problem because there was no real proof that it existed. In other words, the razor blade in the apple is a false threat, and as such, never caused the public hysteria attached to a real threat, like school shootings or terrorist bombings. So if this phenomenon doesn't really exist, why do we all know about it, teach our children about it, and act as if it were true?

Sociologists says that we use urban legends, stories we repeat over and over, to express our doubts about the safety of our kids, our neighborhoods, and our world. Best pinpoints the origin of the razor blades legend to the late 1960s and early 1970s, a time when we became more aware of child abuse as a widespread social problem.

Fear of crime in general grew during that period, as did mistrust of strangers. Television and print journalists to this day publicize the most provocative Halloween stories closest to the holiday, giving credence to rumors and half truths. This vague sense of anxiety congeals into something concrete we can talk about—the "Halloween sadist"—and we tell stories to each other and our kids as a way of saying, "be careful, it's dangerous out there."

In truth, your neighborhood is no more intrinsically dangerous on Halloween night than it is on any other night, and no child to date has been killed by eating a razor blade hidden in an apple by a sadistic stranger on Halloween.

Halloween is a Holiday for Witches. True.

Samhain (sow-en), celebrated on October 31, is one of eight major seasonal holidays marked by men and women who practice a nature-based religion that acknowledges a Goddess and, in some traditions, a Horned God. Known by many names, including Wiccans and members of the Old Religion, most refer to themselves as witches.

Like the ancient Celts before them, modern pagans use solstices and quarter days to mark the turning points of the year. Samhain is reserved for honoring ancestors and remembering loved ones who have died, and for acknowledging the cyclical nature of living and dying.

Although practices vary widely, most witches will gather for a ritual. Witches don't believe in Satan, so there's nothing satanic involved. Nor are there sacrifices, invocations of evil, or naked orgies; this is propaganda leftover from hundreds of years ago.

More likely, this is what you would find at a witch's Samhain ritual. The meeting place (be it inside or out) would be lit with candles, probably jack-o-lanterns, and decorated with harvest fruits and vegetables. People would enter quietly and gather in a circle. There might be a brief invocation of a goddess or god to provide wisdom, or a guided visualization to help understand the process of death and rebirth. Participants might remember people in their lives who have died recently, express grief, and share memories. The ritual might include some scrying (looking into the future) and conclude with everyone dancing to the beat of a drum and chanting. Samhain is a time of death, but within the frozen ground are beginnings of new life, and the goddess will return at the appointed time. The earth will green.

So, if there's nothing intrinsically evil in witchcraft, how did witches get mixed up with the devil in the first place? And why do we think of them as Halloween symbols?

The Halloween Witch

Witches exist not only in history but also in folklore, film, literature, and popular culture. So when you're talking about witches you have to be sure which kind you mean: real or fictional, folkloric or cartoon, ancient or modern?

Most believe that the term witch came from the Old English *wicca* or *wicce*, and referred to the practice of sorcery or magic. Originally, a witch was the local midwife, herbalist, doctor, and advisor. Charms and spells were common medical practice, especially for the poor. A witch was a useful member of society who helped keep the old folkways.

At first, the Christian church lived more or less peaceably with witchcraft. France's first witchcraft trial, for example, was not until 1390; the English were tolerant of witchcraft until the reign of James I in the early fifteenth century.

Then came the Inquisition. People in fifteenth-century Catholic Europe were beginning to question their beliefs: did purgatory really exist? Were the Garden of Eden, original sin, and Virgin birth truth or myth? As feminist scholar Barbara Walker proposes, "the Inquisition was created to win the war between the church and a disillusioned public." Witches were seen as manifestations of the spirit world which up until then, had to be taken on faith. The clergy promoted belief in witchcraft, and made non-belief a heresy. Most importantly, they also redefined the witch to be an agent of Satan.

The Inquisitors began ferreting out witches in every town. At first people scoffed at testimony gathered by the various Inquisitions. Witches, said rational folks, can't raise storms or strike people dead with a glance. But after hundreds of people were imprisoned for disagreeing, then tortured, and eventually forced to confess to the crimes of witchcraft invented by the Inquisitions, others fell silent.

So what was a witch back then? If she lived in Spain where people were dark-haired and dark-eyed, a witch was anyone with blue eyes or red hair. A witch was anyone with special abilities—a poor person who was educated, for example, or someone with a green thumb. Witches were scapegoats for doctors who couldn't help patients, because illnesses caused by witchcraft were believed incurable. They were outcasts, petty criminals, indigents, the insane, or widows; those who were easy to get rid of and often considered a nuisance. They were protesters and dissenters. Witchcraft was used to cover up anything the Inquisitors couldn't explain, and to solicit souls for the Church's war against Satan.

Over the roughly three hundred years of the witch craze in Europe, people came to fear witches. They were wary of witch's pets (cats); witch's tools (brooms); and witch's festivals (the eve of All Hallows). The last witch burning was held as recently as the eighteenth century in Scotland, and the last hanging in the American colonies, 1692.

From this period in history we inherited the image of the witch who flies, kills cattle, curdles milk, and consorts with the Devil at midnight Sabbaths deep in the woods. It is this witch who lives on in fairy tales and folklore and frightens us in film and literature. It is this witch most of us associate with Halloween.

Satanic cults use Halloween to perform ritualistic crimes. False.

There are two questions to address here. First, to what extent do satanic cults or ritualistic crimes really exist? Secondly, what is Satan's connection to Halloween?

Religion scholar J. Gordon Melton calls contemporary Satanism "the world's largest religion that does not exist." The largest organized satanic-style cults such as the Church of Satan or the Temple of Set (never more than a few hundred members) are now largely dormant, and Melton has discovered that most satanic cults usually number three to five people and last only a few months. There is no religious denomination or even any cult today that worships the Devil on Halloween, not even these so-called Satanists. In addition, there are no confirmed statistics, court cases, or studies to support the idea that serious satanic cult crime even exists. (2) It turns out that most of the devil-worshipping activity reported in the media is perpetrated by teenagers based on what they've read in church literature or seen in movies.

So how was Satan tied to Halloween? Satan didn't come into the formula until the fourteenth through seventeenth centuries. This was the time of the Inquisitions, when witches were thought to make a pact with the Devil at their rituals (see the Halloween Witch, above). Fears of witchcraft and satanic rituals abated with the Enlightenment, and by the twentieth century, pointy black hats and red horns were simply part of the fun of Halloween. But films like

Rosemary's Baby, The Exorcist, and all the *Halloween* movies (among many, many others) have etched a more detailed, modern persona for the Devil in our imaginations. Hollywood started to mine Halloween imagery for terror, churches become more vocal about it, and rumors of satanic rituals grew rampant.

It may simply be that Halloween's symbols are incendiary. In our image-based society, somewhere along the line we began to confuse symbols of death with those of evil. Ghosts and goblins, fearsome faces and fire—traditional images for spirits of the dead set free on Halloween—are now often construed as satanic. I suspect it's Hollywood, more than anything else, that helped put the hell in Halloween.

Black cats are in danger on Halloween. Rarely, but yes.

Black cats are the target of age-old superstition: witches can take their shape; they can suck the breath from an infant, curse a corpse, and perform cruelties too numerous to list. Although most of us no longer harbor these beliefs, we do sense that Halloween and black cats go together. And over the past decade or so, newspapers have run many stories about black cats being abducted and used in occult rites on Halloween. Are they?

Since 1997, the American Society for the Prevention of Cruelty to Animals (ASPCA) has instituted a better-safe-than-sorry policy and not allowed the adoption of black cats three days before and after Halloween. In that year, the organization got suspicious when a woman adopted a black cat, but when the ASPCA made a follow-up call to see how the cat was doing, the woman reported the cat was dead. When ASPCA workers came to pick up the body, they discovered she had given a phony address. The investigation of the case halted there. Was the cat harmed? Was it somehow related to Halloween? We won't ever know. But taking a proactive approach seemed the Society's safest choice.

The staff of the Humane Society of the United States (HSUS) to date has not personally witnessed a case of black cat abuse at Halloween (in fact, most shelters report no such cases). It has, however, reported hearing stories, and so recommends protection of black cats around Halloween. In response, shelters and humane societies nationwide have suspended adoptions of black cats. The bans have been in place throughout the 1990s, with some shelters denying adoptions as early as the 1980s. Although HSUS lacks statistics about risk to black cats during this time, anecdotal evidence is enough for it to take a conservative approach. Besides, anyone who wants to adopt a black cat can still do so after the Halloween ban is over, which, for most shelters, is a matter of a few days to a few weeks.

The threat is not all smoke and mirrors. There have been a few, highly publicized incidents of black cat abuse around Halloween. I was able to find and track a dozen reported incidents between 1992 and 1999 (for comparison, in roughly the same time period, an estimated twenty-five hundred dogs and cats had died or suffered during air travel, according to the United States Department of Agriculture). Upon further investigation, some cases turned out to be unrelated to Halloween or black cats. Two of the cats were unharmed, only seven of the incidents involved black cats (as opposed to brown cats or tabbies), and it's difficult to document how many happened on or near Halloween (either the shelters had gone out of business or the staff could not remember). In the only case that was prosecuted, the perpetrators were teenagers. Often confusing the issue, journalists report animal abuse that has taken place at other times in articles about Halloween black cat abuse.

Sadly, animal cruelty happens year-round and to all colors of cats, but we are hyper-aware of anything occult or satanic at Halloween time. In October 1999, for example, there was not one newspaper report of a harmed animal in the dozen Unites States cities I examined. But in that same period, many papers ran articles about suspended adoptions including *USA Today,* the *Washington Post,* and the *Boston Herald.* Most stories quoted shelter personnel who implied that cats are in danger of being used in ritual sacrifice. Consequently, the sense of a crisis exists where there are only unrelated, isolated incidents, none of them involving ritual sacrifice by satanic cults, but rather cruelty and crimes committed by individuals.

The increased media, however, does give the shelters and humane societies a chance to educate the public about pet safety. For those who love and care for cats, saving even one life makes any effort worthwhile.

During Halloween, the Humane Society of the United States recommends that you: (1) keep your cats away from the door and make sure they have on ID tags in case they get spooked and bolt; (2) keep candy out of reach (chocolate is toxic to cats); and (3) keep cats away from flames, and from hanging streamers that could choke them.

Halloween Monsters

Zombies, Goblins and Ghouls

Here's the rundown on what makes a zombie different from a ghoul or a goblin: a zombie, via Haitian folklore, is a corpse who's up and about because a witch doctor has dug it up and stolen its soul. A goblin, from French folklore, plays pranks and steals wine—but can also be occasionally helpful. A ghoul, of Arabic origin, eats corpses and sometimes young children; it was once thought to be the terror of the desert personified. These are all lower creatures of world mythology. Now a ghost—that's a different story. A Gallup poll taken around Halloween 1999 found that roughly one-third of us say we believe in ghosts, three times the number who admitted it twenty years ago.

Ghosts

The first Halloween ghosts were perhaps, as Ray Bradbury suggests in *The Halloween Tree,* memories of our great grandparents. It's not hard to envision ancient tribes camped around a Samhain bonfire telling stories of heroes and battles, strange encounters and unexplained sights. As the night stretched on, we can imagine how the tales grew more vivid, the subjects more supernatural. There would be talk of ghosts.

Although it makes poetic sense for spectral activity to increase on Halloween, most ghost investigators I've talked with say it's just not so. We humans may be more aware of the spirit world on Halloween, but the spirit world appears to treat the holiday as just another night.

Vampires

As for vampires, they have no real tie to Halloween other than as a favorite costume choice and a certain similarity with the other undead characters of Halloween. That said, is the vampire culture more active on this night? Do real vampires even exist?

It depends on how you define vampire. Says Dr. Jeanne Keyes Youngson, lifelong vampirologist, "There is no such thing as the traditional reanimated corpse. I have it from the lips of Milton Helpern, former head of the New York Coroner's Office. It's impossible for a body, once life functions have shut down, to come back to life. There are, of course, vampire 'wannabes' who do their best to emulate the undead." According to Dr. Youngson's Final Twentieth-Century Worldwide Vampire Census, 272 of the 713 respondents claimed to actually be vampires.

Fascination with vampires crosses all age groups and lifestyles, from the little boy ogling a slick black cape and fang set in the Halloween aisle at Wal-Mart to the hordes of adults entrenched in vampire role-playing games. There are those who believe in psychic vampires, individuals who suck the life energy from those around them; human vampires, who claim they experience all the characteristics of fictional vampires except immortality; even in supernatural vampires who inhabit a netherworld also populated by ghosts. But among those who believe themselves to truly be vampires or who live a vampiric lifestyle, Halloween is still a holiday where they can delight in the freedom to be themselves; it's is the only night when the rest of the world looks like them.

Vandalism

Can you imagine answering the door and being hit with a bag full of slimy, stinking muck from the bottom of the street gutter? Can you picture being trapped in your own house by some kids who knotted a rope from your front door to your porch railing? What about finding your front fence hanging from a telephone pole, your cow locked in the schoolhouse, or a six-foot-tall pile of lumber blocking Main Street as you head downtown?

Toilet paper in the trees seems tame by comparison. Yet, all these tricks date from a time when Halloween pranks were considered safe and fun and most people didn't object. Today they would make the papers under headlines such as "Vandals Caught in Halloween Prank Gone Awry" or "Satanic Cult Linked to Cow Theft."

It's true that mischief has become more destructive. A real shift has occurred between then and now, between a time when adults tolerated a certain amount of pranks and now, when angry seniors berate teens on radio talk shows. The change in attitude has less to do with the holiday and more to do with social tensions between classes, races, and generations. Halloween is simply the backdrop for the drama.

When everyone knew their neighbors, pranks were pulled on the local grouch and people smiled guiltily to themselves. But when Americans moved into crowded urban centers full of big city problems like poverty, segregation, and unemployment, Halloween tricks took on a new edge. Vandals struck out blindly against property owners, adults, and authority in general: city kids setting dumpsters on fire didn't know who owned the property they were torching. Tires were slashed without regard to whose car. It wasn't about pulling off a good practical joke any more; it was about doing damage.

The war between kids and property on Halloween has been fought hard over the last twenty years. There are notorious cities like Detroit, where in 1984, a record of eight hundred and ten fires were set during the three-day period around the holiday. Suburban police dealt with broken mailboxes, spray painted cars, and toppled headstones right along with their big city counterparts. "I've got neighbors who are so fed up they're driving around with guns on their dashboards," a spokesperson for a group of homeowners in Wildwood, Illinois, told the *Chicago Sun Times* after the 1986 Halloween season.

Halloween vandalism seemed to reach a peak in the late 1980s. The Halloween "Mall Crawl" in Boulder, Colorado ended in drunken fighting and property damage. There were a record number of arrests in New York City for Halloween-related assaults, and violence erupted in the usually peaceful Castro district of San Francisco. Curfews and community action came into being to fight back against crime.

They scored some dramatic wins. In 1994, Detroit enlisted thirty-five thousand residents to patrol the streets and keep watch over abandoned properties. There were fewer fires reported that Halloween than on an ordinary night, and the city famous for its fiery "Devil's Night" became known for "Angel's Night." Neighborhood crime watches and "Pumpkin Patrols" continue to crop up across the country to help ensure that the little kids get home safely and the bigger kids stay out of trouble. Many cities have started sponsoring concerts and dances for older kids on Halloween.

Arson, vandalism, and harassment are not a normal part of Halloween mischief, and community organizing helps keep the holiday sane for everyone. But that doesn't mean there's no room left for pranks. Pranks and vandalism are apples and oranges, and learning the difference between them is part of growing up.

Traffic

The biggest serious Halloween danger to kids is probably traffic. Former Boston helicopter traffic reporter Judy Paparelli says the accidents start first thing in the morning—it's not just night that's a problem on Halloween. Drunk drivers are part of it; in 1998, more than twenty percent of all fatalities that occurred during Halloween weekend were alcohol-related. The other parts of the problem are low visibility and carelessness.

Halloween costumes make for distracted drivers and excited kids.

Little ones in dark costumes are hard to see, and trick-or-treaters are more apt to run out into streets from between parked cars in their hurry to get to the next house. Experts warn that most little kids aren't ready to handle street-crossing by themselves, and often over-estimate how quickly they can cross or rely too much on the "magi-cal" power of a crosswalk to protect them. The Centers for Disease Control (together with the Division of Unintentional Injury Prevention and the National Center for Injury Prevention and Control) compiled statistics of Halloween-related traffic deaths from 1975 through 1996. They found that "overall, among children aged 5-14 years, an average of four deaths occurred on Halloween during these hours each year, compared with an average of one death during these hours on every other day of the year." An addendum warns the figure may be low, since it does not include accidents that occur in driveways, parking lots and on sidewalks, nor does it include data beyond 10 PM or from another day (for example, when Halloween is on a Sunday and kids trick-or-treat on Saturday instead).

Halloween sadists and satanic psychos don't hurt kids on Halloween. Cars do. No devil-worshipping cult lies in wait for us. But, yes, there are twisted pranksters and angry, unhealthy people in the world. Sometimes Halloween safety restrictions are really a smoke screen for intolerance, and sometimes Halloween mischief masks serious social ills.

The real Halloween monsters are the same monsters we live with every day: bad judgment, anger, and small-mindedness. Maybe we'll learn to define and challenge these everyday threats and leave alone those traditions that strengthen communities and make childhood magical.

CHAPTER NINE

What's Next: Trends in Halloween

Commercial, Communal, Spiritual, Extreme, and Anti-Halloween

Think of Halloween as a tree. Like a sapling, it takes root and shoots up. Through the years, each generation adds a layer, like a series of rings, to the celebration. Although the holiday may look slightly different each time there is new growth, at the core it's the same. It feeds from the same roots, but its branches stretch out in new directions.

On Halloween two hundred years ago, people predicted their marriage partners from the roots of cabbages; no one could have imagined our trick-or-treating, much less the idea that Halloween would become a children's holiday. One hundred years ago, women dressed in fancy gowns at Halloween parties; last year, people were wearing nothing but airbrushed bikinis. I don't think the Victorians saw that coming.

One hundred years from now Halloween may be unrecognizable to us. Maybe stranger danger will be so extreme kids will ride special "Hallo-transit" vehicles down the street, and adults will slip them treats through a pneumatic tube. Downtown there will be a specially designated Halloween zone, where the in vitro, lab-grown pumpkins will be on display in a black and orange decorated vitrine. Perhaps the holiday will become so prepackaged you can only buy the Nostalgia Set (vampire costumes, yard fogger, and a can of garlic soup) or New Dimensions (a coupon good for one night of time travel back to the ancestor of your choice). Maybe we'll come full circle and spend Halloween out on some post-apocalypse hillside pasture, huddled around a peat fire trying to make sense out of sheep guts. Halloween reflects our culture, and will change along with it as long as we have a pulse.

Ancient Celtic Samhain was about death. Medieval All Hallow's was about redemption, and Victorian All Hallowe'en about romance. What is contemporary Halloween about? Some would say consumption. Others would say community or creativity—transforming the ordinary into the extraordinary. Look at my bleeding mask of doom! You think Elvira's the only one who can wear a hydraulic bra and a tight black dress? Watch me! Halloween is growing again, adding another generational layer.

On the one hand, it's almost become a counter-culture holiday— adolescents gain power and adults feel threatened. The celebration has become associated with heavy metal music and gender-bending. And look who's responsible for Halloween's new popularity—baby boomers who came of age in the counterculture of the 1960s. Halloween is counter-reality, a day when dads from the suburbs watch drag queens parade up Sixth Avenue in New York, and people everywhere open their doors to strangers. On Halloween, we walk right up to the threshold of what we can tolerate because we know it's only for one night.

And yet, at the same time, Halloween is evolving from a gently anarchic holiday to an institutionalized one, where corporations try to dictate costume trends and civic organizations regulate hours and days of celebration. Interestingly, 1940s Halloween activities were organized to protect property owners from kids' pranks, but now they're being used to protect kids from adult strangers.

Halloween has gone from being about death as transformation— moving from the physical world to the spirit world—to transformation as presentation—transforming your house, yard, or self for one night and showing it off to the world. This multi-faceted Halloween, this institutionalized rebel, is creative, communal, rule breaking, extravagant, and more than a bit egocentric; in other words, a truly American phenomenon. Halloween has sprouted a few new branches for its twenty-first-century incarnation: commercial Halloween, communal Halloween, spiritual Halloween, extreme Halloween, and anti-Halloween.

Buying and Selling Halloween

The aisles of the Halloween Outlet store in Worcester, Massachusetts, are crowded with clerks trying to unbox the merchandise. A makeshift worktable in the middle is strewn with molded rubber props—bloody fingers, arms, and legs, aliens in jars of viscous liquid—amongst paperwork and calculators. A technician is trying to wire animatronic ghouls in the front window, and the owner, Gary Arvanigian, is up to his elbows in catalog orders at a table in the back room.

"Wait a second, Christine," hollers Gary, "Let me give you the dragon."

Christine wrestles with the front door, trying to balance three big boxes on her hip as she wedges the door open with her foot. She's on her way to a nearby mall to set up a branch store. "I can't fit it in my trunk," she shouts over her shoulder. "The tail hangs out the back of my car."

All seven thousand square feet of the store are packed as full as Christine's arms. But it's only August.

Halloween today is second only to Christmas in activity, say the merchant associations that keep track of retail spending in America, with somewhere around $6.8 billion in estimated annual sales and growing. That's plastic axes, extension cords, cornstalks, and black lights, as well as pumpkin puree, liquid latex, airbrush kits, rubber rats, fog machines, sugar skulls, skeleton bones, cobwebs, and soundtrack CDs—not to mention trailer rentals, motor parts, rotary carving tools and a whole lot more. That figure doesn't include large facets of Halloween, such as the vintage Halloween collectibles business, which, according to dealers, has heated up in recent years. Halloween merchandise and ads are appearing months before the actual day, supplemented by year-round catalog and on-line shopping, all of which has elevated Halloween from a celebration to a whole two month-long season that bridges the gap from back-to-school to Christmas.

The Halloween market has been growing nonstop for over a decade, ever since adults started celebrating seriously in the 1980s, thereby doubling, tripling, and quadrupling the number of people who buy things for Halloween. When the dark attraction industry took off, older teens and twenty-somethings were enticed into the market. Once home decorating caught fire, everyone—whether three or one hundred three, home on Halloween or not—could take part. Halloween is packaged and sold like Christmas now, with the same merchandise categories: decorations, lights, cards, ceramic villages, and the latest, ornaments. Watch out, Santa!

Not only are there more people looking to buy Halloween, but there are also more places than ever to find it. Enterprising companies set up shop in locations unimaginable even ten years ago: in virtual stores in cyberspace, or even vacant storefronts in malls, where they scramble to find personnel and to stock enough product to make it through the three months before Halloween. Although the American market is hardly saturated, entrepreneurs have been inching into the European market on a hunt for new consumers. The Halloween industry is making inroads in France, Germany, Australia, England, even Sweden, to name a few.

"Halloween doesn't belong to our national heritage at all," says Goran Lundstrom, of Helsingborg, Sweden, "We've been celebrating All Saints' Day for hundreds of years, when people go to put a wreath and a candle on their loved ones' graves. But now Halloween has started to make its way into our society."

Which part of Halloween are we exporting to Sweden? Says Goran: "You'll find rubber skeletons, pumpkins, and lots of other things, all in orange. One thing that is different, though, is the trick-or-treating! That isn't done here, I think. Young people just arrange parties in their homes and dress up in Halloween costume."

In Paris, Halloween is just plain hip. Costume companies found their way into the European market in the 1990s, when restaurants and clubs were eager to try anything American. Soon, shops had put out Halloween displays, costume sales were substantial, and even bakeries were hawking "Halloween cakes."

Is Halloween in France a marketing tool or the beginnings of a real holiday? Can other cultures truly celebrate our very American Halloween, or will orange streamers and imported pumpkins fade when the next new thing comes along? And what does exporting our customs do to host country's traditions?

"Creeping Americanization is in fact destroying our Scottish celebration of Halloween," states Ewan McVicar in an editorial in *The Times*, October 25, 1999. "In the grocers' shops you are offered not turnips for lanterns but pumpkins. Trick-or-treat has come here. Instead of a party piece for a reward, you get a threat of harassment and punishment if you do not cough up. Instead of our witches, warlocks, ghosties, and ghoulies, the plastic masks that have invaded news agents' windows are aliens, zombies, vampires, and Frankensteins, all from American cinema imagery."

Community Celebrations: Taking Back Halloween
"We go to the Keene Pumpkin Festival on closing night and collect hundreds of pumpkins, then line them up along the road between

A neighborhood parade in Irvington, New York. Photo by Meg Ruley.

our houses," says Lisa Winant, a New Hampshire mother of three. "Halloween night, we collect all the kids, put them on a wagon and go house to house. The grownups put on skits in the fields and we stop at each one. One year, we had a creature from the black lagoon crawl out of the pond, and this year we're going to make trees come to life. We started doing this with just our family several years ago, but now it's become a community celebration."

This is not an isolated incident. Many individuals, believing that the commercialization of Halloween is flatlining our most creative holiday, are finding new ways to celebrate. Doing something together satisfies a need for community intensified by the busy nature of our lives.

In Medfield, Massachusetts, Bonnie and Stephen Burgess began an impromptu Halloween parade on a whim: "I stuffed mailboxes on our street with fliers inviting everyone to march in a neighborhood parade." recalls Bonnie. "We set the start time and the route and held our breath. I had no idea how many would come . . . a dozen? We had seventy people march with us, then we all went back to our house for cider and treats. We'll definitely do it again next year."

One or two people with a good idea can bring a community together and inspire a whole new generation of trick-or-treaters. This is how neighborhood legends are made. Take Leafman, for example, a simple dummy stuffed with leaves and topped by a big orange pumpkin head. Leafman sat on the screened-in porch of a Newton, Massachusetts home for sixteen years. At first, he was just a decoration until his creator, Michael Norman, decided to make him talk. Leafman rocked in his chair, lit up, and magically knew every single child's name. Once word got out, Norman got five hundred children trick-or-treating at his house. Though other houses had better decorations, and even better treats (Mrs. Leafman has been known to give out pencils), the children growing up nearby wouldn't think of missing Leafman on their rounds. In fact, when he retired, the entire neighborhood grieved. He was Halloween to them. He knew their names.

> "I've always decorated my yard for Halloween: tombstones, dummies, and even a dead Elvis. Last year I had a young mom and her two tiny kids in tow. She told me that she had always come trick-or-treating at my house as a child, and now she made a point of bringing her kids. I couldn't believe I'd done this—that it had already passed to another generation." —Debra Wyman-Whitehead, Manchester, Washington

Dr. Steve DeFossez and son Chris in their Giant Pumpkin Regatta. Photo by Steve Martin.

Steve Defossez, a medical doctor and member of the New England Pumpkin Growers Association, has created an entirely different agenda for his Halloween tradition: a pumpkin regatta. Defossez produced his first annual Giant Pumpkin Regatta for Parkinson's Research at Stiles Beach in Boxford, Massachusetts in October 1999.

"I was nurturing two promising pumpkins that summer," he recalls. "Drought, vine borers, fertilizer burn, blossom rot, stem splitting and breaking, and overactive vine training had yet to grace my humble plot. Gazing at Bert and Gert with my eldest son Christopher, the idea of organizing a fundraiser for Parkinson's Disease research was born. Chris and I could collect sponsors for our boats, sail, and survive."

Defossez, whose father suffers from the disease, reaped nearly four thousand dollars for Parkinson's Research in the inaugural year—he was also able to spread the joy of growing, building and sailing giant pumpkin motorboats.

In each of these cases, one person or family took the impetus to create a Halloween that was unique and consequently, launched a new tradition. It's this kind of generosity that takes the sting out of commercialized Halloween.

Halloween's Spiritual Side

Here and there, the dead are coming back to live with us. Drive by a cemetery around Halloween, and you'll catch a glimpse of Mylar balloons and bright orange pumpkins decorating the graves of children. Even roadside memorials to victims of car accidents are done up for Halloween in my town. I may not know who died at that spot, but I know the person is still somehow a part of the holiday celebration. You can see this same impulse—remembering the dead at holiday time—in the growing popularity of Mexican Day of the Dead celebrations in the United States.

The Days of the Dead, or *Los Dias de muertos,* blend pre-Columbian and Spanish Catholic cultures. There are many regional variations, but usually October 31 is a night of preparation for cooking food and assembling home altars; November 1 is *Dia de los angelitos* (Day of the Little Angels), when souls of children are welcomed home; and November 2 is *Dia de los muertos* (Day of the Dead), a time to welcome those who died as adults and celebrate them with picnics in cemeteries, storytelling, and cleaning up gravesites. Along the United States/Mexican border, the Days of the Dead and Halloween have mingled: pumpkins and witches are for sale in Mexican shops, and people can now buy sugar skulls in American bakeries.

Public Day of the Dead celebrations are gradually making their way into mainstream America. Self-Help Graphics in East Los Angeles, a Latino organization, has hosted a citywide Day of the Dead celebration each year since 1972. Its popularity has grown exponentially, say organizers, because it's not just a party, but has personal relevance to anyone who has lost a loved one. Over the past decade, major museums and art galleries in Milwaukee, New York, Chicago, Houston, and Miami have hosted Day of the Dead exhibits by living Chicano artists inspired by the Mexican *ofrenda,* a home altar created especially for Days of the Dead to hold offerings for loved ones. These exhibitions feed the American public's growing interest in multicultural celebrations and folk art, as well as in the more spiritual, meaningful aspects of the holiday. It's this spiritual connection that attracts thousands of American tourists to Day of the

Dead celebrations in Mexico, especially in the small, pretty-as-a-movie-set Oaxaca City, where the smell of marigolds wafts from the cemeteries in early November.

> "In the evening, some cemeteries slowly fill with people. They carry flowers and candles to decorate the graves of the dead. At the little cemetery of San Felipe del Agua near Oaxaca City, there is a painted wooden altar in the center of the graveyard. It is filled with flowers and candles, offered by the faithful on the night of All Souls'. . . . At the few unattended gravestones, small children play the traditional board games—*El Ancla* and *La Oca*—by the waning light of a single vigil candle . . . Close to midnight the musicians gather in the middle of the pantéon to play *Las Golondrinas* (The Swallows) and *Dios Nunca Muere* (God Never Dies). Then slowly the families collect their baskets and candles and leave the little cemetery."
> —description of Day of the Dead by Judith Strupp Green, Curator of Mexican Ethnology, San Diego Museum of Man, Balboa Park in *Popular Series* No. 1, May 1969

Just as Latin Americans are reclaiming their spiritual holiday right next to, or on top of Halloween, many of an estimated one million neopagans [1] in the United States are celebrating their October 31 holiday more publicly. Modern day witches now open their Samhain rituals to the public in gatherings all across the nation from Portland, Oregon to New York City; Laramie, Wyoming to Memphis, Tennessee; and Sterling Heights, Michigan to St. Petersburg, Florida. And, according to leaders, the numbers of participants have been growing over the past ten years.

Halloween, for many, has become a time to touch down and find our place in a long line of generations.

Extreme Halloween

> "Today's Hallmark-approved, TV special-packed, sanitized and ready-to-go Horror Lite is missing something. Like the rest of the major holidays (and quite a few of the minor ones), Halloween today seems to be a slicked-up, white bread, Disney-fied version of its former self."
> —James Lileks, in his editorial column, "Backfence," for the *Minneapolis Star Tribune*

For those of you who side with Mr. Lileks, you're not alone. Over the past two decades, Hollywood, in tandem with the dark entertainment industry, has created a sophisticated clientele that demands vivid, increasingly graphic, sensational scares. Enter the Halloween prop business, barely existent in the 1970s.

In haunted houses, windpipes made of cold, cooked lasagna noodles have given way to items like the Colorado-based Distortions Unlimited's Gallows, a realistic replica of a hanging, or their Electric Chair, a detailed animatronic man writhing in an electric chair. Crowds eat it up: mostly twelve to twenty-four year-olds, and surprisingly, often more women than men. The industry shows no signs of getting any less sophisticated; each new season brings more intense visuals, unique tortures, and real life, pump-your-blood, it's-gonna-get-you scares.

If the adults who grew up in the 1950s and 1960s try to preserve trick-or-treating to honor Halloween, those who came of age in the 1970s with heavy metal, slasher movies, and the fear of razor blades in their apples just might get nostalgic for a scarier, more extreme Halloween. These folks drive much of the dark attraction industry— the businesses that create and supply haunted entertainment, gory costumes, decorations, and realistic effects.

Graphic gore is not new, nor is our appetite for it. Think of the blood-smeared Judith waving the severed head of Holofernes above the Hebrews, or Oedipus gouging out his own eyes, and even the televised image of Nicole Simpson's bloody neck; we rarely look away. If Jaycees haunted houses were the equivalent of PG, most professional haunted houses today have become R-rated. Commercial haunts are more realistic, more engaging, and more interactive. Customers want to be someplace where the unexpected will pop up, where they're terrified of what's around the corner.

"It's like boot camp for the psyche," said horror film director Wes Craven to David Blum in a *New York Times* interview. "In real life human beings are packaged in the flimsiest of packages, threatened by real and sometimes horrifying dangers, events like Columbine. But the narrative form puts those fears into a manageable series of events. It gives us a way of thinking rationally about our fears."

Haunted attractions give people the experience of being safe and afraid at the same time. We know it's not real. In fact, professional haunters know that if you tread too hard on that fine line of reality/unreality and even hint that something's really wrong, the fun goes flat like a busted party balloon. Being spooked, says psychologists, is even good for us. Haunted houses, like roller coasters, provoke anxiety. If we get anxious enough times and see that we really don't get hurt, then we become less afraid in general.

But it's not just the fear, the surprise, and the adrenaline—you can get all that in a movie. Haunters know you have to balance your effects with the right amount of actors. Human contact is key to a successful scare. By adding the element of performance, they hit on what hooks people: the possibility that something real could happen.

Anti-Halloween

HALLOWEEN IN THE PULPIT

Is Halloween sacrilegious or secular? Lest you think ours is the only time in which folks protest Halloween, here's a the holiday envisioned by a priest at St. John's Rectory in Hartford, Connecticut before the Civil War:

> "Instead of the profane rites by which it has been desecrated, I have supposed it [Halloween] observed in Christian homes, by fire-side tales and recollections of the departed, and conversations about the state of Intermediate Repose."
> —Arthur Cleveland Coxe, "Halloween, A Romaunt" (1846)

Every October some pastors will rail against Halloween and the Devil and others will just as passionately defend the holiday. The media loves this particular battle: if our culture was destroyed tomorrow and all that was left were television talk show videotapes, future archeologists would think Halloween was a satanic ground war. Yet the fact is the huge majority of folks mark Halloween as they always have, and it's a well-publicized minority who speak out against it. It's also important to note that religious beliefs vary church by church, and that many have no problem with Halloween.

"I would say that just as Peter Cottontail does not summarize the meaning of Easter and Rudolph the Rednosed Reindeer does not summarize the meaning of Christmas, witches and goblins don't summarize the meaning of All Saints' Day," stated Reverend George Niederauer, Bishop of Salt Lake City's Roman Catholic Diocese, in a 1999 interview with the *Salt Lake Tribune.*

"Being overly concerned with Halloween and its pagan origins is not in keeping with Christian faith," United Methodist Minister Rev. Ronald Hodges agreed. "If we believe fully in the omnipotence of God, then concern about witches, ghosts and goblins . . . is misplaced. It is God alone who rules creation, and persons need not fear the dark side of the human experience."

A HALLOWEEN HOW-TO

Halloween doesn't register with the Jewish faith or among Buddhists because it's viewed as a secular holiday. But Seventh Day Adventists boycott the holiday completely, many Muslims don't celebrate it, and some Protestant Evangelical churches are adamantly opposed to it. It's because Halloween's origin is pagan, and its symbols can be regarded as Christian-related, that it gets into so much trouble in the pulpit.

Churches that oppose Halloween respond by hosting "trunk-or-treat" parties, where people park their cars in the church lot, give out treats, then throw a party for the kids. Some urge children to dress as saints or heroes on Halloween, and some substitute a fall festival, all peaceable alternatives. But there are also blatant, anti-Halloween crusades, perhaps the most volatile of which is the haunted house in drag: Christian Hell Houses.

> "Hell House is not a glorification or observation of Halloween! This outreach happens during the 'Halloween' time of year because that is when the average, unsaved American is conditioned to visit haunted-house type attractions. Hell House simply capitalizes on the seasonal opportunity for the sake of the gospel."
> —Introduction to The Hell House Outreach Manual

Christian Hell Houses create realistic horrors to proselytize: if you do these sorts of things—have abortions, drive drunk, contract AIDS, or, in a few churches, wear trench coats and shoot fellow students—you will go to Hell. Satan himself welcomes unrepentant sinners at the end of the show, and an angel redeems the saved. Hell Houses are billed as "spiritually based haunted houses" for which you can buy a kit: a two hundred and eighty-page how-to manual, video, CD of sound effects and scripts. Hell House creators, the Pentecostal Abundant Life Christian Center in Arvada, Colorado, believe the concept demonstrates how actions have consequences, and that death is forever. But the shows, as the manual states, have nothing to do with Halloween, and often polarize towns unnecessarily into tense, pro- and anti-Halloween factions.

Halloween in the Principal's Office

"Youngsters at the West Jordon [Utah] school can wear plaid shirts, overalls, and straw hats this Friday and will learn how to square dance and line dance instead of parading through the halls as Darth Vader or Pokemon characters. When children wear blue jeans, [principal] Berrett doesn't worry they will bring guns or knives."   —*Salt Lake Tribune,* October 27, 1999

> "We're trying to get away from Halloween's connotations. We find that we stay away from a lot of the objections that might be surrounding us. It's a kind of preventative thing."
> —Principal of Belle Chasse Primary School, New Orleans, Louisiana, in an interview with the *Times Picayune,* 1997

Often Halloween's iconography is used as a backdrop for an obvious political or moral agenda. Sometimes it's more subtle. Regulating Halloween costumes in school, for example, is ostensibly for kids' safety, but it's also a way to make kids conform.

"We do a lot with schools around Halloween; not so much Halloween costumes, but story costumes instead," said Natalya Haden, who with husband Jack Cody owns Creatures of Habit, a vintage clothing and costume shop in Paducah, Kentucky. "It takes the Halloween out of Halloween. Witches, ghosts, and ghouls are Halloween characters. The scariness is what makes it different from any other dress-up occasion. The fear of hurting someone's feelings or being PC [politically correct] doesn't allow children to be as creative."

Jack agrees. "I'd be surprised if Halloween lasts another ten years. It used to be whole wheat and now it's white bread with the crusts cut off."

Our public schools need to serve every single student, be they Haitian immigrant, fundamentalist Christian, Quaker, Buddhist, Muslim, or Jew. School officials need to answer to parents. If Halloween is perceived as religious or anti-religious, principals will hear from them. If it's viewed as taking up too much valuable academic time, or if older kids' costumes scare the younger children, they'll hear about it. Most recently, if a Halloween costume is seen as an opportunity to conceal a weapon or drugs, principals may even be held responsible. No devils, no witches, no black lipstick or white, Goth face makeup, no baggy pants or hats, please. School officials under fire opt for the choice that offends the least number of people. But to what extent are we letting a vocal few dictate the pleasures of the majority? Has everyone really been heard?

The whitewashing of Halloween celebrations in our schools may simply be a sign of the times. It's not just Halloween; celebrating holidays in school in general is being downplayed. Some schools

A HALLOWEEN HOW-TO

eschew all holidays or invent new, secular ones to take the place of the traditional quasi-religious ones. For example, the Hillsborough, New Jersey schools initiated Special Persons Day to take the place of St. Valentine's Day. May Day celebrations in school have all but died out in the past thirty years, and a new, generic "celebration of light" has begun to crop up to cover all the winter religious holidays— Christmas, Kwanzaa, and Hanukkah—together.

There may always be people who have no use for Halloween. So be it. One of the hallmarks of an enlightened society is that it respects all beliefs, majority or minority. There's no reason why those who don't celebrate Halloween should be punished for it. Moreover, there's no reason why those who do should be restricted. We have to find ways to make our celebrations flexible enough to let anyone in, or out, without giving up the heart and soul of Halloween.

Designer Trick-or-Treat

Come to the Mall-o-ween carnival! A twenty-five-cent ticket lets you play games for great prizes! Enter the costume contest! Win!

Trade your Halloween candy for cash! Dentist X will pay one dollar for every pound of candy you turn over to him, up to five pounds!

Come to the Health Center and tour our haunted house, where nice folks hand out candy from inside office doorways (don't tell Dr. X)!

Trick-or-treat over on our street, where the sidewalks are wide and well lit, and every house gives out full-size bars (no snack-size miniatures here)!

Celebrate Halloween indoors, in stores, in malls, in office buildings, in upscale neighborhoods!

Somewhere along the way, we've become convinced that when it comes to trick-or-treating, our own neighborhoods are not as much fun as the fancy ones, and that shops and malls are safe havens, while the streets outside our own houses are not. That homemade treats are dangerous, and store-bought, wrapped candies are not. We've become suspicious: of strangers, of cookies baked by someone else's grandma, of older kids in masks and hoods. The dark makes us nervous, and because we love our kids so much, we transfer our fears to them.

It doesn't matter if we know deep down that there are no satanists looking to kidnap our kids, and no crazy person trying to hide blades in their treats. We still fear for our kids, and act as if these things might be true. Even trick-or-treating gives us pause.

I distributed a questionnaire to 50 adults in the fall of 1999. They were of all ages, lived in rural, urban and suburban areas, and came from 11 states coast to coast. One of the questions I asked was this: would you allow your 10-year-old to go trick-or-treating in your own neighborhood without a parent? Forty-one respondents answered this question. Only 8 said yes: 3 were parents with grown children, 1 was in her 20s with no children, and the other 4 lived in areas where they knew all their neighbors. The other respondents said no (21), or only if they were with friends (12). The reasons? It's too dangerous/you can't trust people (15); I live on a busy street (3); there are wild teenagers out (4); and it's too dark (3).

The sense of fear around Halloween has spawned a host of preventive measures designed to keep kids safe. Some towns hold community-wide parties on Halloween night, making families choose whether kids will go out trick-or-treating or attend the party. This attempt to eliminate trick-or-treating seems to occur only in communities that have serious reservations about Halloween already. Such towns have prominent conservative religious groups, or have had a recent child-related crime spill over into the Halloween season that made everyone nervous about stranger danger. Some towns and cities regulate the hours for Halloween activities; since Halloween is not recognized by the federal government, each municipality can establish its own rules. They post trick-or-treating hours that tend to be earlier, some even in the afternoon, before dark. The newly formed Halloween Association, a national trade organization based in Maryland, has a campaign to set Halloween on the last Saturday of October, before daylight savings time ends. It's safer, says the organization: the day will be lighter longer, and will never be a school night. Many others are adamantly opposed to this proposal, from parents who resent government intrusion to businesses, like costume shops, who make more money when Halloween falls midweek.

But does it work? Does regulating Halloween hours for trick-or-treating keep kids safer? We really don't know yet. There's no hard data proving such rules have an effect on Halloween accidents. The National Safety Council does not keep statistics on trick-or-treating hours, and the Centers for Disease Control traffic child fatality figures for Halloween do not include any numbers indicating a significant change since 1975. Rather, dictating hours when kids can trick or treat gives the illusion of safety: adults feel better when kids go out earlier, and during specified times. It also makes it easier to plan and structure the night.

Another common reaction is to go trick-or-treating in confined, controlled environments. Mall trick or treating arose soon after the tampered-treat scares of the 1970s; many communities still offer it. But a newer trend is developing along these lines, which is to take kids to affluent neighborhoods, or "good Halloween neighbor-hoods"—areas that give really great treats, and all the houses partic-ipate. Or to do a prearranged trick or treat route, where you stop only at friends' houses, even if it means getting in the car and driv-ing all over town. Let's call it designer trick-or-treat.

There are many advantages to designer trick-or-treating: going to a special area of town that's famous for its Halloween celebration means there'll be lots of other folks around, increasing the feeling of safety as well as the fun. Affluent neighborhoods are usually better lit, with wide walkways leading up to the front door; it's easier to keep watch on your little ones. Morevoer, trick-or-treating only at friends' houses means you know and trust everyone your child comes into contact with.

But what you lose with designer trick-or-treating is an essential aspect of modern Halloween: an opportunity to build community, to turn strangers into acquaintances. Nothing permanent is gained. You've missed your one chance a year to visit with the people on your own block, choosing instead to visit those you already know, or those you'll probably never see again. Case in point: children in my town often trick-or-treat across the city line in an upscale neighborhood in Cambridge, Massachusetts, where the houses are huge and always being remodeled. Last Halloween, workmen—not the owners—were handing out candy!

One last thought on safety: I think it's interesting that most of us support zero tolerance on terrorists; even when they're holding a plane full of hostages, we support a firm refusal to negotiate. Yet we will, almost without a fight, let the specter of the Halloween danger terrorize us into giving up a ritual we dearly love and clearly need.

The Importance of Halloween

The Brazilian kids in my neighborhood are stunned by Halloween. They have just come to America and are learning English; they don't know yet to say trick-or-treat, or even thank you. But I can see their shy smiles and unbelieving eyes; this unexplainable generosity on the part of strangers sets their heads spinning.

There's a deeper value in knocking on your neighbor's door. Historians always describe Halloween as the one night a year when the veils between the worlds of the living and the dead are lifted. Perhaps in our culture today, Halloween is the one night a year when the barriers between people can be lifted: between classes, races, and generations.

Halloween is also full of milestones. The first time we don't trick-or-treat is as significant as unmasking Santa: it's the end of child-hood. Years later there's another marking: the first time we trick-or-treat with our children we become acutely aware of ourselves as adults, walking in the same responsible footsteps of our own parents.

People adapt customs to their needs, and they'll keep a holiday if it fits in with their values. Right now, preserving childhood is some-thing parents care about. Trick-or-treating, pageants, haunts, parades, and parties are all popular now because there's a need for community. People want to experience something real, a connec-tion with each other and with forces beyond all of us, and an outgo-ing, exhibitionist holiday like Halloween is a perfect vehicle.

Yes, Halloween is becoming more popular, commercial, and adult, as well as more spiritual, creative, and extreme. But when you open the frame and stand way back, you can see how everything's connected. Halloween isn't evolving in a vacuum, it reflects who we are and what we value. Halloween is a touchstone for every one of us through time and across continents. As Jack Santino writes in *All Around the Year*:

> "Celebration, symbol, ritual, festival, holiday, folk custom—all too often these are viewed as fun, pleasant, perhaps even beautiful upon occasion, but also as frivolous, never as primary to life. I suggest that in fact they have to do with those parts of life, both biological and social, that are of the most importance to us, with birth and death, with life and growth . . .Where we find elaborate symbol and ritual we find issues and events that are of central importance to human beings."

Maybe future generations will look back with nostalgia to our time, when death separated generations and people had to imag-ine what good and evil looked like on this night once called Halloween. They may chuckle to themselves at both our cynicism and our innocence. But I'm willing to bet they still have a Halloween. Because as long as the earth goes around the sun, there will be the coming of the dark season, and with it, the need to cele-brate all that remains hidden in the shadows.

Notes

CHAPTER 1

1. Anyone interested in Halloween traditions would enjoy Jack Santino's many books on holidays and American culture, particularly *Halloween and Other Festivals of Death and Life*, from the University of Tennessee Press, 1994.

CHAPTER 4

1. Statistic from the International Mass Retail Association, 1999.
2. For years, many thought Samhain was not only a time (summer's end), but also the name of a death god who ruled the festival. This idea likely emerged in the nineteenth century, and is now disregarded. Scholars currently agree that there was no Celtic Lord of Death known as Samhain.
3. For more vampire poems, check out *The Vampire in Verse, An Anthology*, edited by Steven Moore, a Count Dracula Fan Club publication (see Resources).

CHAPTER 7

1. For an extensive vampire chronology and vampire information in general, read J. Gordon Melton's *The Vampire Book: The Encyclopedia of the Undead*, (Visible Ink Press, Detroit, 1994).
2. Statistics are from hauntedamerica.com. Co-director Sharon Marzano also notes that many older attractions (in operation for

fifteen to twenty years) have recently closed due to an increase in competition from giant theme parks as well as from a lack of affordable, permanent space. Others in the industry cite the expense of complying with new, more stringent fire codes as the major reason many smaller haunts have closed.

CHAPTER 8

1. Joel Best and Gerald T. Horiuchi, "The Razor Blade in the Apple: the Social Construction of Urban Legends," *Social Problems,* Vol. 32, June 1985. Best updated his research twice: in 1990 and in 1999. His findings remain the same.
2. For a good study of satanic cult activity in America today, read Jeffrey Victor's *Satanic Panic,* Open Court Publishing Company, Chicago, 1993.

CHAPTER 9

1. The Witches' Voice, the largest Internet site for the neopagan community, quotes this one million figure; earlier, pre-Internet estimates were anywhere from thirty thousand to five hundred thousand, depending on the source.

Halloween Resources

All Things Halloween

Organizations

•Global Halloween Alliance
Rochelle Santopoalo, President
1228 Dewey Avenue
Evanston, Illinois 60202-1123
847-328-3605
www.halloweenalliance.com
Organization devoted to the celebration of Halloween; hosts an annual convention each June in a different city. Publishes *Happy Halloween Magazine.*

•Halloween Online, LCC
1027 South Rainbow Boulevard #113
Las Vegas, Nevada 89145
760-321-9335
www.halloween-online.com
Internet site featuring Halloween how-to's, safety info, food, news, ghost stories, screensavers, fangs, spooky fonts, and clip art.

Halloween Stories

•*Harvest Tales and Moonlight Revels: Stories for the Waning of the Year,* Michael Mayhew, editor, Mona Caron, illustrator, Bald Mountain Books, 1998.
Collection of nineteen stories and poems written by different authors for their annual Halloween storytelling party.

Halloween Collectibles

• *Halloween in America* by Stuart Schneider, Schiffer Publishing, Atglen, Pennsylvania, 1995. www.wordcraft.net.

Large format book containing over eight hundred and fifty color photographs of Halloween collectibles.

• *More Halloween Collectibles: Anthropomorphic Vegetables and Fruit of Halloween* by Pamela E. Apkarian-Russell, photos by Christopher J. Russell, Schiffer Publishing, Atglen, Pennsylvania, 1998.

Ms. Apkarian-Russell has published several large format, full-color books on Halloween and Salem Witchcraft collectibles; she also edits the *Trick or Treat Trader,* a newsletter for Halloween collectors.

Contact:

Chris Russell and the Halloween Queen Antiques

PO Box 499

Winchester, New Hampshire 03470

603-239-8875

halloweenqueen@cheshire.net

http://cheshire.net/~halloweenqueen/home.html

Costume and Prop Catalogs

• *Anatomical Chart and Model Catalog*

8221 Kimball

Skokie, Illinois 60076-2956

1-800-621-7500 x235 (Halloween extension)

www.anatomical.com

Everything from brain, heart and hand molds to chocolate ears to all sizes of Buckys (skeletons). Ask for fourth class bones and skeletons— they're irregulars, sold for much less than the bones that go to schools and medical organizations, but perfect for Halloween decorating.

• *Death Studios Catalog*

431 Pine Lake Avenue

La Porte, Indiana 46350

219-362-4321

www.deathstudios.com

Quality latex masks, props, and materials for making monsters. Website includes links to books on latex mask-making, sculpting tools, mold-making materials, artificial eyeballs, and dental materials (for fangs).

• *The Fright Catalog*
The Halloween Outlet
246 Park Avenue
Worcester, Massachusetts 01609
1-800-HALWEEN
www.halween.com
Costumes, masks and props, large and small.

• *Oriental Trading Company*
1-800-875-8480
www.oriental.com
Catalog and on-line store. Has a huge Halloween selection each year with everything from striped witch socks to candy to costumes, glow sticks, jewelry, and things you never knew existed.

• *Terror by Design*
632 Oriole Drive
Streamwood, Illinois 60107
630-830-9561
www.btprod.com
Books, fog machines, masks and prop building books, props, glow paints, latex special effects, web shooters ("shoot a roomful of flame-retardant cobwebs in minutes"), thunder and lightning control boxes, and much more.

Costume and Prop How-To's

•http://www.deviousconcoctions.iwarp.com
On-line listing of prop projects with detailed instructions for each one. Includes information for making candlesticks, cemeteries, coffins, fog, pneumatic props, and much more.

•http://terrorsyndicate.com
Features designs and how-to's for prop-building projects; includes Monster Mud Playground (they say they coined the name for this latex paint and joint compound mixture) with instructions for how to build creatures.

Collections of Halloween Folklore

(Find these at your library)
• *The Frank C. Brown Collection of North Carolina Folklore,* edited by Wayland D. Hand, volumes VI and VII especially, Duke University Press, Durham, North Carolina, 1961.

•*Folklore in America: tales, songs, superstitions, proverbs, riddles, games, folk drama and folk festivals.* Selected and edited by Tristram P. Coffin and Hennig Cohen from the *Journal of American Folklore,* Doubleday, New Jersey, 1966.

•*Observations on the Popular Antiquities of Great Britain,* Vol I and II especially, compiled by John Brand, Bell and Daldy, London, 1872.

•*The New Golden Bough,* written by Sir James George Frazer and edited by Dr. Theodore H. Gaster, Criterion Books, New York, 1959.

Miscellaneous Resources

• *Vintage Holiday Clip Art*
381 Old-Fashioned Holiday Vignettes in Full Color, selected and arranged by Carol Blanger Grafton, Dover Publications, Inc., New York, 1993.

• *Sugar Skull Kits*
CRIZMAC, Inc.
P.O. Box 65928
Tuscan, Arizona 85728
1-800-913-8555

• *Free Spooky Sound Clips*
•http://13thtrack.com (Halloween radio)
Website has all sorts of Halloween sounds and music, an on-line magazine, and general Halloween information and links.
To Predict the Phase of the Moon on Halloween
•http://tycho.usno.navy.mil/vphase.html
From the Time Service Department at the United States Naval Observatory in Washington, D.C., view the phase of the moon for any date and time from 1800 to 2199 A.D.

Haunted Houses

Organizations
•International   Association   of   Haunted   Attractions: http://www.iahaweb.com. Go to the Visitor Area to find a "haunt lookup" option that lists member attractions by state.

Books
•*Give Them a Real Scare This Halloween. A Guide to Scaring Trick or*

Treaters, and Haunting Your House, Yard or Party by Joseph Pfeiffer, Chessmore Publishing Co., Chapel Hill, North Carolina, 1997.

Lots of great ideas plus a reference section.

•*The Complete Haunted House Book* by Tim Harkelroad, Moonlighting Publications, 420 Taylor Street, Bristol, Tennessee 37620.

A step-by-step how-to from brainstorming through publicity to building scenes.

Magazines

•*Haunted Attraction Magazine,* Leonard Pickel, Editor
P.O. Box 220286
Charlotte, North Carolina 28222
704-366-0875
www.hauntedattraction.com
Industry news, how-to's and reviews of attractions coast to coast. Also publishes *Haunted Attraction Industry Buyer's Guide* (contacts and listings for everything from consultants to props to masks to electronics, tents, fog machines and insurance).

HAUNTED ATTRACTION LISTINGS

• *www.HauntedAmerica.com*
773-342-0771
Website featuring the Haunted House Directory, a huge database of haunted attractions listed by state, industry news, message boards, virtual haunted house, ghost stories, and home haunting guide.

• *www.hauntedhouse.com*
Website listing attractions by state, some reviews; includes some private yard listings.

• *www.hauntworld.com*
Website lists more than one thousand haunted attractions coast to coast.

CYBER-COMMUNITIES FOR HALLOWEEN HAUNTERS

• HOWL 2000
www.WildRice.com/Howl2000
Chat and postings all about Halloween by people who love it; mostly how-to for yard haunters and professionals.

Ghosts

Organizations:

• *American Ghost Society, Troy Taylor, President*
515 East Third St., Alton, Illinois 62002
618-465-1086/1-888-GHOSTLY
http://www.prairieghosts.com
Society with just under five hundred members known for rational approach. Publishes *Ghost of the Prairie Magazine* (quarterly), and holds an annual conference. Offers free investigative service; if they determine the activity is genuine, they refer you to someone who can help you. Also affiliated with:
The Haunted Museum (a tribute to ghost hunting throughout history), open Monday through Friday 10 AM-6 PM; Saturday 10 AM-4 PM, free); Whitechapel Press (Haunted America Ghost Book Catalog with over three hundred titles) and Riverboat Molly's Book Company (ghost stories for ghost enthusiasts).

•*International Ghost Hunters Society, Dr. Dave Oester and Rev. Sharon Gill, Founders*
IGHS Headquarters
Crooked River Ranch, Oregon 97760
541-548-4418
www.ghostweb.com
A society of ghost researchers, ghost hunters, and ghost believers of around twelve thousand members. Offers memberships, on-line weekly newsletter, and workshops.

•*International Society of Paranormal Researchers*
Organization uses technological equipment to investigate paranormal phenomenon. Offers "Expeditions" led by Dr. Larry Montz, parapsychologist; visit haunted sites and learn how to use various equipment.
4712 Admiralty Way
#541
Marina Del Rey, California 90292
323-644-8866
info@ispr.net
http://www.ispr.net

Pumpkins

Organizations

• **The Great Pumpkin Commonwealth**
c/o Hugh Wiberg, spokesperson
445 Middlesex Avenue
Wilmington, Massachusetts 01887
Twenty-two sites in North America; publishes the New England
Pumpkin Growers Association Newsletter.

• **World Pumpkin Confederation**
Ray Waterman, President
14050 Rte. 62
Collins, New York 14034
716-532-5995
www.pandpseed.com/wpc.html
Annual weigh-offs, prizes for growing the biggest giant pumpkin.
•*http://www.backyardgardener.com/wcgp*
Website dedicated to giant pumpkins including statistics, weigh-off
sites, festivals, techniques, stories, and links.

Tombstones

Books
•*The Tombstone Tourist: Musicians* by Scott Stanton, 3T Publishing,
Portland, Oregon, 1998.
A collection of the final resting places of the famous and infamous
in the music world.
•*Grave Matters: A Curious Collection of 500 Epitaphs from Which We
Learn of Grieving Spouses, Fatal Gluttony, Vengeful Relations,* by E.R.
Shushan, Ballantine Books, 1990.
Pre-1900 tombstones in categories much like those listed in the
title.

Websites
•City of the Silent (http://alsirat.com/silence/)
Includes information about cemetery symbols, epitaphs, history,
burials, tombstone rubbings, and other aspects of mortuary culture.
•Find a Grave (http://www.findagrave.com)
A database of 2.5 million non-famous and famous graves.

Urban Legends

Books

• *Curses! Broiled Again! The Hottest Urban Legends Going* (W.W. Norton, 1989) or *Too Good to be True* (W.W. Norton, 1999), both by Jan Brunvand.

Websites

• http://www.snopes.com

Urban Legends reference pages listed by topic and updated often.

Vampires

Organizations

• **The Vampire Empire, *formerly known as* The Count Dracula Fan Club**
Penthouse North
29 Washington Square West
New York, NY 10011-9180

Founded in 1965 by Dr. Jeanne Keyes Youngson. Dedicated to Bram Stoker and his sanguinary Count Dracula, as well as other noteworthy horror personalities; also actively promotes and encourages, by club members, the study of vampirism in its many forms. Maintains a delicate balance between the serious aspects of the subject and a light-hearted approach; appeals to all age groups.

• *Anne Rice's Vampire Lestat Fan Club*
ARVLFC
P.O. Box 58777
New Orleans, Louisiana 70158-8277

Membership gives you first dibs on tickets for the Gathering, among other things.

Books

• *The Vampire in Verse, An Anthology,* edited by Steven Moore, Adams Press, Chicago, 1985 (A Count Dracula Fan Club Publication). Useful for finding good verse for invitations, this collection of more than fifty poems also has a good bibliography for other readings.

• *VideoHound's Vampires on Video,* J. Gordon Melton, Visible Ink Press, 1997.

A comprehensive guide and listing of over over six hundred films and documentaries.

Witchcraft

Books

•*Drawing Down the Moon: Witches, Druids, Goddess-Worshippers and other Pagans in America Today,* by Margot Adler, Penguin Books, 1997.
Often cited as the best overall introduction to the subject.

Websites

•www.neopagan.net
Excellent Halloween information compiled by neopagan scholar and practitioner Isaac Bonewits.

•www.witchvox.com (the Witches Voice)
"A proactive educational network dedicated to correcting misinformation about witches and witchcraft." Largest site for the witch and neopagan community; includes lots of Halloween information around October.

Bibliography

Allen, A. "Toads: the Biochemistry of the Witches' Cauldron." *History Today* 29 (1979).

Babineck, Mark. "Poisoned Treats Haunt Halloween." *AP Wire* (1999).

Band, Carol. "Halloween on Parade." *The Boston Parent's Paper* (1999).

Banks, M. MacLeod. *British Calendar Customs*. London: William Glaisher Ltd., 1946.

Bannatyne, Lesley. *Halloween: An American Holiday, An American History*. Gretna: Pelican Publishing Company, 1998.

Best, Joel. "The Myth of the Halloween Sadist." *Psychology Today* 35 (1985).

_____ and Gerald Horiuchi. "The Razor Blade in the Apple: the Social Construction of Urban Legends." *Social Problems* 32, no. 5 (1985).

Bierce, Ambrose. *Tales of Soldiers and Civilians*. New York: The Heritage Press, 1943.

Black, Maggie. "Saints and Soul-Caking." *History Today* (1981).

Blain, Mary E. *Games for Halloween*. New York: Barse and Hopkins Publishers, 1912.

Blum, David. "Embracing Fear as Fun to Practice for Reality." *New York Times* (1999).

Brand, John. *Observations on the Popular Antiquities of Great Britain*. Vol. I and III. London: Bell and Daldy, 1872.

Brunvand, Jan. *Curses! Broiled Again!* the Hottest Urban Legends Going. New York: WW Norton, 1989.

_____, *Too Good To Be True.* New York: WW Norton, 1999.

Carr-Gomm, Phillip, ed. *The Druid Renaissance: The Voice of Druidry Today.* London, San Francisco: Thorsons, 1996.

Cole, Caroline Louise. "Pumpkin Boats for Charity." *Boston Globe* (1999).

Convery, Eric. "Religious Groups Reject Holiday's Dark Trappings." *Boston Herald* (1999).

Curtis, Mary. "California Reigns tonight as Party King." *Los Angeles Times* (1998).

Dart, John. "Recasting Halloween in a Different Light." *Los Angeles Times* (1998).

Davies, Robertson. "Haunted by Halloween." *New York Times* (1990).

Dolan, Beth. "Black Magic." *Tampa Tribune* (1999).

Edwards, Cliff. "Halloween's Not Just for Kids Anymore, As Sales Figures Show," *AP Wire* (1997).

Eliade, Mircea. *A History of Religious Ideas.* Chicago: U of Chicago P, 1978.

Ellis, Bill. "Death by Folklore: Ostension, Contemporary Legend, and Murder." *Western Folklore* 48 (1989).

Ensalaco, Carol A. *Samhain and Halloween: Tradition and Transformation in an Ancient Celtic Festival.* Harvard University, Ph.D. thesis, 1987.

Falcome, Lauren Beckham. "Frights of Fancy. Adults Join Kids to Make Halloween a Retail Smash." *Boston Herald* (1999).

Foster, Mary. "Halloween is Big in New Orleans, America's 'Most Haunted' City." *AP Wire* (1999).

Frazer, Sir James George. *The New Golden Bough.* New York: Criterion Books, Inc., 1959.

Frazier, Lisa. "Trick or Treaters Get an Early Start." *Washington Post* (1999).

Garciagodog, Juanita. *Digging the Days of the Dead: A Reading of Mexico's Dias de Muertos.* Colorado: UP of Colorado, 1998.

The Good Wife's Cookbook. London: Selfridge and Co., Ltd., 1911.

Grider, Sylvia. "The Razor Blades in the Apple Syndrome." *Perspectives in Contemporary Legend* CECTAL Conference Paper Series 34, Sheffield, England: University of Sheffield (1984).

Green, Judith Strupp. *The Days of the Dead. Laughing Souls: The Days of the Dead in Oaxaca, Mexico.* San Diego Museum of Man, Popular Series No. 1 (1969).

Hand, Wayland D. "Will o' the Wisps, Jack-o'-Lanters and Their Congeners: A Consideration of the Fiery and Luminous Creatures of Lower Mythology." *Fabula: Journal of Folklore Studies* 18 (1977).

Haining, Peter, ed. *Gothic Tales of Terror: Classic Horror Stories from Great Britain, Europe and the U.S. 1765-1840.* New York: Taplinger Publishing Co., 1972.

Haliburton, R. G. *New materials for the history of man, derived from a comparison of the calendars and festivals of nations.* 1863, published privately (in the Houghton Library collection of Harvard College Libraries).

Hackney, Wayne. "The World's first Pumpkin Regatta." *Ottawa-St. Lawrence Grower's Newspaper* (1998).

Harlow, Tim. "Halloween: Too Fun or Too Far?" *Minneapolis Star Tribune* (1999).

Harbach, Louise. "Walking Among the Dead Proves to be a Popular Attraction." *Philadelphia Inquirer* (1999).

Harkelroad, Tim. *The Complete Haunted House Book.* Bristol, Tennessee: Moonlighting Productions, 1998.

Henning, John."The Meaning of All the Saints." *Medieval Studies* 10 (1948).

Howe, John W. "What is Happy About Halloween?" *Christianity Today* 22 (1977).

Irwin, Florence. *Irish County Recipes.* Belfast, Ireland: The Northern Way, Ltd. (no pub. date).

Jacobs, W.W. *The Monkey's Paw.* Suffolk, England: The Boydell Press, 1983.

Kahler, Susan C. "Natasha's Story." *Journal of Veterinary Medicine* 209, no. 10 (1996).

Kellett, Arnold. *The Dark Side of Guy de Maupassant: A Selection and Translation.* New York: Caroll and Graf Publishers, 1989.

King, John. *The Celtic Druids' Year, Seasonal Cycles of the Ancient Celts.* New York and London: Blandford Publishing, 1994.

Knight, Jennifer. "Adoptions of Black Cats Halt for Halloween." *Los Angeles Times* (1998).

Kondratier, Alexei. "Samhain: Season of Death and Renewal." *An Tribhis Mhor: The IMBAS Journal of Celtic Reconstructionism* 2 (1997).

Kugelmass, Jack. *Masked Culture: The Greenwich Village Halloween Parade.* Columbia UP, 1994.

_____, "Backfence: What's So Scary about Halloween Anyhow?" *Minneapolis Start Tribune* (1999).

Lacher, Irene. "Saying Boo! to Halloween." *Los Angeles Times* (1999).

Loiselle, Jeff. "Great Gourd Local Team Catapults Pumpkin 1200 Feet Over Bog." *The Quincy Patriot Ledger* (1999).

Macdonald, Lorraine. "Samhain Customs in Scotland." *Dalriada Magazine* (1997).

Matthews, John and Philip Carr-Gomm. *Book of Druidry.* Northamptonshire, England: The Aquarian Press, 1990.

McNeill, F. Marion. *The Scot's Kitchen.* London and Glasgow: Blackie and Son, Ltd., 1930.

_____, *Halloween Its Origins, Rites and Ceremonies in the Scottish Tradition.* Edinburgh: Albyn Press, 1970.

McVicar, Ewan. "Tradition in Decay, Dark Force of Political Correctness Threatens Scotland's Traditional Halloween." *The Edinburgh Times* (1999).

Melton, J. Gordon. *Encyclopedic Handbook of Cults in America.* New York: Garland Publishing, Inc., 1986.

_____, *The Vampire Book: The Encyclopedia of the Undead.* Detroit, Michigan: Visible Ink Press, 1994.

Mooney, Chris. "Who's There? Not Houdini—Not Yet." *Boston Herald* (1999).

Moore, Stephen, ed. *The Vampire in Verse.* Chicago: Adams Press, 1985.

Moran, Richard. "The Myth of the Halloween Sadist." *Philadelphia Inquirer* (1987).

Morrow, Bradford and Patrick McGrath, ed. *The New Gothic.* New York: Random House, 1991.

Narciso, Dean. "Abused Cat Now Teaching Aid for Halloween Safety." *Columbus Ohio Dispatch* (1996).

Oates, Joyce Carol, ed. *American Gothic Tales.* New York: Plume, 1996.

O'Connor, Anne-Marie. "Day of the Dead Crosses Borders." *Los Angeles Times* (1999).

O'Hanlon, Ann. "Frenzy of Fear." *Washington Post* (1999).

Pilcher, James. "Haunted Houses Pushing Limits." *AP Wire* (1999).

Rowland, Pam."Headless Horseman Haunted Hayride and Haunted House." *Happy Halloween Magazine* 3, no. 1 (2000).

Ruane, Michael E. "Locked Into Halloween." *Washington Post* (1999).

Santino, Jack. *The Hallowed Eve, Dimensions of Culture in a Calendar Festival in Northern Ireland.* Lexington, Kentucky: UP of Kentucky, 1998.

_____, ed. *Halloween and Other Festivals of Death and Life.* Knoxville: The U of Tennessee P, 1994.

_____. *All Around the Year, Holidays and Celebrations in American Life.* Urbana and Chicago: U of Illinois P, 1995.

_____. *New Old Fashioned Ways: Holidays and Popular Culture.* Knoxville: U of Tennessee P, 1996.

Santopoalo, Rochelle. *Halloween: Play Time for Adults.* The Fielding Institute, (Ph.D. thesis) 1996.

Schwartz, Alvin, ed. *When I Grew Up Long Ago.* Philadelphia: JB Lippincott Co., 1978.

Sloan, David L. *Ghosts of Key West.* Key West, Florida: Phantom Press, 1998.

Smith, Joan Lowell. "The Trick for Halloween? Keep Pets Inside." *NJ Star-Ledger* (1999).

Starkey, Marion L. *The Devil in Massachusetts.* New York: Alfred A. Knopf, 1949.

Stein, Jeannine. "Toil and Trouble." *Los Angeles Times* (1999).

Stewart, R. J. *Celtic Myths, Celtic Legends.* London: Blandford Publishing, 1994.

Stone, Gregory P. "Halloween and the Mass Child." *The American Culture.* Boston: Houghton Mifflin, 1968.

Sullivan, Jim. "Spookyworld Scares up Some New Haunts." *Boston Globe* (1999).

Tomsho, Robert. "Hauntrepreneurs Find Ghouls Golden, But the Competition Can Be Very Scary." *Wall Street Journal* (1991).

Victor, Jeffrey. *Satanic Panic.* Chicago: Open Court Publishing Co., 1993.

Walker, Barbara. *Women's Encyclopedia of Myths and Secrets.* San Francisco: Harper and Row, 1983.

Walker, Sam and Daniel Costello. "America's Most Haunted." *Wall Street Journal* (1999).

White, Newman Ivey et. al. *Frank C. Brown Collection of North Carolina Folklore.* Durham, North Carolina: Duke UP, 1952-1964.

Willing, Richard and Jayne O'Donnell. "Shelters Guard Black Cats During Halloween Season." *USA Today* (1999).

Youngson, Jeanne Keyes. *Private files of a Vampirologist: Case Histories and Letters.* Chicago: Adams Press, 1997.

_____. *The Bizarre World of Vampires,* Chicago: Adams Press, 1996.

_____ and Shelley Leigh-Hunt, ed. *Do Vampires Exist?.* Dracula Press, 1993.

Index